Lighting Design
on
BROADWAY

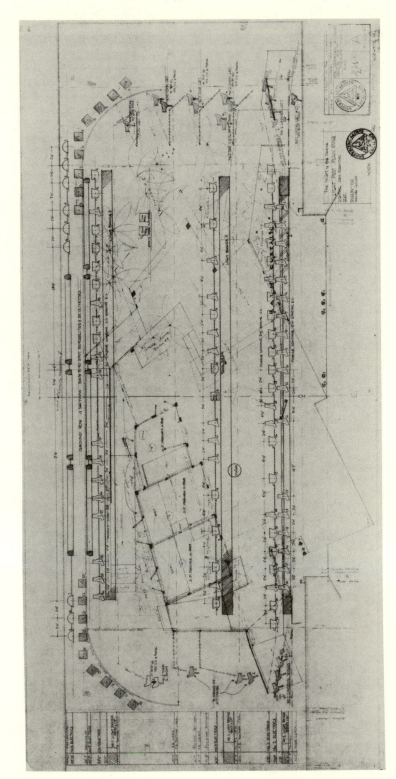

Light plot by Jean Rosenthal for *The Night of the Iguana*, 1961

Lighting Design
on
BROADWAY

Designers and Their Credits, 1915-1990

Bobbi Owen

Bibliographies and Indexes in the Performing Arts, Number 11

Greenwood Press
New York • Westport, Connecticut • London

Library of Congress Cataloging-in-Publication Data

Owen, Bobbi.
   Lighting design on Broadway : designers and their credits,
1915-1990 / Bobbi Owen.
     p. cm.—(Bibliographies and indexes in the performing arts,
ISSN 0742-6933 ; no. 11)
   Includes bibliographical references and index.
   ISBN 0-313-26533-X (alk. paper)
   1. Stage lighting designers—New York (N.Y.)—Biography—
Dictionaries.   I. Title.   II. Series.
PN2091.E4094   1991
792'.025'09227471—dc20   91-24007
  [B]

British Library Cataloguing in Publication Data is available.

Library of Congress Catalog Card Number: 91-24007
ISBN: 0-313-26533-X
ISSN: 0742-6933

First published in 1991

Greenwood Press, 88 Post Road West, Westport, CT 06881
An imprint of Greenwood Publishing Group, Inc.

Printed in the United States of America

The paper used in this book complies with the
Permanent Paper Standard issued by the National
Information Standards Organization (Z39.48-1984).

10 9 8 7 6 5 4 3 2 1

The author and publisher gratefully acknowledge the State Historical
Society of Wisconsin for permission to use a light plot of *Night of the
Iguana*, from the Jean Rosenthal Collection.

Contents

Preface

When I began working on this book, I thought that finding biographical information about lighting designers would be a reasonable task, if only because the profession is relatively new. It was comparatively easy to obtain biographical information about the designers who have been practicing their art on Broadway in the last thirty to forty years. These designers were especially cooperative when I or one of my assistants reached them and they provided information about themselves willingly. However, information on the pioneers of the field and those active during the early years of this century was more difficult to locate or research. When electricity was coming into general use, companies began to specialize in theatrical lighting, and many individuals gradually took more responsibility for designing instead of simply illuminating the stage. Louis Hartmann, David Belasco's lighting designer, and the Kliegl Brothers are part of theatre history in twentieth-century America and are generally known, but details about the other pioneers were skimpy and difficult to access. Those individuals I located and was fortunate enough to talk with regaled me with stories about the early years of lighting design, and provided enough information for several volumes of anecdotes. In general, however, I wish that all newspapers were indexed as thoroughly as *The New York Times*, and that all designers (and illuminating engineers) deposited information in the Billy Rose Theatre Collection at the New York Public Library at Lincoln Center. Then, life for an author, at least this author, would be simpler.

My task was made easier because of the diligent searching efforts of my research assistant, Lynn Roundtree, and I am satisfied that if information was to be discovered, he found it. We have worked together for the past two years on both this project and *Scenic Design on Broadway*. I dread moving on to my next project without his assistance, and I hope that he may be blessed with such capable assistance in his own writing career.

In addition to Lynn, this book was possible because of assistance from the University of North Carolina at Chapel Hill through the Scholarly Publications Committee in the College of Arts and Sciences, and from the Institute for the Arts and Humanities and the staff of the Humanities Reference Division of the Academic Affairs Library. Becket Royce, Cynthia Stewart, Ann Oldham, Aaron Carlos, Shelle Wheless, Joel Reider and Sheketha Hauser all helped make this book possible, as did the wonderful pages at the Billy Rose Theatre Collection at Lincoln Center: Louis Paul, Evelyn Lyman, Adeline Maxineau and Scherece Williams, and my excellent friends Judy and David Adamson. My husband, Gordon Ferguson, never blanches when I mention my next project, and his ability to manage the computer technology is invaluable.

One of the most inspiring teachers I had while studying costume design in graduate school was a lighting designer, Gilbert Helmsley. This book is dedicated to him, and to all lighting designers, especially those who, while the profession was developing, contributed to productions but received no credit or acknowledgment of their contribution in theatre playbills.

Introduction

"What light through yonder window breaks..."
Romeo and Juliet

When theatre performances took place during the day and primarily out of doors, lighting, except for special effects or winter afternoon performances, was not a critical element. The move to indoor theatres in the seventeenth and eighteenth centuries created the need for general illumination. Interior lighting was achieved initially with wax candles, several hundred in front of the proscenium arch and two or three thousand behind the proscenium opening to illuminate the actors, and coincidentially the audience. Made daily from tallow distilled from mutton fat and cooked in boiler rooms in the theatres, these candles created a haze that hung between the audience and the stage. An adage of long standing in the theatre is "an actor not seen is an actor not heard." Therefore, lines of dialogue were sometimes shouted by the actors so they could be heard through the fog. In addition, smoke from the candles got into the actors' lungs and caused them to cough and spit. Because this became an enormous problem, spittoons were built into theatres on both sides of the proscenium for the actors to use. Wicks required continual attention, so candle boys would move about on stage trimming wicks without regard for the scene being played. They were often applauded for effective trimming.

The introduction of clean-burning gas into theatres was obviously welcomed. Curiously, gas lights and, subsequently, electric lights were used in the foyers, lobbies and exteriors of theatres long before they were used to light the stage. The first English theatre to use gas lighting was Drury Lane in London around 1817. Gas was controllable through dimmers, but this feature was not exploited until Henry Irving used it for special effects together with general illumination in the 1880s. Limelight, created by burning lime or calcium, was developed in 1816 and used at Covent Garden in 1837. It provided a brilliant white light and, again, was mainly used for special effects, such as sun rays streaking through clouds or lightning.

Electricity was first used on stage in 1846 at the Paris Opera to create a rising sun, but was not generally used until 1878 when electric arcs (Jablochkoff candles) were introduced into the Paris Hippodrome. Incandescent bulbs made an appearance in the Savoy Theatre in London in 1881, one year after being introduced at the Paris Opera. Kliegl Brothers, the first company devoted to stage lighting, was formed in 1896 to provide lighting equipment to theatres. Few additional innovations were introduced until the 1920s, when footlights, reflectors, spotlights, dimmers, and lighting control panels all began to appear, for general light, and to focus attention on particular places on stage. The years between 1915 and 1920 were crucial in the development of the field of lighting design because it was then that "illuminating engineers" began to look on stage lighting as a branch of their industry. Innovations such as reflectors and colored light were introduced into the theatre, and lighting effects were used more often to help manipulate the audience's emotions.

Only during the last sixty to seventy years has lighting design come into its own. Theodore

Fuchs described the "deplorable" early lighting system in *Stage Lighting* (1929):

> The usual procedure of play production in the professional theatre is, roughly, as follows: the producer appoints a director (who directs only the actors), a cast is chosen, and rehearsals begin; a specialist is commissioned to design the settings, which are constructed by one company and painted by another; properties are furnished by a third company, and costumes, when necessary, are often designed by a second specialist and are furnished by still another company. The highly specialized activities of the various stage workers – the director, the scenic designer, the costume designer, and others – being executed each apart from the others, lack a unifying element, and often do not jibe, do not form a harmonious whole. Hence light would be at a disadvantage and its possible effectiveness greatly reduced, even were it planned and carried out with the utmost care. But at this point in the production of a play the lighting has not yet been thought of. In fact the playhouse has not yet been assigned by the theatre real-estate "interests." The lighting is left until the dress rehearsal, for the stage electrician (who has seen the production for the first time) to work out as best he can. Under this deplorable system, which is the result of economic conditions, good lighting is usually accidental, and in many productions is just as one would expect it to be – utterly inadequate, meaningless, and ugly.

The movement toward a strong visual format in the theatre, which began in the early 1920s, helped encourage the specialization of designers. At that time it was standard practice for a single designer to control all of the visual elements of a production, including scenery, lighting and costumes, and to have assistants follow the various elements through the building process. The process was especially complex when the same designers were involved with many productions as the same time. Gradually, designers such as Jo Mielziner and Robert Edmond Jones admitted the difficulty of maintaing control over such a wide range of activities and initiated a trend toward specialization.

Another influence that emerged during the early days of the Depression was the Federal Theatre Project created to provide employment for all varieties of theatre professionals. Having many different individuals doing specialized jobs meant that more individuals were paid, however little, for their work. Therefore, the Federal Theatre Project encouraged specialization. Once the specializations were developed, there was little possibility of returning to the format used in the past.

Master electricians and their assistants were often employed by theatres, or producers. The successful Broadway producer David Belasco, for whom the Belasco Theatre is named, worked for many years with Louis Hartmann, initially an electrician. Hartmann is remembered primarily as Belasco's lighting designer and between 1901 and 1931 they created many innovative stage lighting techniques, including incandenscent spotlights and silvered reflectors. Many Broadway theatres also employed electricians as permanent staff members to create lighting effects.

Even as the number of designers who specialized in lighting increased in the middle of this century, they continued to take the "all-category" exam for membership in United Scenic Artists. Designers including Jean Rosenthal, Abe Feder, and Peggy Clark were admitted into United Scenic Artists in the general category and gradually specialized in lighting, although all were capable designers of scenery and/or costumes. Arguably, a talented lighting designer might not be able to render designs for costumes or scenery and so, in the early 1960s, a separate category was created. In response to a movement by the International Association of Theatrical and Stage Employees (I.A.T.S.E.) to organize lighting designers, a committee of United Scenic Artists members was formed, which included Elmon Webb, Tharon Musser, Abe Feder, Peggy Clark, Jean Rosenthal, Donald Oenslager, and Jo Mielziner; they recommended that a separate category for lighting designers be created. In November 1962 the first entrance exam specifically for lighting designers was held, and Gilbert Helmsley and Patricia Collins were among those subsequently admitted.

The purpose of this book is to focus attention on the individuals who have practiced the art of lighting design in the twentieth century. The production of *The Man Who Married a Dumb Wife* in 1915 is generally recognized as the beginning of the modern era of Broadway. By examining theatre playbills over the following seventy-five years, a partial history of the profession of lighting designers is revealed. Playbills of the early years of the century reveal that designers were rarely regarded as a critical element of a production. The references that do exist in these early playbills are difficult to find, included in the back along with acknowledgments, if mentioned at all. Often there are references to lighting equipment companies, illuminating engineers and electricians, but no clear indication of a designer's contribution, however evident the need may have been within a production.

Gradually, very gradually, more recognition was given to the contribution of the lighting designer. As this happened the personalities of individual designers emerged along with their unique styles and their work became recognizable. Today, designers even have their own following and may often play a role in bringing audiences into the theatre.

With the passing of each year since 1915, more designers have received credit for their designs in Broadway plays. At the turn of the century only one lighting designer was mentioned for approximately every one hundred productions (usually indicated as "electrical effects by..."). By the 1943-44 season, one quarter of the productions list lighting designers. When United Scenic Artists acknowledged lighting designers as a separate membership category in 1962, they finally began receiving consistent credit on the title page. It is now extremely rare for a program not to list the full slate of designers.

As revealed in the biographical sketches in this volume, the individuals who work as lighting designers come from various backgrounds. In the early decades of the twentieth century, many of the lighting specialists were illuminating engineers, or master electricians, who gradually began to focus on design rather than the technical aspects of illuminating the stage. Some were designers of scenery or costumes who gradually specialized in lighting. Currently, however, many are specialists in lighting design, trained through an apprenticeship with another designer, in a theatre, or in one of the growing number of university graduate programs offering a degree in design.

This relatively new area of theatrical design is developing rapidly. Many theatrical lighting designers also work as architectural lighting specialists and have created techniques for lighting motion pictures and animated films. Innovations in lighting technology are also continuing, and the advent of computerization has made the tools of the trade more powerful. Less than a century has passed since Kliegl Brothers, the first company devoted to stage lighting equipment, was formed in 1896. Louis Hartmann and other pioneers of the field of design helped begin the profession, which will undoubtedly continue its rapid advance and integration into theatrical production. Lighting designers have already had a profound effect on theatre in the twentieth century, and their role and recognition can be expected to grow.

Lighting Design
on
BROADWAY

Designers and Their Credits

Lowell Achziger

Lowell Achziger was born in 1949 in Denver, Colorado and received a B.F.A. at Carnegie-Mellon University. A specialist in lighting for film and television, he designed lights for the original off-Broadway production of *Godspell*. His credits include designs for the Mc-Carter Theatre in Princeton, New Jersey and the Academy Theatre in Lake Forest, Illinois.

Lighting Designs:
1982: *Eminent Domain*

Mitch Acker

Mitch Acker first designed lighting on Broadway in 1981. He has designed lights for rock concerts, night clubs in Atlantic City, New Jersey, and for the Yarmouth Playhouse in Yarmouth, Massachusetts and the Hollywood Playhouse in Ft. Lauderdale, Florida. Off-Broadway he designed lights for plays including *Live at Crystal Six*.

Lighting Designs:
1981: *Marlowe*

P. Dodd Ackerman

Philip Dodd Ackerman (a.k.a. Ackermann) initially received credit for the scene designs of a Broadway show in 1916, after which his name appeared in numerous playbills during the 1920s and 1930s. His design expertise was generally used for scenery, although he contributed lighting designs to two productions in the late 1920s.

He was also the principal designer of P. Dodd Ackerman Scenic Studio.

Lighting Designs:
1927: *Honor Be Damned* 1929: *Hot Chocolates*

Scenic Designs:
1916: *Any House*; *Her Soldier Boy*; *Passing Show of 1916, The*; *Pay-Day*; *Robinson Crusoe, Jr.* 1917: *De Luxe Annie*; *Furs and Frills*; *Grass Widow, The* 1918: *Passing Show of 1918, The* 1919: *Carnival*; *Lonely Romeo, A*; *Take It from Me* 1920: *Broken Wing, The*; *Guest of Honor, The*; *Her Family Tree*; *Little Miss Charity*; *Passion Flower, The*; *Three Live Ghosts* 1921: *Danger*; *Ghost Between, The*; *Nightcap, The*; *Nobody's Money*; *Skirt, The*; *Title, The* 1922: *Advertising of Kate, The*; *For Goodness Sake*; *Frank Fay's Fables*; *Go Easy, Mabel*; *Kempy*; *Rotters, The* 1923: *Chicken Feed*; *Ginger*; *Little Jessie James*; *Magnolia*; *Polly Preferred*; *Stepping Stones*; *Thumbs Down*; *Wasp, The* 1924: *Alloy*; *Betty Lee*; *Conscience*; *Lady Killer, The*; *My Girl*; *Pigs*; *Sitting Pretty*; *Stepping Stones* 1925: *Alias the Deacon*; *All Dressed Up*; *Green Hat, The*; *Kiss in a Taxi, A*; *Merry, Merry*; *No, No Nanette*; *Pelican, The*; *Piker, The* 1926: *2 Girls Wanted*; *Castles in the Air*; *Climax, The*; *Ghost Train, The*; *Girl Friend, The*; *Twinkle, Twinkle*; *Up the Line*; *Weak Woman, A*; *What's the Big Idea*; *Woman Disputed, The* 1927: *Barker, The*; *Crime*; *Excess Baggage*; *Half a Widow*; *Honor Be Damned*; *It Is to Laugh*; *Just Fancy*; *Kempy*; *Lady Alone*; *Lost*; *Madame X*; *My Princess*; *Sinner*; *Spring Board, The*; *Trial of Mary Dugan*; *Window Panes* 1928: *Caravan*; *Crashing Through*; *Cross My*

Heart; Father, The; Hello, Yourself; Jealousy; Just a Minute; La Gringa; Lady of the Orchids, The; Marriage on Approval; Relations **1929:** *Conflict; Freddy; Headquarters; Humbug, The; Mountain Fury; Murder on the Second Floor* **1930:** *Challenge of Youth, The; Courtesan; Dear Old England; Farewell to Arms, A; Five Star Final; Frankie and Johnnie; I Want My Wife; Long Road, The; Ninth Guest, The; Phantoms; Recapture; Tyrant, The* **1931:** *Cold in Sables; Divorce Me, Dear; It Never Rains; Nikki; Steel* **1932:** *Budget, The; Devil Passes, The; East of Broadway; Girl Outside, The; Inside Story, The; Life Begins; Nona* **1933:** *Marathon; Move On, Sister; Sailor, Beware; Strange Gods; Undesirable Lady, An* **1934:** *Birthday; Brittle Heaven; Divine Moment, A; Hotel Alimony; No Questions Asked; Picnic; Queer People; Red Cat, The; Richard of Bordeaux; Strangers At Home; Yesterday's Orchids* **1935:** *Abide with Me; How Beautiful with Shoes; Lady Detained, A; Little Shop; Macbeth; Othello; Sailor, Beware; Stick-in-the-Mud; Touch of Brimstone, A* **1936:** *Among Those Sailing; In the Bag* **1937:** *House in the Country, A* **1938:** *Happiest Days, The; Time and the Conways*

"Acknowledgments"

Even in the days before producers acknowledged the need for lighting designers, they were aware of the need to illuminate actors. When electricity became generally available producers employed electricians and rented or purchased lighting equipment. Playbills in the early years of the twentieth century Broadway stage occasionally mention the name of an electrician and his staff, but more often credit an equipment company, some of which specialized in theatrical lighting. Therefore the acknowledgements which appear in numerous programs are often for lighting equipment companies, although scanning the names of the individuals involved leads generally to a realization that there was more than supplying equipment involved. Since the early 1960s, lighting designers have been more often recognized for their contribution to productions. Prominent lighting equipment companies, generally listed with other acknowledgements in the back of playbills before then, include:

Century Lighting Company, founded by Edward Kook and Joseph and Isidore "Ted"

Levy, was located at 351 West 52nd Street in 1931. Edward Kook, who died September 29, 1990, was president of Century Lighting Company from 1929 to 1968. Levy and Kook developed an elipsoidal spotlight, the "leko," which is named after them. They were also responsible for innovative lighting systems, effects, controls and instruments, often working with inventor George Izenour.

Display Stage Lighting Company was later known as Display & Stage Lighting Company. John Higham, President, Michael E. Kelly, Vice President, and William E. Price, Secretary, operated the business at 270 West 44th Street beginning in 1919.

DuWico was operated by Gus Durkin and Haral Williams and was located at 313 West 41st Street beginning in the teens and through the 1940s. For additional information, see "DuWico".

Fulton Stage Lighting Company, run by Francis F. Fox, President, Thomas Fitzgerald, Vice President, and William Remlinger, Secretary, was located at 419 W. 42nd Street, New York in 1927.

Kliegl Brothers, the oldest American company specializing in stage lighting equipment, was founded in 1896 by brothers John H. and Anton Kliegl. For additional information, see "Kliegl Brothers" and "John H. Kliegl."

New York Calcium Lighting Company was a company with general illumination as its primary purpose but which also served theatres.

Often these companies were formed to provide general illumination for homes and businesses and they drifted into a theatrical specialization. In the current theatre, a company will supply the lighting instruments and technical expertise, leaving a designer, hired by a producer, to design. Lighting designers have been receiving credit on the title page of playbills since the early 1960s and credits acknowledging contributions of all kinds are listed together in the back of programs.

Because the focus of this book is on designers, the index focuses on plays which acknowledged a designer by name. A few representative credits list "Ack Only" as an indication that playbills often did not list the individual responsible for the lighting design by name. Prior to the 1960s hundreds of Broadway productions make no mention of lighting designers and the number of playbills with acknowledgements are excessive. Plays which do not appear in the index of this volume either had playbills which made no reference to lighting designers or only listed acknowledgements. Biographies are included for a few representative lighting equipment companies such as "Kliegl Brothers" and "DuWico" among others, as examples of the contributions made by lighting equipment companies.

Daniel Adams

Daniel Adams is responsible for the lighting design of numerous tours, concerts and appearances by stars of the entertainment business. His credits include David Bowie's 1974 tour, Diana Ross' return engagement at Caesar's Palace, and the 1977 United States tour *Evening with Diana Ross*.

Lighting Designs:
1977: *Lily Tomlin in "Appearing Nightly"*

Christopher Akerlind

Christopher Akerlind designed lights for the first time on Broadway in 1990. He was born in Hartford, Connecticut on May 1, 1962, the son of Raymond and Gail Akerlind. He received a B.A. from Boston University where he launched his design career with *Hamlet*. His M.F.A. is from the Yale University School of Drama. He has worked extensively as an assistant to Jennifer Tipton, whom he credits as an influential force in his career along with Mark Lamos. A nomination for a Marharam Award accompanied his Broadway debut with *The Piano Lesson*.

Lighting Designs:
1990: *Piano Lesson, The*

Fred Allison

The lighting designer Fred Allison has been represented on Broadway twice, in 1969 and 1970.

Lighting Designs:
1969: *Three Men on a Horse* **1970:** *Norman, Is That You?*

Al Alloy

Although you will find his name only rarely in playbills, Al Alloy was involved with the lighting for over two hundred productions during his Broadway career, including many directed and produced by David Merrick, Brady and Wyman and Max Gordon, and many designed by Jo Mielziner. He was born Oscar Alloy in 1887 in New Orleans to a Spanish family recently emigrated from Gibraltar. At age seventeen he ran away from home, joining a brother in Philadelphia who worked as a theatre electrician. Al soon became involved with the theatre and quickly surpassed his brother with his expertise and flair with lighting effects. He met his wife, actress Barbara Grace, while creating lights for *Most Immoral Lady* starring Alice Brady, in which she played a small part. They were married on November 27, 1928 and had two children, including a son, Anthony Alloy, who followed his father into the theatre business, initially as a lighting designer. Al Alloy developed from electrician to lighting designer at the same time the field was developing. He did his job, professionally and creatively, and did not care about receiving credit or seeing his name in playbills. His influence remains evident however, not only in the productions he lit but with the colleagues he influenced. During his association with the annual "Festival of Music" in Philadelphia from 1948 to 1960 Al created the 'dancing waters' lighting effect. He also designed numerous industrial and Las Vegas shows during his remarkable career which occurred as lighting design was becoming a profession. Al Alloy died in Sunrise, Florida in 1976.

Lighting Designs:
1936: *Women, The* **1943:** *Bright Lights of 1943* **1944:** *Late George Apley, The* **1957:** *Good As Gold* **1960:** *Good Soup, The* **1961:** *Ross*

Ralph Alswang

Ralph Alswang made his debut on Broadway as a set designer for *Comes the Revelation* in 1942, as a lighting designer for *Home of the Brave* in 1945, and as a costume designer for *Beggars Are Coming to Town* in 1945. He was born in 1916 and raised in Chicago where he attended classes at the Chicago Art Institute and the Goodman Theatre. He also studied with Robert Edmond

Jones. For the majority of his distinguished career Mr. Alswang concentrated on scenery and lighting, but he also designed costumes for twelve shows between 1945 and 1966. In addition he designed theatres (including the Uris in New York City), guided restorations of theatres (including the Palace Theatre in New York City), directed and produced. He developed a theatre technique called "Living Screen" which integrated live action and motion pictures, and produced *Is There Intelligent Life on Earth?* using the method, for which he held three patents. Ralph Alswang was married in 1944 to Betty Taylor, an interior designer, and they had three children. He died in New York City on February 15, 1979 at age 62.

Lighting Designs:
1948: *Small Wonder*

Scenic Designs:
1948: *Story for Strangers, A; Strange Bedfellows; Trial By Jury* 1949: *How Long Till Summer; Mikado, The; Pirates of Penzance, The; Trial By Jury* 1959: *Hostile Witness* 1950: *Julius Caesar; Kathryn Dunham and Her Company; King Lear; Legend of Sarah; Let's Make An Opera; Peter Pan; Pride's Crossing; Tickets, Please* 1951: *Courtin' Time; Love and Let Love; Number, The; Out West of Eighth* 1952: *Conscience; Iolanthe; Mikado, The; Pirates of Penzance, The; Trial By Jury/ H.M.S. Pinafore; Two's Company* 1953: *Bat, The; Be Your Age; Ladies of the Corridor, The; Pink Elephant, The; Sing Till Tommorrow* 1954: *Fragile Fox; Magic and the Loss, The; Rainmaker, The* 1955: *Catch a Star; Deadfall; Southwest Corner, The* 1956: *Affair of Honor; Best House in Naples, The; Hot Corner, The; Time Limit; Uncle Willie* 1957: *First Gentleman, The; Hide and Seek; Tunnel of Love, The* 1958: *Love Me Little; Sunrise At Campobello* 1959: *Girls Against the Boys, The; Hostile Witness; Raisin in the Sun, A* 1961: *Come Blow Your Horn* 1963: *Advocate, The* 1964: *Comedy in Music Opus 2; Fair Games for Lovers* 1965: *Ken Murray's Hollywood; World of Charles Aznavour* 1966: *At the Drop of Another Hat; Committee, The* 1967: *Halfway Up the Tree* 1972: *Fun City*

Costume Designs:
1945: *Beggars Are Coming to Town; Home of the Brave* 1947: *Whole World Over, The* 1948: *Happy Journey, The/ Respectful Prostitute, The; Last Dance, The* 1955: *Deadfall* 1964: *Comedy in Music Opus 2; Fair Games for Lovers* 1965: *Ken Murray's Hollywood* 1966: *At the Drop of Another Hat* 1945: *Home of the Brave* 1946: *Lysistrata; Swan Song* 1947: *Gentlemen from Athens, The; Our Lan'; Young Man's Fancy, A* 1948: *Play's the Thing, The; Story for Strangers, A; Strange Bedfellows; Trial By Jury* 1949: *How Long Till Summer; Mikado, The; Pirates of Penzance, The; Trial By Jury* 195: *Hostile Witness* 1950: *Daphne Laureola; Julius Caesar; King Lear; Let's Make An Opera; Peter Pan; Pride's Crossing* 1953: *Anna Russell and Her Little Show; Bat, The; Ladies of the Corridor, The; Pink Elephant, The; Sing Till Tommorrow* 1954: *Fragile Fox; Rainmaker, The* 1955: *Deadfall; Southwest Corner, The* 1956: *Affair of Honor; Best House in Naples, The; Hot Corner, The; Time Limit; Uncle Willie* 1957: *First Gentleman, The; Hide and Seek; Tunnel of Love, The* 1958: *Epitaph for George Dillon; Sunrise At Campobello* 1959: *At the Drop of a Hat; Girls Against the Boys, The; Hostile Witness; Raisin in the Sun, A* 1961: *Come Blow Your Horn* 1963: *Advocate, The; School for Scandal, The* 1964: *Comedy in Music Opus 2; Fair Games for Lovers* 1965: *Beyond the Fringe; Ken Murray's Hollywood; World of Charles Aznavour* 1966: *At the Drop of Another Hat; Committee, The* 1967: *Halfway Up the Tree* 1942: *Comes the Revelation* 1945: *Home of the Brave* 1946: *I Like It Here; Lysistrata; Swan Song* 1947: *Gentlemen from Athens, The; Our Lan'; Whole World Over, The; Young Man's Fancy, A* 1948: *Jenny Kissed Me; Last Dance, The; Seeds in the Wind; Set My People Free; Small Wonder*

John Murray Anderson

John Murray Anderson, a native of St. John's, Newfoundland, was born on September 20, 1886 and died at the age of 67 on January 30, 1954. He came to the United States in 1910 after studying in Lausanne, Switzerland and Edinburgh. He served the theatre in a variety of functions: dancer, producer, writer, director, and lyricist. He devised six *Greenwich Village Follies*, also serving as a costume designer on one of the productions and a set designer on another. He occasionally also designed lights. In fact in all of the productions for which he received credit as a designer he had an additional role, often as director. "Murray" also worked as a producer for Radio City Music Hall, the New York Hippodrome, and Metro-Goldwyn-Mayer as well as on Broadway, and encouraged the talents of young theatre aspirants, including E. Carleton Winckler.

Lighting Designs:
1939: *One for the Money* **1940:** *Two for the Show* **1948:** *Heaven on Earth*

Scenic Designs:
1923: *Greenwich Village Follies*

Costume Designs:
1924: *Greenwich Village Follies*

Kathleen Ankers

Kathleen Ankers is known as an art director on television, with credits including *Late Night with David Letterman* and *F.Y.I.* on ABC-TV, and numerous specials and series. Born in London, she has designed for the Old Vic in Bristol, London and Liverpool, the Citizen's Theatre in Glasgow and in London's West End among other theatres. Kathleen Ankers began her career in the theatre in her teens with a repertory company in Farnham, where she went hoping to work on scenery and costumes but was hired to work in the box office. When the designer came down with the mumps, she got her start creating sets and costumes. In addition to her designs on Broadway she has designed sets and costumes off-Broadway and for regional theatres, including the Hartford Stage.

Lighting Designs:
1952: *Mr. Pickwick*

Scenic Designs:
1952: *Mr. Pickwick*

Costume Designs:
1952: *Fancy Meeting You Again; Mr. Pickwick* **1974:** *My Sister, My Sister*

Julie Archer

Julie Archer, a designer of lights and sets, was born on May 5, 1957 in Minneapolis, Minnesota. She studied at the School of Visual Arts at the University of Minnesota before moving to New York City at age 18. She quickly found work (in various capacities) with Mabou Mines and remains closely associated with the company. Her career has been influenced by Ruth Malaczeck, one of the founding members. In 1980 she designed the settings for *Vanishing Pictures* with Ruth Malaczeck and received an Obie award. Her set and lighting designs for *Hajj*, also for Mabou Mines, won the Joseph Maharam Award in 1983.

Lighting Designs:
1988: *Gospel at Colonus, The*

Will Steven Armstrong

Will Steven Armstrong specialized in scenic design during his career in theatre although he also designed lights and costumes. He was awarded the Tony for outstanding scene design in 1962 for *Carnival*. Mr. Armstrong was born in New Orleans in 1930 and died August 12, 1969. He studied both at Louisiana State and Yale Universities. Mr. Armstrong designed the stage of the American Shakespeare Festival in Stratford, Connecticut as well as sets, lights and costumes for that company.

Lighting Designs:
1959: *Andersonville Trial, The* **1961:** *Carnival; Cook for Mr. General, A; I Can Get It for You Wholesale; Kwamina; Subways Are for Sleeping* **1962:** *Tchin-Tchin* **1963:** *Dear Me, the Sky Is Falling; Nobody Loves An Albatross; One Flew Over the Cuckoo's Nest; Rehearsal, The; Semi-Detached* **1964:** *I Had a Ball; Passion of Joseph D, The; Ready When You Are* **1966:** *Three Bags Full* **1967:** *Something Different* **1969:** *Front Page, The; Zelda*

Scenic Designs:
1959: *Andersonville Trial, The* **1960:** *Caligula* **1961:** *Carnival; Cook for Mr. General, A; I Can Get It for You Wholesale; Kwamina; Subways Are for Sleeping* **1962:** *Tchin-Tchin* **1963:** *Dear Me, the Sky Is Falling; Nobody Loves An Albatross; One Flew Over the Cuckoo's Nest* **1964:** *I Had a Ball; Passion of Joseph D, The; Ready When You Are; Three Sisters, The* **1966:** *Lion in Winter, The; Pousse-Cafe; Three Bags Full; Wayward Stork* **1967:** *Imaginary Invalid, The; Something Different; Tonight At 8:30; Touch of the Poet, A* **1968:** *Forty Carats* **1969:** *Front Page, The; Zelda*

Costume Designs:
1959: *Andersonville Trial, The* **1960:** *Caligula* **1964:** *Girl Could Get Lucky, A* **1966:** *Lion in Winter, The*

William Armstrong

William Armstrong graduated from the Yale School of Drama. In addition to credits as a lighting designer on Broadway, he has contributed designs to the Williamstown Theatre Festival, the American Repertory Theatre and the Indiana Repertory Theatre. Recent credits include *Hedda Gabbler* and *'night, Mother* at The Guthrie Theatre and *The Mother of Us All* at the Lenox Arts Center.

Lighting Designs:
1980: *Lesson from Aloes, A* **1981:** *Scenes and Revelations* **1982:** *Macbeth*

Barry Arnold

Barry Arnold, a native of New York City, was production designer for one show in 1970. He started designing in summer stock at Eagles Mere Playhouse and first worked in New York at the Equity Library Theatre. Off-Broadway designs include *Curley McDimple, The Millionairess,* and *Love and Maple Syrup.*

Lighting Designs:
1970: *President's Daughter, The* **1976:** *Bubbling Brown Sugar* **1982:** *Joseph and the Amazing Technicolor Dreamcoat*

Scenic Designs:
1970: *President's Daughter, The*

Costume Designs:
1970: *President's Daughter, The*

Boris Aronson

Boris Aronson, painter, scenic designer and occasionally a costume and lighting designer, was born in Kiev, Russia in 1900 and studied at the State Art School, the School of Modern Painting, and with Alexandra Exter at the School of Theatre. He created sets and costumes in the United States for the first time at the New York City Yiddish Theatre in 1924, beginning five decades of outstanding design. Among the many prizes won by Mr. Aronson were several Tony Awards for outstanding scenic design for *The Rose Tattoo, Follies, Company, Zorba, Cabaret* and *Pacific Overtures.* He designed extensively for the theatre, ballet and film. The breadth and creativity of his work has received belated recognition since his death on November 16, 1980. The lavishly illustrated *The Theatre Art of Boris Aronson* by Frank Rich was published by Knopf in 1987, and his designs continue to be collected and featured in exhibitions.

Lighting Designs:
1945: *Stranger, The* **1948:** *Survivors, The* **1950:** *Country Girl, The*; *Season in the Sun* **1952:** *I've Got Sixpence* **1953:** *Frogs of Spring, The* **1957:** *Rope Dancers, The*; *Small War on Murray Hill*

Scenic Designs:
1927: *2x2=5* **1930:** *Josef Suss* **1932:** *Walk a Little Faster* **1934:** *Ladies' Money*; *Small Miracle* **1935:** *Awake and Sing*; *Battleship Gertie*; *Body Beautiful, The*; *Paradise Lost*; *Three Men on a Horse*; *Weep for the Virgins* **1937:** *Western Waters* **1938:** *Merchant of Yonkers, The* **1939:** *Awake and Sing*; *Gentle People, The*; *Ladies and Gentlemen* **1940:** *Cabin in the Sky*; *Heavenly Express*; *Unconquered, The* **1941:** *Clash By Night*; *Night Before Christmas, The* **1942:** *Cafe Crown*; *R.U.R.*; *Russian People, The* **1943:** *Family, The*; *South Pacific by Rigsby*; *What's Up* **1944:** *Sadie Thompson* **1945:** *Assassin, The*; *Stranger, The* **1946:** *Gypsy Lady*; *Truckline Cafe* **1948:** *Love Life*; *Skipper Next to God*; *Survivors, The* **1949:** *Detective Story* **1950:** *Bird Cage, The*; *Country Girl, The*; *Season in the Sun* **1951:** *Barefoot in Athens*; *I Am a Camera*; *Rose Tattoo, The* **1952:** *I've Got Sixpence* **1953:** *Crucible, The*; *Frogs of Spring, The*; *My Three Angels* **1954:** *Mademoiselle Colombe* **1955:** *Bus Stop*; *Diary of Anne Frank, The*; *Once Upon a Tailor*; *View from the Bridge, A* **1956:** *Girls of Summer* **1957:** *Hole in the Head, A*; *Orpheus Descending*; *Rope Dancers, The*; *Small War on Murray Hill* **1958:** *Cold Wind and the Warm, The*; *Firstborn, The*; *J.B.* **1959:** *Flowering Cherry*; *Loss of Roses, A* **1960:** *Do Re Mi*; *Semi-Detached* **1961:** *Garden of Secrets, The*; *Gift of Time, A* **1963:** *Andorra* **1964:** *Fiddler on the Roof* **1966:** *Cabaret* **1968:** *Price, The*; *Zorba* **1970:** *Company* **1971:** *Follies* **1972:** *Creation of the World and Other Business,*; *Great God Brown, The* **1973:** *Little Night Music, A* **1976:** *Fiddler on the Roof*; *Pacific Overtures* **1981:** *Fiddler on the Roof*

Costume Designs:
1927: *2x2=5* **1937:** *Western Waters* **1938:** *Merchant of Yonkers, The* **1940:** *Cabin in the Sky*; *Heavenly Express* **1968:** *Price, The* ·

Martin Aronstein

Martin Aronstein is well known as a lighting designer both on and off-Broadway. He was born on November 2, 1936 in Pittsfield, Massachusetts and studied at Queens College of the City of New York. In 1960 he became lighting designer for the New York Shakespeare Festival. His designs have been nominated for five Tony Awards and he has received two awards for lighting from the Los Angeles Drama Critics Circle. His list of lighting credits is long and includes productions in New York, in regional theatres, for dance companies, and as American lighting supervisor for foreign companies at the Kennedy Center in Washington, D.C.

Lighting Designs:
1964: *I Was Dancing*; *Milk Train Doesn't Stop Here Anymore, The*; *Severed Head, A*; *Tiny Alice* 1965: *Cactus Flower*; *Impossible Years, The*; *Royal Hunt of the Sun* 1966: *Investigation, The*; *Slapstick Tragedy*; *Those That Play the Clowns* 1967: *Astrakhan Coat, The*; *How Now Dow Jones*; *Marat/Sade*; *Song of the Grasshopper* 1968: *Education of H.Y.M.A.N. K.A.P.L.A.N., The*; *Forty Carats*; *George M!*; *Guide, The*; *Her First Roman*; *I'm Solomon*; *Morning Noon and Night*; *Promises, Promises* 1969: *Billy*; *Buck White*; *Dozens, The*; *La Strada*; *Penny Wars, The*; *Play It Again, Sam* 1970: *Chinese, The/ Dr. Fish*; *Gingerbread Lady, The*; *Grin and Bare It!/ Postcards*; *Paris Is Out*; *Park* 1971: *Ain't Supposed to Die a Natural Death*; *And Miss Reardon Drinks a Little*; *Four in a Garden*; *Incomparable Max, The* 1972: *Ambassador*; *Different Times*; *Don't Play Us Cheap*; *Hurry, Harry*; *Little Black Book, The*; *Moonchildren*; *Much Ado About Nothing*; *Promenade, All!*; *Sugar* 1973: *Au Pair Man, The*; *Beggar's Opera, The*; *Measure for Measure*; *Nash At Nine*; *Scapin*; *Tricks* 1974: *American Millionaire, An*; *Fame*; *My Fat Friend*; *Next Time I'll Sing to You* 1975: *Kennedy's Children*; *Ritz, The* 1976: *I Have a Dream*; *Poison Tree, The* 1977: *Dirty Linen/ New Found Land* 1978: *Hello, Dolly*; *Players* 1979: *Grand Tour, The* 1980: *Blackstone!*; *Division Street*; *Home*; *Mixed Couples* 1982: *Ghosts*; *Medea*; *Whodunnit* 1983: *Noises Off* 1984: *Beethoven's Tenth*; *Woman of Independent Means, A* 1985: *Benefactors* 1986: *Wild Honey* 1987: *Pygmalion*

Costume Designs:
1990: *Accomplice*

Mason Arvold

In September 1967 Mason Arvold, a painter and scenic designer, exhibited his paintings and collages in a one-man show at the Morris A. Mechanic Theatre Lounge in Baltimore, Maryland. His works of art have also been exhibited at the Galerie Internationale and Parke Bernet in New York City. He was born in Fargo, North Dakota and learned to design while working with his father, who ran the Little Country Theatre at North Dakota State University. After moving to New York City he also assisted A.A. Ostrander with the development of lighting and projection techniques for fashion shows.

Lighting Designs:
1950: *Alive and Kicking*

William F. Ash

William F. Ash was lighting designer for a show on Broadway in the 1920s. An electrician, he was associated with Illo Equipment Company and Illo Frank Theatrical Supplies, both located on West 47th Street in New York City in 1932.

Lighting Designs:
1924: *Badges*

Adrian Awan

Adrian Awan spent the majority of his professional life on the West Coast. At the time of his death on June 10, 1968, he had recently retired from 20th Century Fox where he had been employed as exploitation manager. He also supervised the technical aspects of productions for the Hollywood Bowl and musicals for the Los Angeles and San Francisco Civic Light Opera Associations.

Lighting Designs:
1945: *Red Mill, The* 1946: *Gypsy Lady*

Scenic Designs:
1945: *Red Mill, The*

Lemuel Ayers

Lemuel Ayers was both a designer of sets, lights and costumes and a theatrical producer. He was born in New York City on January 22, 1915. He received a degree in architecture from Princeton

University and one in drama from the University of Iowa. Mr. Ayers received the Donaldson Award for both sets and costumes for *Kiss Me Kate* in 1943 and for *Camino Real* in 1952. He also received the Donaldson Award for *My Darlin' Aida* in 1952 and *Kismet* in 1953. He was married in 1939 and had two children. Mr. Ayers died in 1955 after a brief but brilliant career. His credits on Broadway as a set designer were extensive and include *High Button Shoes* and *Oklahoma!*. He served as art director for the film *Meet Me in St. Louis*.

Lighting Designs:
1944: *Bloomer Girl* 1951: *Music in the Air* 1952: *My Darlin' Aida* 1953: *Camino Real*

Scenic Designs:
1939: *Journey's End; They Knew What They Wanted* 1941: *Angel Street; As You Like It; Eight O'Clock Tuesday; They Walk Alone* 1942: *Autumn Hill; Pirate, The; Plan M; Willow and I, The* 1943: *Harriet; Oklahoma!* 1944: *Bloomer Girl; Peepshow; Song of Norway* 1946: *Cyrano De Bergerac; St. Louis Woman* 1948: *Inside U.S.A.; Kiss Me Kate* 1950: *Out of This World* 1951: *Music in the Air; Oklahoma!* 1952: *Kiss Me Kate; My Darlin' Aida; See the Jaguar* 1953: *Camino Real; Kismet* 1954: *Pajama Game, The*

Costume Designs:
1941: *Angel Street; As You Like It; Macbeth* 1946: *Cyrano De Bergerac; St. Louis Woman* 1948: *Kiss Me Kate* 1950: *Out of This World* 1951: *Music in the Air* 1952: *Kiss Me Kate; My Darlin' Aida; See the Jaguar* 1953: *Camino Real; Kismet* 1954: *Pajama Game, The*

Ballou

David R. (Tex) Ballou was born in Manila, The Philippines in 1925, the son of Charles Nicholas Senn Ballou and Emily Barnes Smith Ballou. His family includes a portrait artist, Bertha Ballou. Ballou received an M.F.A. at the Goodman Art Institute where he later spent six years as head of the costume program, teaching among others Theoni V. Aldredge. Ballou credits Mordecai Gorelik as a major influence on his career, along with Richard Whorf and his other teachers while studying at Biarritz. His debut was for *Bachelor Born* for the Lynchburg (Virginia) Little Theatre. Ballou, who designs scenery, lights and costumes, has been awarded

almost every professional prize in the New York theatre, including a Tony nomination for the scenic design for *The Legend of Lizzie* in 1959, the Vernon Rice Award for *Machinal*, and Obie awards for *Machinal, A Doll's House* and the design of the off-Broadway Theatre Four. He is also an active industrial designer and has over three hundred credits for productions for Coca-Cola, I.B.M., Chevrolet, McDonald's, Charles of the Ritz and many others.

Lighting Designs:
1956: *Wake Up, Darling*

Scenic Designs:
1956: *Wake Up, Darling* 1959: *Legend of Lizzie*

Costume Designs:
1954: *Flowering Peach, The* 1955: *Red Roses for Me* 1959: *Legend of Lizzie*

Bill Ballou

Bill Ballou has designed sets, sound, and lights and worked as a technician throughout New England, beginning with musicals in high school and followed by productions at the Rockland County Community Theatre. His credits include productions at Hartford Stage Company, American Place Theatre, Smith College, StageWest and Shakespeare and Company. His credits also include sound design off-Broadway and in regional theatres. He was born in Manhattan on April 26, 1950 and received a B.A. in theatre from Hampshire College in 1978. His mother, Billie Ballou, is a storyteller. He maintains a shop specializing in metal work and woodwork for theatres and also consults on the conception and coordination of feature films.

Lighting Designs:
1981: *Heartland*

Scenic Designs:
1981: *Heartland*

Watson Barratt

Watson Barratt was a prolific scenic designer who occasionally also designed costumes and lights. He was born in Salt Lake City, Utah, on June 27, 1884 and studied in New York and Wilmington, Delaware. He began professional life as an illustrator, specializing in magazine covers. He entered the theatre as a scenic artist, later becoming the chief scenic designer for the Shuberts. His first scene designs on Broadway were seen in 1917 and he debuted as a costume designer on Broadway in 1926, after which he did numerous productions, including lighting for one in 1950. Mr. Barratt, who also served as director of the St. Louis Municipal Opera for several years, died in 1962.

Lighting Designs:
1950: *With a Silk Thread*

Scenic Designs:
1917: *Night in Spain, A* **1918:** *Girl O' Mine; Ideal Husband, An; Little Journey, A; Little Simplicity; Melting of Molly, The; Passing Show of 1918, The; Sinbad; Sleeping Partners* **1919:** *Dancer, The; Monte Cristo, Jr; Oh, What a Girl; Passing Show of 1919, The; Shubert Gaieties of 1919; Sleepless Night, A* **1920:** *Cinderella on Broadway; Floradora; Outrageous Mrs. Palmer, The; Tick-Tack-Toe* **1921:** *Blossom Time; Bombo; In the Night Watch; Last Waltz, The; Mimic World, The; Silver Fox, The; Whirl of New York, The* **1922:** *Goldfish, The; Hotel Mouse, The; Lady in Ermine, The; Make It Snappy; Passing Show of 1922, The; Rose of Stamboul, The; Springtime of Youth; Thin Ice* **1923:** *Artists and Models; Caroline; Dancing Girl, The; Dew Drop Inn; For All of Us; Passing Show of 1923, The; Topics of 1923* **1924:** *Artists and Models; Blossom Time; Dream Girl, The; Farmer's Wife, The; Innocent Eyes; Passing Show of 1924, The; Student Prince, The; Vogues of 1924; Werewolf, The* **1925:** *Artists and Models; Big Boy; Gay Paree; June Days; Lady's Virtue, A; Love Song, The; Mayflowers; Princess Flavia; Virgin of Bethulia, The* **1926:** *Blossom Time; Countess Maritza; First Love; Gay Paree; Great Temptations; Katja; Merry World, The; Night in Paris, A; Padre, The; Pearl of Great Price, The* **1927:** *Artists and Models; Cherry Blossoms; Circus Princess, The; Crown Prince, The; Immortal Isabella?; Love Call, The; Mixed Doubles; My Maryland; Night in Spain, A; Nightingale, The; Scarlet Lily, The* **1928:** *12,000; Angela; Countess Maritza; Greenwich Village Follies; Kingdom of God, The; Luckee Girl; Red Robe, The; Silent House, The; Sunny Days; Young Love* **1929:** *Boom Boom; Broadway Nights; Lady from the Sea, The; Love Duel, The; Music in May; Night in Venice, A; Pleasure Bound; Street Singer; Wonderful Night, A* **1930:** *Artists and Models;*

Lost Sheep; Meet My Sister; Nina Rosa; Royal Virgin, The; Scarlet Sister Mary; Three Little Girls **1931:** *As You Desire Me; Blossom Time; Cynara; Experience Unnecessary; If I Were You; Peter Ibbetson; School for Scandal, The; Student Prince, The; Wonder Bar, The* **1932:** *Little Rocketeer, A; Marching By; Smiling Faces* **1933:** *Mikado, The; Ten Minute Alibi* **1934:** *Music Hath Charms; No More Ladies; Perfumed Lady, The; Roman Servant, A; Shatter'd Lamp, The; So Many Paths; Ziegfeld Follies: 1934* **1935:** *Knock on Wood; Laburnum Grove; Living Dangerously* **1936:** *Black Limelight; Case of Clyde Griffiths, The; Come Angel Band; Golden Journey, The; Green Waters; Lady Precious Stream; Laughing Woman, The; Mid-West* **1937:** *Frederika; Hitch Your Wagon; Lady Has a Heart, The; Merely Murder; Tell Me, Pretty Maiden; Three Waltzes; Wise Tomorrow* **1938:** *Bachelor Born; Blossom Time; Come Across; Madame Capet; Outward Bound; You Never Know* **1939:** *Billy Draws a Horse; Clean Beds; Close Quarters; Foreigners; Importance of Being Earnest, The; Time of Your Life, The; White Steed, The* **1940:** *Kind Lady; Leave Her to Heaven; Love's Old Sweet Song; Romantic Mr. Dickens; Time of Your Life, The; Walk with Music* **1941:** *Ah, Wilderness; Golden Wings; Hope for a Harvest; My Fair Ladies; Night of Love* **1942:** *Little Darling; Magic/ Hello, Out There; Rivals, The; Yesterday's Magic* **1943:** *Artists and Models; Ask My Friend Sandy; Blossom Time; Student Prince, The; This Rock; Ziegfeld Follies: 1943* **1944:** *Bright Boy; Pick-Up Girl; Sheppy* **1945:** *Happily Ever After; Lady Says Yes, A; Rebecca* **1946:** *Flamingo Road; January Thaw* **1947:** *Heads Or Tails; Little A; Louisiana Lady* **1948:** *Ghosts; Hedda Gabler; My Romance* **1950:** *With a Silk Thread* **1954:** *Starcross Story, The* **1955:** *Righteous Are Bold, The*

Costume Designs:
1926: *Pearl of Great Price, The* **1930:** *Hello, Paris* **1935:** *Living Dangerously* **1939:** *Importance of Being Earnest, The* **1942:** *Magic/ Hello, Out There; Rivals, The* **1950:** *With a Silk Thread*

William H. Batchelder

William H. Batchelder studied stagecraft with Harry Feldman and at the Yale School of Drama after receiving a B.A. at Harvard in 1958. He was born on June 27, 1937 in New York City and is known primarily as a lighting designer and a production manager. He has served as stage manager for productions New York City Center Light Opera Company at the New York City Center and on Broadway starting with *The Right Honorable Gentleman* in 1965. He worked as an assistant to Jean Rosenthal and has worked as production manager and lighting designer for Elliot Feld, as well as stage manager and lighting designer for the Martha Graham Dance Company.

Lighting Designs:
1972: *Captain Brassbound's Conversion*

Howard Bay

Howard Bay, well known as a scenery and lighting designer, was involved with nearly two hundred productions during his career. Originally from Centralia, Washington where he was born on May 3, 1912, he directed and taught as well as designed for the theatre after his professional debut in 1933 with *There's a Moon Tonight*. Mr. Bay also designed for television, film, and industrial shows. He lectured, wrote books about design and was active in professional associations, serving as President of United Scenic Artists. Occasionally during his long, prolific career Mr. Bay also contributed costume designs to a production in addition to the sets and lights, including *Man of La Mancha* which he designed with Patton Campbell, and with whom he shared a Tony nomination. He won a Tony Award for *Toys in the Attic*, a Maharam Award for *Man of La Mancha* and Donaldson Awards for *Carmen Jones* and *Up in Central Park*. Mr. Bay died on November 21, 1986 at age 74 while working on a production of *The Music Man* to be presented at the Peking Opera House.

Lighting Designs:
1944: *Chicken Every Sunday; Follow the Girls; Men to the Sea* 1945: *Up in Central Park* 1948: *Magdalena* 1949: *Magnolia Alley* 1951: *Autumn Garden, The; Flahooey* 1953: *Midsummer* 1955: *Desperate Hours, The; Red Roses for Me* 1956: *Night of the Auk; Very Special Baby, A* 1957: *Look Back in Anger; Music Man, The; Romanoff and Juliet* 1958: *Interlock* 1959: *Desert Incident, A; Fighting Cock, The* 1960: *Cool World, The; Cut of the Axe; Toys*

in the Attic; Wall, The 1961: *Isle of Children; Milk and Honey* 1963: *Bicycle Ride to Nevada; My Mother, My Father and Me* 1964: *Never Live Over a Pretzel Factory* 1969: *Fire!* 1970: *Cry for Us All* 1976: *Home Sweet Homer; Poor Murderer* 1977: *Man of La Mancha* 1979: *Utter Glory of Morrissey Hale, The*

Scenic Designs:
1936: *Battle Hymn; Chalk Dust* 1937: *Marching Song; Native Ground; One Third of a Nation; Power* 1938: *Life and Death of An American; Merry Wives of Windsor, The; Sunup to Sundown; Trojan Incident* 1939: *Little Foxes, The* 1940: *Corn Is Green, The; Fifth Column, The; Morning Star* 1941: *Brooklyn, U.S.A.; Man with Blond Hair, The* 1942: *Count Me in; Eve of Saint Mark, The; Great Big Doorstop, The; Johnny 2x4; Moon Is Down, The; Strings, My Lord, Are False, The; Uncle Harry* 1943: *Carmen Jones; Corn Is Green, The; Merry Widow, The; New Life, A; One Touch of Venus; Patriots, The; Something for the Boys* 1944: *Catherine Was Great; Chicken Every Sunday; Follow the Girls; Listen Professor; Men to the Sea; Searching Wind, The; Storm Operation; Ten Little Indians; Violet; Visitor, the* 1945: *Deep Are the Roots; Devil's Galore; Marinka; Polonaise; Up in Central Park* 1946: *Show Boat; Woman Bites Dog; Would-Be Gentleman, The* 1948: *As the Girls Go; Magdalena* 1949: *Big Knife, The; Magnolia Alley; Montserrat* 1950: *Come Back, Little Sheba; Hilda Crane; Michael Todd's Peep Show* 1951: *Autumn Garden, The; Flahooey; Grand Tour, The; Two on the Aisle* 1952: *Shrike, The* 1953: *Children's Hour, The; Mid-summer* 1955: *Desperate Hours, The; Red Roses for Me* 1956: *Night of the Auk; Very Special Baby, A* 1957: *Music Man, The* 1958: *Interlock* 1959: *Desert Incident, A* 1960: *Cool World, The; Cut of the Axe; Toys in the Attic; Wall, The* 1961: *Isle of Children; Milk and Honey* 1963: *Bicycle Ride to Nevada; My Mother, My Father and Me* 1964: *Never Live Over a Pretzel Factory* 1969: *Fire!* 1970: *Cry for Us All* 1976: *Home Sweet Homer; Poor Murderer* 1977: *Man of La Mancha* 1979: *Utter Glory of Morrissey Hale, The*

Costume Designs:
1938: *Merry Wives of Windsor, The; Sunup to Sundown; Trojan Incident* 1950: *Hilda Crane* 1957: *Look Back in Anger* 1976: *Home Sweet*

Homer 1977: *Man of La Mancha*

Mr. Beardsley

Mr. Rudolph Beardsley, partner with Alexander Grinager in the scenic studio Grinager and Beardsley, was a painter and illustrator. He was born in 1875 in New York City and died there on August 15, 1921. In addition to the productions he worked on in collaboration with Alexander Grinager, he also designed lighting for a production in 1914.

Lighting Designs:
1914: *Silent Voice, The*

Cecil Beaton

Cecil Beaton designed many handsome costumes and sets during his lifetime and will always be remembered for his contribution to both the stage and film versions of *My Fair Lady*. Cecil Walter Hardy Beaton was born in London in 1904 and began sketching costumes at a very young age, dressing himself and his family for playlets which he also staged. Cecil Beaton's designs for opera, stage and film were regularly seen in the United States and England. He specialized in settings and costumes and for one production on Broadway in 1946 also designed the lighting. Details of his life as a photographer and designer have been well documented through publications of his diaries, reminiscences, and photographs. He selected an official biographer, Hugo Vickers, shortly before his death in 1980 at the age of 76. The book, *Cecil Beaton, A Biography* was published in 1986. He was nominated for six Tony awards and received four: *Quadrille* in 1955, *My Fair Lady* in 1957, *Saratoga* in 1960, and *Coco* in 1970.

Lighting Designs:
1946: *Lady Windermere's Fan*

Scenic Designs:
1946: *Lady Windermere's Fan* 1950: *Cry of the Peacock* 1952: *Grass Harp, The* 1954: *Quadrille* 1955: *Chalk Garden, The*; *Little Glass Clock, The* 1956: *Glass Clock, The* 1959: *Look After Lulu*; *Saratoga* 1960: *Tenderloin* 1969: *Coco*

Costume Designs:
1946: *Lady Windermere's Fan* 1950: *Cry of the Peacock* 1952: *Grass Harp, The* 1954: *Portrait of a Lady*; *Quadrille* 1955: *Chalk Garden,*

The; *Little Glass Clock, The* 1956: *My Fair Lady* 1959: *Look After Lulu*; *Saratoga* 1960: *Dear Liar*; *Tenderloin* 1969: *Coco* 1976: *My Fair Lady* 1981: *My Fair Lady*

Jeffrey Beecroft

Jeffrey Beecroft was born on April 1, 1956 in Sacramento, California, the son of M.T. and Judith Beecroft. He received an M.F.A. at New York University Tisch School of the Arts and has been influenced by John Gleason, Dean Tavolaris, and Ridley Scott. He works extensively in the United Kingdom where he debuted with *We Won't Pay! We Won't Pay!* in London's West End. He has also designed *Cherry Orchard* and *Three Sisters* in London, *Troilus and Cressida, Hamlet, Edipus Rex, Cyrano de Bergerac* and *Much Ado about Nothing* for the Royal Shakespeare Company, and *After Aida* at the Old Vic. He has taught seminars in design at Oxford. Prizes for design include the Evening Standard Award in the United Kingdom, Outer Drama Critics Award, and two San Francisco Drama Critics Awards. Off-Broadway he has designed productions such as *The Transfiguration of Benno Blimpie* at Playwrights Horizon. Jeffrey Beecroft was production designer for the 1990 Kevin Costner film *Dances with Wolves*.

Lighting Designs:
1984: *Cyrano De Bergerac*; *Much Ado About Nothing*

Ben Beerwald

Benjamin Beerwald (a.k.a. Bierwald) was chief electrician of the Century Theatre in New York City and as such was responsible for the illumination of many productions, although he did not officially receive design credit nor function as a designer in the same sense as contemporary lighting designers. The September 1913 issue of *Theatre Magazine* featured "Benny" in an article entitled "A Maker of Moons" recounting his creation of moonlight and moonrise for the Broadway production of *Joseph and his Brethren*.

Lighting Designs:
1916: *Miss Springtime* 1917: *Ziegfeld Follies: 1917*

Norman Bel Geddes

Norman Bel Geddes was a designer of sets, lights and costumes, a producer and an industrial designer. He was born in 1893 in Adrian, Michigan and died in 1958. He began designing in 1916 in California and in 1918 designed sets for a production at the Metropolitan Opera, marking his debut in New York City. Mr. Bel Geddes never created costumes without also designing the sets for a production. His career was remarkable, and although his list of credits on Broadway is not long, he was involved in well over two hundred productions during his lifetime, designing, writing about design and producing. His creativity was well used in the theatre where he designed such innovative productions as The Miracle for Max Reinhardt and was important in the development of the New American Stagecraft movement. He also designed and consulted on the design of theatres around the world. Norman Bel Geddes was married to the costume designer Edith Lutyens, and is the father of the actress Barbara Bel Geddes.

Lighting Designs:
1917: I.O.U. **1918:** I.O.U. **1924:** Miracle, The **1931:** Hamlet **1932:** Flying Colors **1937:** Eternal Road, The **1940:** It Happens on Ice

Scenic Designs:
1917: I.O.U. **1918:** I.O.U. **1921:** Ermine **1922:** Orange Blossoms; Truth About Blayds, The **1923:** Will Shakespeare **1924:** Lady, Be Good; Miracle, The; Quarantine; She Stoops to Conquer **1925:** Arabesque **1926:** Devil in the Cheese **1927:** Creoles; Damn the Tears; Five O'Clock Girl; John; Julius Caesar; Spread Eagle **1928:** Patriot, The; She Stoops to Conquer **1929:** Fifty Million Frenchmen **1930:** Change Your Luck **1931:** Hamlet **1932:** Flying Colors **1935:** Dead End **1936:** Iron Men **1937:** Eternal Road, The; Seige **1940:** It Happens on Ice **1941:** It Happens on Ice **1943:** Sons and Soldiers **1944:** Seven Lively Arts

Costume Designs:
1921: Ermine **1923:** Will Shakespeare **1924:** Miracle, The **1925:** Arabesque **1926:** Devil in the Cheese **1930:** Change Your Luck **1931:** Hamlet **1935:** Dead End **1936:** Iron Men **1937:** Eternal Road, The **1940:** It Happens on Ice **1941:** It Happens on Ice **1943:** Sons and Soldiers

Benrimo

J. Harry Benrimo was an actor, playwright, and producer who was active in the theatre in California, London and New York. His acting career began in California, but he soon moved to New York where he first appeared in The First Born in 1897, later performing the same role in London. He co-authored several plays, including The Yellow Jacket with George C. Hazelton, which he also designed. Born in San Francisco on June 21, 1874, he died on May 26, 1942.

Lighting Designs:
1928: Yellow Jacket, The

Scenic Designs:
1917: Willow Tree, The **1928:** Yellow Jacket, The

Costume Designs:
1917: Willow Tree, The **1928:** Yellow Jacket, The

Emanuel Berian

Emanuel Berian (a.k.a. Emil František Burian) designed lighting for one production on Broadway in 1936. He lived from 1904 to 1959 and founded his own theatre in 1933 in his native Czechoslovakia, the "D34" where he created sophisticated theatrical effects including combinations of live action and projection. He was deported from Czechoslovakia in 1941 but returned to restore the avant-garde theatre after World War II.

Lighting Designs:
1936: Battle Hymn

Aline Bernstein

Aline Bernstein had a distinguished career as the first prominent female scenic and costume designer. She was born on December 22, 1882, the daughter of actor Joseph Frankau, and originally hoped to follow in his footsteps. However, she began designing dresses for the Neighborhood Playhouse and soon left behind all thoughts of performing. In addition to designing on Broadway for thirty-four years, she helped found the Museum of Costume Art at Rockefeller Center (now at the Metropolitan Museum of Art). In 1926 she became the first woman to attain membership as a scenic designer in the Brotherhood of Painters, Decorators and Paperhangers of the American Federation of Labor, the union which at that time represented designers. In 1950 she received a Tony Award for the costumes for *Regina*. Mrs. Bernstein, in addition to a busy career designing, also wrote two novels, *Three Blue Suits* and *The Journey Down*. Her relationship with novelist Thomas Wolfe was recorded by Wolfe in many of his books. Their correspondence was collected in *My Other Loneliness*, edited by Suzanne Stutman and published in 1983 by the University of North Carolina Press. Married to Theodore Bernstein and the mother of two children, Aline Frankau Bernstein died in 1955 at the age of 72.

Lighting Designs:
1924: *Little Clay Cart, The*

Scenic Designs:
1924: *Little Clay Cart, The* 1925: *Critic, The; Dybbuck, The; Legend of the Dance, The* 1926: *Apothecary, The; Grand Street Follies; Lion Tamer, The; Little Clay Cart, The; Ned Mc Cobb's Daughter; Romantic Young Lady, The* 1927: *Commedia del'Arte; Grand Street Follies; If; Love Nest, The; Lovers and Enemies; Tone Pictures/The White Peacock* 1928: *Caprice; Cherry Orchard, The; First Stone, The; Grand Street Follies; Hedda Gabler; Improvisations in June; L'Invitation Au Voyage; Maya; Peter Pan; Would-Be Gentleman, The* 1929: *Cherry Orchard, The; Game of Love and Death, The; Grand Street Follies; Katerina; Lady from Alfaqueque, The; Living Corpse, The; Mademoiselle Bourrat; On the High Road; Seagull, The* 1930: *Alison's House; Grand Hotel; Green Cockatoo, The; Lady from Alfaqueque, The; Romeo and Juliet; Siegfried; Women Have Their Way/ The Open Door* 1931: *Getting Married; Reunion in Vienna; Tommorrow and Tomorrow* 1932: *Animal Kingdom, The; Clear All Wires; Firebird; Jewel Robbery; Late Christopher Bean, The; Lenin's Dowry; Liliom* 1933: *Cherry Orchard, The; Good Woman, Poor Thing, A; Thunder on the Left; We, the People* 1934: *Between Two Worlds; Children's Hour; Judgement Day; L'Aiglon; Mackerel Skies* 1935: *Camille; Night in the House; Sunny Morning, A/ The Women Have Their Way/ etc.* 1936: *And Stars Remain; Days to Come* 1937: *Storm Over Patsy; To Quito and Back* 1938: *American Landscape* 1940: *Male Ani-*mal, The 1950: *Happy Time, The*

Costume Designs:
1916: *Inca of Perusalem, The; Queen's Enemies, The* 1921: *Great Brozopp, The* 1922: *Fashions for Men* 1924: *Little Clay Cart, The; She Stoops to Conquer* 1925: *Caesar and Cleopatra; Dybbuck, The; Grand Street Follies; Hamlet; Legend of the Dance, The* 1926: *Apothecary, The; Grand Street Follies; Lion Tamer, The; Little Clay Cart, The; Ned Mc Cobb's Daughter; Romantic Young Lady, The; White Wings* 1927: *Commedia del'Arte; Doctor's Dilemma, The; Grand Street Follies; If; Love Nest, The; Lovers and Enemies; Tone Pictures/The White Peacock* 1928: *Cherry Orchard, The; First Stone, The; Grand Street Follies; Hedda Gabler; Improvisations in June; Maya; Peter Pan; Would-Be Gentleman, The* 1929: *Game of Love and Death, The; Grand Street Follies; Lady from Alfaqueque, The; Living Corpse, The; On the High Road; Seagull, The* 1930: *Alison's House; Grand Hotel; Green Cockatoo, The; Lady from Alfaqueque, The; Romeo and Juliet; Siegfried; Women Have Their Way/ The Open Door* 1932: *Clear All Wires; Dark Hours, The; Liliom* 1933: *Cherry Orchard, The* 1934: *L'Aiglon* 1935: *Camille; Night in the House; Sunny Morning, A/ The Women Have Their Way/ etc.* 1937: *To Quito and Back* 1938: *American Landscape* 1939: *Little Foxes, The* 1942: *Willow and I, The* 1943: *Harriet; Innocent Voyage, The* 1944: *Feathers in a Gale; Searching Wind, The* 1947: *Eagle Has Two Heads, The* 1949: *Regina* 1950: *Burning Bright; Enemy of the People, An; Happy Time, The; Let's Make An Opera*

Ken Billington

Ken Billington learned the craft of lighting design through study at the Lester Polakov Studio and Forum of Stage Design and by assisting Tharon Musser, Thomas Skelton, William Rittman, and Pat Collins. His first designs in New York were for *Fortune and Men's Eyes* off-Broadway in 1969. He was born on October 29, 1946 in White Plains, New York. He has been honored with numerous awards, including five Tony nominations, two Los Angeles Drama Critics Awards, one Boston Drama Critic Association Award, three New York Drama Desk Awards, and a Lumen Award for lighting the

Red Parrot nightclub. Just as he had learned through being an assistant, he hires assistants (currently Clifton Taylor, John McKernon and Jason Kantrowitz) to work with him as he designs projects around the country. Recent designs include many projects for major opera companies, industrial promotions, interiors, and extravaganzas.

Lighting Designs:
1973: *Chemin De Fer*; *Holiday*; *Visit, The*
1974: *Bad Habits*; *Love for Love*; *Rules of the Game, The* 1975: *Member of the Wedding, The*; *Rogers and Hart*; *Skin of Our Teeth, The*; *Sweet Bird of Youth* 1976: *Checking Out*; *Fiddler on the Roof* 1977: *Knickerbocker Holiday*; *She Loves Me*; *Side By Side By Sondheim*; *Some of My Best Friends* 1978: *Do You Turn Somersaults*; *On the Twentieth Century*; *Working* 1979: *Madwoman of Central Park West, The*; *Magnificent Christmas Spectacular, The*; *Snow White and the Seven Dwarfs*; *Sweeney Todd* 1980: *Happy New Year*; *It's Spring*; *Magnificent Christmas Spectacular, The*; *Perfectly Frank*; *Rockette Spectacular with Ginger Rogers, A* 1981: *America*; *Copperfield*; *Fiddler on the Roof*; *Foxfire*; *My Fair Lady*; *Talent for Murder, A*; *Wally's Cafe* 1982: *Blues in the Night*; *Doll's Life, A* 1984: *End of the World*; *Play Memory*; *Shirley Maclaine on Broadway*; *Three Musketeers, The* 1985: *Grind*; *Home Front* 1986: *Jerome Kern Goes to Hollywood*; *Little Like Magic, A* 1987: *Late Nite Comic*; *Roza*; *Stardust*; *Sweet Sue* 1988: *Christmas Spectacular, The* 1989: *Meet Me in Saint Louis*; *Tru* 1990: *Lettice & Lovage*

Paul Bismarck

Paul Bismarck designed lighting for two productions on Broadway in the late teens. He was an electrician, residing at 328 West 44th Street in New York City in 1932.

Lighting Designs:
1917: *Chu Chin Chow* 1919: *Aphrodite*

Jack Blackman

Jack Blackman studied at Columbia University and with Lester Polakov at the Studio and Forum of Stage Design. Mr. Blackman is known as a set and lighting designer who works in theatre,

film and television, especially for ABC-TV. He designed the off-Broadway theatre Stage 73 and was art director for the 1985 film *The Ultimate Solution of Grace Quigley*.

Lighting Designs:
1965: *Postmark Zero*

Scenic Designs:
1964: *Sign in Sidney Brustein's Window, The*
1965: *Postmark Zero*

Costume Designs:
1965: *Postmark Zero*

John E. Blankenchip

John E. Blankenchip was born in Independence, Kansas on November 14, 1919. He received a B.F.A. in Scene Design and Directing from the Carnegie Institute of Technology in 1941, where he studied with Lloyd Weninger and Bess Schraeder Kimberly. In 1943 he received an M.F.A. from Yale University after studying with Donald Oenslager, Frank Bevan, George Eisenhower and Stanley McCandless. Mr. Blankenchip worked as assistant designer under Harry Horner for shows including *Winged Victory*. He designs all elements of a production when possible, and in his debut on Broadway created sets, lights and costumes. Mr. Blankenchip, who teaches design and directing at the University of Southern California, continues to design occasionally, including sets, costumes and lights for a recent production of *Pal Joey* in La Jolla.

Lighting Designs:
1951: *Angel in the Pawnshop*

Scenic Designs:
1951: *Angel in the Pawnshop* 1952: *Long Watch, The*

Costume Designs:
1951: *Angel in the Pawnshop* 1952: *Long Watch, The*

Norman Blumenfield

Norman Blumenfield designed lights for a play in 1957 on Broadway.

Lighting Designs:
1957: *Simply Heavenly*

Mel Bourne

Mel Bourne was born on November 22, 1923 and was reared in Chicago. After studying electrical engineering at Purdue University and subsequently at LeHigh University he turned his attention to design. He studied with Frank Bevan at the Yale University School of Drama and worked as an assistant to Robert Edmond Jones for four years. He made his New York debut with the Theatre Guild's production of *Seagulls over Sorento*. Mr. Bourne currently spends most of his time designing films. His credits as art director include *Rude Awakening, Manahttan, Annie Hall, Still of the Night, Fatal Attraction* and *Reversal of Fortune*, among many others. His designs have been regularly honored with Academy Award nominations for Art Direction. Mel Bourne also designs commercials and television productions.

Lighting Designs:
1952: *Seagulls Over Sorrento*

Scenic Designs:
1952: *Male Animal, The; Seagulls Over Sorrento* 1953: *End As a Man*

Costume Designs:
1953: *End As a Man*

John Boyt

John Boyt has designed sets, costumes and/or lights for numerous productions in New York since 1946. Besides his designs for the theatre, he has created costumes and scenery for ballets, operas, and television. He designed the world premier of Aaron Copeland's *The Tender Land* and many other productions at the New York City Center. John Boyt was born in Newark, New Jersey on April 19, 1921 and was graduated from the University of Iowa in 1942. He also attended Northwestern University and studied at the Mohawk Drama Festival in Schenectady, New York.

Lighting Designs:
1956: *Debut*

Scenic Designs:
1946: *Playboy of the Western World, The* 1956: *Debut*

Costume Designs:
1946: *Flag Is Born, A; Playboy of the Western World, The; Years Ago* 1947: *Anthony and*

Cleopatra 1955: *Wooden Dish, The* 1956: *Debut; Lovers, The*

Bob Brannigan

Bob Brannigan designed lighting for one production in 1962 on Broadway.

Lighting Designs:
1962: *Egg, The*

Eugene Braun

Eugene Braun was a lighting designer active from 1918 to 1949. He was born in Tisza-Ujlak, Hungary and studied electricity in a Budapest technical school prior to emigrating to New York City at age sixteen. At the time of his death on April 9, 1965 at age 77 he was head electrician at Radio City Music Hall, where he had been a member of the electrics staff from the time of its opening in 1932. Earlier he was an electrician for New York Calcium Company, on the electrical staff of Lew Fields' Theatre, and had also worked an assistant electrician at the Winter Garden and Roxy Theatres. The 1918 playbill for *Oh, Land! Lady!* credits him as a member of the Princess Theatre Studios.

Lighting Designs:
1918: *Oh, Lady! Lady!; Oh, My Dear* 1942: *Stars on Ice* 1944: *Hats Off to Ice* 1946: *Icetime* 1947: *Icetime of 1948* 1948: *Howdy, Mr Ice* 1949: *Howdy Mr. Ice of 1950*

Andrew Bridge

Andrew Bridge was born on July 21, 1952 in England, the son of Peter Bridge, a theatrical producer, and his wife Roslyn. He studied at Port Regis and Bryanston Schools, as well as the London Academy of Music and Drama, and has been influenced by Richard Pilbrow. He has won Tony, Drama Desk and Outer Cricle Critics Awards for *The Phantom of the Opera*, and a Lighting Industry Federation Award for architectural lighting for the Lloyd's of London Headquarters. His designs include the *Siegfried and Roy* spectacular in Las Vegas and *Shirley Bassey in Concert*. West End credits include *Time, Billy Bishop Goes to War, Canterbury Tales, The Boyfriend*, and *Little Me*. In London he is also a consultant for commerical presentations, industrial promotions, and architectural projects through a design company, "Imagination". He lives in London with wife, Susan and son, Oliver.

Lighting Designs:
1984: *Oliver!* **1988:** *Phantom of the Opera, The* **1990:** *Aspects of Love*

Herbert Brodkin

Herbert Brodkin, who died at age 77 on October 31, 1990, received an M.F.A. from Yale University in 1940. He was born on November 9, 1921 in New York City and studied at the University of Michigan, receiving a B.A. there in 1934. He designed scenery and lights for theatre and Hollywood studios prior to beginning in television, initially as a set designer but primarily as a producer in a career lasting some forty years. He was responsible for *The Defenders* as well as shows for *Playhouse '90, The Elgin Hour*, and *Studio One*. With Robert Berger he formed Titus Productions in the 1960s and continued producing provocative productions, including *Skokie, Mandela, Sakarov* and *Pueblo* until dissolving the company in 1989. A retrospective show in 1985 at the Museum of Broadcasting featured productions from his television career.

Lighting Designs:
1947: *Volpone* **1948:** *Silver Whistle, The*
Scenic Designs:
1947: *Caribbean Carnival; This Time Tomorrow* **1948:** *Silver Whistle, The*

Jack Brown

Jack Brown is a lighting and scenic designer who has designed for the Opera Society of Washington and Boston Arts. Off-Broadway credits include *Stephen D, Dylan* and *Slow Dance on the Killing Ground*. After graduating from Carnegie Tech with a major in acting, he operated the White Barn Theatre near Pittsburgh in 1963. For the Broadway production of *Invitation to a March* he served as assistant to William Pitkin.

Lighting Designs:
1963: *Natural Affection* **1964:** *Beeckman Place; Ben Franklin in Paris; Dylan; Slow Dance on the Killing Ground*

Scenic Designs:
1972: *Heathen!*

Patrika Brown

Patrika Brown designed lights for one play on Broadway in 1975. With dancer Karin Dwyer she opened The Erotic Baker at 73 West 83rd Street in New York City. They have also published *The Erotic Baker Cookbook*.

Lighting Designs:
1975: *Boccaccio*

Catherine Browne

Catherine Browne designed sets, lights and costumes for a 1966 production which originated in London's West End and subsequently moved to Broadway.

Lighting Designs:
1966: *Killing of Sister George, The*
Scenic Designs:
1966: *Killing of Sister George, The*
Costume Designs:
1966: *Killing of Sister George, The*

Fred Buchholz

Fred Buchholz was born on September 27, 1954 in Arlington, Virginia and studied at SUNY-Purchase. He served on the staff at the Arena Stage in Washington, D.C. and the New York Shakespeare Festival, and includes Jennifer Tipton and Bill Mintzer as influences on his career. His New York debut came with *Frimbo* at the Grand Central Terminal. He has designed many productions off-Broadway and has created special effects for dance and theatre companies. Productions include: *Mary Stuart* for the Dodger Theatre's first production at New York Shakespeare Festival, *How It All Began* and *Maybe I'm Doing It Wrong*.

Lighting Designs:
1982: *Pump Boys and Dinettes*

John Burlingame

John Burlingame created one Broadway lighting design in 1972.

Lighting Designs:
1972: *Via Galactica*

Lloyd Burlingame

Lloyd Burlingame has been production designer for plays both on and off-Broadway since he debuted in New York City with the opening of *Leave it to Jane*. Born in Washington, D.C. on December 31, 1934, the son of Harry and Estelle Burlingame, he had an early introduction to the arts by his uncle, Lloyd Embry, a portrait painter. After study at Carnegie-Mellon he spent a year at La Scala in Milan on a Fulbright Scholarship initiating his study of opera, which has remained of particular interest. Mr. Burlingame prefers to have responsibility for all of the design elements for a production, after the example set by Robert Edmond Jones, and has had that responsibility with all of his Broadway credits. Mr. Burlingame, in addition to actively designing, is a Master Teacher of Design and Chair of the Department of Design at New York University. In 1985 a retrospective show of his scenic designs and touchable art was held in New York City, and a one-man show of recent work, "Once More with Feeling," was held at the Wadsworth Atheneum in Hartford, Connecticut in 1988.

Lighting Designs:

1963: *Lady of the Camellias, The* 1965: *Boeing-Boeing*; *Inadmissable Evidence*; *Right Honorable Gentleman, The* 1966: *First One Asleep, Whistle*; *Help Stamp Out Marriage*; *Loves of Cass Mc Guire, The*; *Philadelphia, Here I Come* 1967: *Brief Lives*; *There's a Girl in My Soup* 1968: *Day in the Death of Joe Egg, A*; *Flip Side, The*; *Rockefeller and the Red Indians*; *Woman Is My Idea* 1969: *Hadrian VII*; *Love Is a Time of Day* 1970: *Not Now, Darling* 1971: *Midsummer Night's Dream, A*; *Philanthropist, The* 1972: *Vivat! Vivat Regina!*

Scenic Designs:

1964: *Alfie* 1966: *First One Asleep, Whistle*; *Loves of Cass Mc Guire, The*; *Philadelphia, Here I Come* 1967: *Astrakhan Coat, The*; *Keep It in the Family* 1968: *Woman Is My Idea* 1969: *Love Is a Time of Day* 1970: *Not Now, Darling*

Costume Designs:

1964: *Alfie* 1966: *Philadelphia, Here I Come* 1967: *Astrakhan Coat, The* 1968: *Woman Is My Idea* 1969: *Love Is a Time of Day* 1970: *Not Now, Darling*

John Bury

John Bury was born in Aberystwyth, Wales on January 27, 1925. Originally an actor, he progressed to design work through various technical positions. His career began in 1946 at Joan Littlewood's Theatre Workshop and designed for many productions between 1954 and 1964. His first designs for the Royal Shakespeare Company in Stratford-upon-Avon were sets and costumes for *Julius Caesar* in 1963, and from 1964 until 1968 he was head of design for the RSC. Mr. Bury was appointed Head of Design at the National Theatre of Great Britain in 1973. Mr. Bury's work was first seen in New York City in 1974 when he designed the sets and lights for *Oh, What a Lovely War*. Mr. Bury has also designed for films and opera and consulted on the design of theatres. In 1975 he received a Gold Medal for design in Prague which was followed by a Golden Troika in Prague, in 1979. He was elected a fellow of the Royal Society of the Arts in England in 1968 and also has been honored with the Order of the British Empire (O.B.E.). *Amadeus* brought Mr. Bury a Tony nomination for outstanding costume design, and a Tony Award for the set in 1981.

Lighting Designs:

1964: *Oh What a Lovely War*; *Physicists, The* 1967: *Homecoming, The* 1971: *Old Times* 1976: *No Man's Land* 1980: *Betrayal* 1986: *Petition, The*

Scenic Designs:

1964: *Oh What a Lovely War*; *Physicists, The* 1967: *Homecoming, The* 1970: *Rothschilds, The* 1971: *Old Times* 1972: *Via Galactica* 1976: *No Man's Land* 1980: *Amadeus*; *Betrayal* 1986: *Petition, The*

Costume Designs:

1964: *Physicists, The* 1967: *Homecoming, The* 1970: *Rothschilds, The* 1972: *Via Galactica* 1976: *No Man's Land* 1980: *Amadeus*; *Betrayal* 1986: *Petition, The*

Ian Calderon

Ian Calderon was born on July 20, 1948. He received a Bachelor of Arts from Hunter College in 1970 and an Master of Fine Arts from the Yale University School of Drama in 1973 after studying with Donald Oenslager and Ming Cho Lee. He began designing lights while in high school and has continued designing lights ever since. In addition to his designs on the Broadway stage he has numerous credits off-Broadway, in regional theatres, and for rock concerts. He is also a production supervisor, producer and lighting consultant. Two Tony nominations have been awarded to Ian Calderon, for *That Championship Season* in 1973 and *Trelawney of the "Wells"* in 1976.

Lighting Designs:
1972: *Sticks and Bones*; *That Championship Season* **1975:** *Lieutenant, The* **1976:** *Trelawney of the "Wells"* **1978:** *Cheaters*; *Effect of Gamma Rays on Man-in-the-Moon Marigolds, The*; *Paul Robeson*; *Timbuktu* **1983:** *Breakfast with Les and Bess*

Patton Campbell

Born in Omaha, Nebraska on September 10, 1926, Patton Campbell received both a B.A. and an M.F.A. at Yale. His career has been principally as a costume designer, but he began as a scenic, lighting and costume designer in various summer stock theatres and as an assistant to Rouben Ter-Arutunian. He has designed for many companies, including the New York City Opera, the Santa Fe Opera and the Opera Company of Boston. He has also designed national tours and productions at the New York City Center. His list of extensive costume and scenery credits includes many operas, both world premieres and works from the standard repertory. His designs for opera have also been broadcast on television, principally by WNET. Mr. Campbell was nominated for a Tony Award in 1977 for *Man of La Mancha*, which he designed with Howard Bay. In addition to his design activity Mr. Campbell is an educator, having taught at Barnard College, Juilliard, Columbia University, and the State University of New York at Purchase.

Lighting Designs:
1955: *Grand Prize, The*

Scenic Designs:
1955: *Grand Prize, The*

Costume Designs:
1955: *All in One, Trouble in Tahiti*; *Twenty Seven Wagons Full of Cotton* **1956:** *Fallen Angels* **1957:** *Hole in the Head, A*; *Makropoulos Secret, The* **1958:** *Howie* **1960:** *There Was*

a Little Girl **1961:** *All American*; *Conquering Hero, The* **1965:** *Glass Menagerie, The* **1966:** *Agatha Sue, I Love You* **1967:** *Come Live with Me*; *Natural Look, The* **1968:** *Loot* **1977:** *Man of La Mancha*

Daniel J. Carey

Daniel J. Carey (a.k.a. D. J. Carey) was staff electrician for Equity Players, Inc. in the 1920s. In the mid-1920s he also designed lights for two productions on Broadway. *Cole's New York City Directory* lists him as an electrician as early as 1915, when he resided at 272 West 154th Street. In 1932 he remained employed as an electrician and lived with his wife Odette at 69 Tiemann Place in New York City.

Lighting Designs:
1925: *Brother Elks*; *Candida*

Frank Carrington

Frank Carrington was an actor who appeared on stage and screen. He contributed the lighting designs to one production on Broadway in the mid-1920s. He is best remembered however, as the co-founder, producer and director of the Paper Mill Playhouse in Millburn, New Jersey which he founded in 1938 with Antoinette Scudder. In 1972 the Paper Mill Playhouse was named the State Theater of New Jersey. Mr. Carrington died on July 3, 1975 at age 73.

Lighting Designs:
1925: *Wild Birds*

Don Casey

Don Casey was lighting designer for a Broadway play in the early 1920s. In 1919 he maintained an office at 1493 Broadway in New York City.

Lighting Designs:
1923: *Lullaby, The*

Richard Casler

The lighting designer Richard Casler has worked as an assistant for many outstanding American designers including Jo Mielziner, Rouben Ter-Arutunian, William and Jean Eckart, Donald Oenslager, Boris Aronson and George Jenkins. He received his undergraduate education at

Stanford University and an M.F.A. from Yale in 1958. Some of his many off-Broadway designs are *The Saving Grace* and *Thistle in my Bed*. He also designed and installed a "Baroque Christmas Creche" at the White House for its permanent collection.

Lighting Designs:
1965: *Anya* **1969:** *Red White and Maddox*

Stewart Chaney

Stewart Chaney designed sets, sometimes costumes, and occasionally lights on Broadway. He was born in Kansas City, Missouri, and studied at Yale with George Pierce Baker and also in Paris with André L'Hote. He began his career as a scene designer in summer stock and made his Broadway debut with the opening of *The Old Maid* in 1935. For the following thirty years his designs for scenery, costumes and lights were seen regularly in plays, operas and ballets. During the 1940s Mr. Chaney designed two films, *Up in Arms* and *The Kid From Brooklyn*. He also worked in television during its early years. Mr. Chaney died on November 9, 1969 at the age of 59. His designs are included in the collections of the Smithsonian Institution in Washington, D.C.

Lighting Designs:
1944: *Down to Miami* **1946:** *Obsession* **1947:** *Bathsheba; Druid Circle, The; Inspector Calls, An* **1948:** *Doctor Social* **1949:** *I Know My Love* **1950:** *Design for a Stained Glass Window* **1951:** *King of Friday's Men, The; Lo and Behold!; Moon Is Blue, The* **1953:** *Late Love; Sherlock Holmes* **1957:** *Hidden River, The* **1960:** *Forty-ninth Cousin, The*

Scenic Designs:
1934: *Bride of Torozko, The; Dream Child; Kill That Story* **1935:** *Ghosts; Old Maid, The; On to Fortune; Parnell; Times Have Changed* **1936:** *Aged 26; Hamlet; Hedda Gabler; New Faces of 1936; O Evening Star; Parnell; Spring Dance* **1937:** *But for the Grace of God; Having Wonderful Time* **1938:** *Wuthering Heights* **1939:** *Life with Father* **1940:** *International Incident, An; Suzanna and the Elders; Twelfth Night* **1941:** *Blithe Spirit; More the Merrier, The; Sunny River* **1942:** *Lady Comes Across, The; Morning Star* **1943:** *Blythe Spirit; Dark Eyes; Innocent Voyage, The; Three's a Family; Voice of the Turtle, The; World's Full*

of Girls, The **1944:** *Down to Miami; Dream with Music; Duke in Darkness, The; Embezzled Heaven; House in Paris, The; Jacobowsky and the Colonel; Laffing Room Only; Late George Apley, The; Pretty Little Parlor; Public Relations; Trio* **1945:** *Dunnigan's Daughter; Many Happy Returns; Mr. Strauss Goes to Boston; One Man Show; Signature* **1946:** *Joy Forever, A; Obsession; Winter's Tale, The* **1947:** *Bathsheba; Craig's Wife; Druid Circle, The; Inspector Calls, An; Laura* **1948:** *Doctor Social; Life with Mother; Red Gloves; You Never Can Tell* **1949:** *I Know My Love; Ivy Green, The; My Name Is Aquilon* **1950:** *Design for a Stained Glass Window; Great to Be Alive* **1951:** *King of Friday's Men, The; Lo and Behold!; Moon Is Blue, The; Seventeen* **1952:** *Much Ado About Nothing* **1953:** *Girl Can Tell, A; Late Love; Sherlock Holmes* **1957:** *Hidden River, The* **1960:** *Forty-ninth Cousin, The* **1964:** *Severed Head, A*

Costume Designs:
1935: *Ghosts; Old Maid, The; Parnell* **1936:** *Aged 26; Hamlet; Hedda Gabler; New Faces of 1936; Parnell* **1938:** *Wuthering Heights* **1939:** *Life with Father* **1940:** *Twelfth Night* **1942:** *Lady Comes Across, The* **1944:** *Duke in Darkness, The; Embezzled Heaven; Jackpot; Late George Apley, The* **1945:** *Dunnigan's Daughter* **1946:** *Joy Forever, A; Winter's Tale, The* **1947:** *Bathsheba; Inspector Calls, An* **1948:** *Doctor Social; You Never Can Tell* **1949:** *I Know My Love; Ivy Green, The* **1950:** *Design for a Stained Glass Window; Great to Be Alive* **1951:** *King of Friday's Men, The; Lo and Behold!* **1952:** *Much Ado About Nothing* **1953:** *Sherlock Holmes* **1964:** *Severed Head, A*

Nick Chelton

Nick Chelton was born in the Paddington area of London on June 18, 1946 and learned lighting design through training at Theatre Projects, where he served as lighting designer from 1971 to 1975. *Hamlet*, starring Alan Bates, was his London debut in 1971. His designs are often seen throughout England in plays and operas. He has designed lighting for the Greenwich and Royal Court Theatres, the Royal Shakespeare Company and in the West End. His designs for opera have been seen at the Kent Opera among others.

Lighting Designs:
1989: *Shirley Valentine*

Dawn Chiang

The daughter of Franklin Chiang and Julienne Lay Chiang, Dawn Chiang was born in Palo Alto, California, on July 19, 1953. She received a Bachelor of Arts at Oberlin College in 1975 and honed her talents as a lighting designer by assisting H. R. Poindexter, Tharon Musser and John Gleason and by working at theatres on the West Coast, including the Mark Taper Forum, the Ahmanson Theatre and South Coast Repertory. In both 1978 and 1980 she received Drama Logue Critics Awards for lighting design at South Coast Repertory. In New York her design for *A Man for All Seasons* in 1987 at the Roundabout Theater was nominated for an American Theatre Wing Award. In addition to her other responsibilities she is resident lighting designer for the New York City Opera, State Theatre, Lincoln Center in New York City.

Lighting Designs:
1979: *Zoot Suit*

Chipmonck

E.H. Beresford Monck uses "Chipmonck" as his professional name. Additional credits for this California-based designer include designs for Delores Del Lago. He received a nomination for a Tony Award for the lighting design of *The Rocky Horror Show*.

Lighting Designs:
1975: *Rocky Horror Show, The*

Peggy Clark

As with many designers, Peggy Clark's initial exposure to the theatre was as a performer. She gave up acting, however, and became a major force in the establishment of theatrical lighting design as an independent profession. Born in Baltimore, she graduated from Smith College and in 1938 received an M.F.A. at Yale University, where she was introduced to all areas of design. Only three months after graduation Peggy Clark made her debut on Broadway, designing the costumes for *The Girl From Wyoming*. Although she continued to design costumes for a time, she also served in various technical positions and designed scenery while developing an expertise in stage lighting. During her career she has lit over one hundred productions on Broadway. Teaching has also been part of her life: at her alma mater, Smith College; at Yale; and at Lester Polakov's Studio and Forum of Stage Design. In 1968 Peggy Clark became the first woman elected President of United Scenic Artists Local 829. She was named a fellow of the United States Institute for Theatre Technology in 1978. Married to Lloyd R. Kelley from 1960 until his death in 1972, she is also known as Peggy Clark Kelley.

Lighting Designs:
1926: *Gentlemen Prefer Blondes* **1946:** *Beggar's Holliday* **1947:** *Brigadoon; High Button Shoes; Medea; Topaz* **1948:** *Love Life; Rape of Lucretia, The* **1949:** *Along Fifth Avenue; Gentlemen Prefer Blondes; Touch and Go* **1950:** *All You Need Is One Good Break; Bless You All* **1951:** *High Ground, The* **1952:** *Of Thee I Sing; Pal Joey* **1953:** *In the Summer House; Kismet; Maggie; Trip to Bountiful, The; Wonderful Town* **1954:** *On Your Toes; Peter Pan* **1955:** *No Time for Sergeants; Plain and Fancy; Righteous Are Bold, The; Will Success Spoil Rock Hunter?* **1956:** *Auntie Mame; Bells Are Ringing; Mr. Wonderful; New Faces of '56* **1957:** *Eugenia; Nude with Violin; Potting Shed, The* **1958:** *Flower Drum Song; Present Laughter; Say, Darling* **1959:** *Billy Barnes Revue; Cheri; Goodbye Charlie; Juno* **1960:** *Bye, Bye, Birdie; Distant Bell, A; Under the Yum-Yum Tree; Unsinkable Molly Brown, The* **1961:** *Mary, Mary; Sail Away; Show Girl* **1962:** *Romulus* **1963:** *Girl Who Came to Supper, The* **1964:** *Bajour; Poor Richard* **1966:** *Best Laid Plans, The* **1968:** *Darling of the Day* **1969:** *Jimmy; Last of the Red Hot Lovers* **1971:** *How the Other Half Loves* **1980:** *Musical Chairs*

Scenic Designs:
1941: *Gabrielle* **1951:** *High Ground, The*

Costume Designs:
1942: *Great Big Doorstop, The; Uncle Harry* **1944:** *Ramshackle Inn* **1945:** *Dark of the Moon; Devil's Galore* **1951:** *High Ground, The*

Norman Coates

The lighting designer named Norman Coates (as distinguished from the British designer of sets and costumes with the same name) was born in Norristown, Pennsylvania on January 25, 1952 and received his B.A. at Temple University. He began designing at Temple with a production of *Pale Horse, Pale Rider*. Since then he has designed lights for dance, regional theatres and off-Broadway. His lighting designs for *Limbo Tales* were honored with a Villager Award. During the 1990-91 academic year he was in residence at the North Carolina School of the Arts in Winston-Salem. He is resident lighting designer for the North Carolina Theatre in Raleigh, North Carolina, where he has designed twenty-four musicals over four seasons.

Lighting Designs:
1985: *News, The* 1989: *Prince of Central Park*

Steve Cochrane

Steve Cochrane served as lighting design consultant to a Broadway production in the late 1980s.

Lighting Designs:
1987: *Oba Oba*

S.A. Cohen

S.A. Cohen was a lighting designer on Broadway in 1979.

Lighting Designs:
1979: *Got Tu Go Disco*

Pat Collins

Pat Collins has been designing lights on Broadway regularly since her debut in 1977. Credits off-Broadway include *How I Got that Story* and *A Life in the Theatre*. Her designs have been honored with a Tony Award for *I'm Not Rappaport* in 1985, a Drama Desk Award for *Execution of Justice* in 1986, a Los Angeles Drama Critics Award for *The Dybbuck*, and a Marharam Award for *A Life in the Theatre*. After studying at Brown University and the Yale University School of Drama, she has worked extensively in opera as well as theatre. Credits in regional theatres include *The Illusion* at Hartford Stage, where she frequently collaborates with artistic director Mark Lamos and scenic designer John Conklin.

Lighting Designs:
1977: *Threepenny Opera, The* 1978: *Ain't Misbehavin'*; *King of Hearts*; *Stages* 1980: *Bacchae, The*; *Charlotte* 1981: *Floating Light Bulb, The* 1982: *Steaming* 1983: *Baby*; *Moose Murders* 1985: *Boys of Winter, The*; *I'm Not Rappaport* 1986: *Arsenic and Old Lace*; *Execution of Justice,* 1987: *Death and the King's Horseman*; *Sherlock's Last Case* 1988: *Ain't Misbehavin'* 1989: *Heidi Chronicles, The*

William Conway

William Conway died at age 36 on February 10, 1950 in London where he was general manager of a theatrical production company, H. M. Tennent, Ltd. From 1930 to 1939 he was theatre correspondent for *The London Daily Mail*, a position he left to become business manager and director for John Gielgud. In 1947 he directed and designed lights for two productions on Broadway in which John Gielgud appeared.

Lighting Designs:
1947: *Importance of Being Earnest, The*; *Love for Love*

John Marshall Coombs

John Marshall Coombs designed the sets and lights for a production on Broadway in 1930.

Lighting Designs:
1931: *No More Frontier*

Scenic Designs:
1931: *No More Frontier*

Pamela Cooper

The daughter of the prominent Hollywood agent Frank Cooper, Pamela Cooper literally grew up in the theatre. She was born in Los Angeles, California on March 25, 1952 and received a Bachelor of Arts from Ithaca College. After receiving her Master of Fine Arts in 1976 at the University of California at Los Angeles, she worked as an assistant lighting designer at the Mark Taper Forum. She acknowledges Gordon Davidson (who gave her a start in the business) as a mentor along with Jean Rosenthal and Tharon Musser. With extensive experience designing for rock concerts and pop artists, she also has numerous credits in Las

Vegas and Atlantic City, for dance companies, and for regional theatres including the Denver Theatre Center. Her Broadway debut was directed and choreographed by Michael Peters, a frequent collaborator. She also designed lights for dances which Michael Peters recently choreographed for the Royal Winnipeg Ballet and the National Ballet of Canada. While continuing to design occasionally, she is currently a personal manager for performers including Ben Vereen, writers and choreographers.

Lighting Designs:
1985: *Leader of the Pack*

Theodore Cooper

Theodore Cooper has created sets and lights for two productions on Broadway.

Lighting Designs:
1949: *Texas, Li'l Darlin'* **1950:** *Story for Sunday Evening, A*

Scenic Designs:
1949: *Texas, Li'l Darlin'* **1950:** *Story for Sunday Evening, A*

Sol Cornberg

Sol Cornberg began an apprenticeship at the Cleveland Play House in 1926 while in high school and became technical director of the theatre in 1930. While retaining this position in Ohio he was also a theatre consultant, lighting consultant and technical director for other theatres. He also served as technical advisor for the Federal Theatre in Ohio, Michigan and Kentucky and taught at Case Western Reserve University. Sol Cornberg published *A Stage Crew Handbook* (in collaboration with Emanuel L. Gebauer) in the late 1930s and became Director of Studio and Play Planning for the National Broadcasting Company in New York City in the early 1940s. After serving in World War II he returned to his career in television production. In 1954 Sol Cornberg revised *Television Techniques*, originally published by Hoyland Bettinger in 1947.

Lighting Designs:
1933: *Growing Pains*

Peter Cotes

Peter Cotes, an actor, director and occasional designer of sets and lights, was born Sydney Boulting in Maidenhead, England on March 12, 1912. He appeared on stage for the first time when he was four years old, as a page in *Henry V*. His credits as a director of plays in England are lengthy, and in addition he has directed *A Pin to See the Peepshow* and *Hidden Stranger* in New York. Television and films have also been within his domain, and he has adapted many of the works he has directed.

Lighting Designs:
1963: *Hidden Stranger*

Scenic Designs:
1963: *Hidden Stranger*

Larry Crimmins

As resident lighting designer at Hartford Stage in Connecticut, Larry Crimmins designed numerous plays in the early 1970s. His work was seen on the Broadway stage, beginning in 1974.

Lighting Designs:
1974: *My Sister, My Sister* **1977:** *Gemini*

Audrey Cruddas

Audrey Cruddas designed sets and costumes on Broadway for several plays by Shakespeare staged in the mid-1950s. She was born in Johannesburg, South Africa on November 16, 1914 and studied at the St. John's Wood School of Art. Her first professional designs were the sets for *The White Devil* in 1948. Shortly after the opening of that production she was invited to design *King John* for the Royal Shakespeare Festival in Stratford-upon-Avon, which led in turn to numerous additional credits. Audrey Cruddas usually designs both sets and costumes for productions, as she has done for each of her shows on Broadway. She also occasionally designs lights. Her designs for the opera, ballet and theatre have been seen around the world. She received the Donaldson Award for *Caesar and Cleopatra* in the 1951-52 season.

Lighting Designs:
1958: *Hamlet; Henry V*

Scenic Designs:
1956: *Macbeth* **1958:** *Hamlet; Henry V*

Costume Designs:
1951: *Antony and Cleopatra; Caesar and Cleopatra* **1956:** *Macbeth* **1958:** *Hamlet; Henry V*

F. Mitchell Dana

Lighting designer F. Mitchell Dana was born Frank Livingston Mitchell, II on November 14, 1942. He was educated at Utah State University where he received a B.F.A. in 1964 and the Yale School of Drama where he received an M.F.A. in 1967. His credits in regional theatre in the United States read like a who's who of regional theatres, including fifty productions at A.C.T. between 1972 and 1980, the 1972 Stratford (Ontario) Festival and productions at the Goodman Theatre among many, many others. Off-Broadway he has designed at the Manhattan Theatre Club and the Brooklyn Academy of Music. In addition he has designed lights for television and industrials and has lectured on lighting design at many universities. Recent credits include *The Kingfish* in the 1990-91 Broadway season.

Lighting Designs:
1970: *Charley's Aunt* **1974:** *Freedom of the City, The* **1978:** *Inspector General, The; Man and Superman; Once in a Lifetime* **1980:** *Suicide, The* **1981:** *Mass Appeal* **1982:** *Monday After the Miracle* **1984:** *Babe, The* **1986:** *Oh Coward!*

Jack Daniels

Jack Daniels was the lighting designer for a play on Broadway in 1944.

Lighting Designs:
1944: *Dark Hammock*

Robert Darling

Robert Darling is from Oakland, California where he was born on October 1, 1937. He received a B.A. from San Francisco State University and in 1973 an M.F.A. from the Yale School of Drama. He worked as an assistant to Will Steven Armstrong and Ming Cho Lee, and studied with and was influenced by Robert Edmond Jones, Donald Oenslager and the opera producer Kurt Herbert Adler. His New York debut

occurred with the opening of *Another Evening with Harry Stoones* in 1962. He also has extensive credits lighting ballet, opera and musical theatre for companies such as the San Francisco, New York City, Houston and Santa Fe Operas. He has served as producer and artistic director for the Central City Opera House.

Lighting Designs:
1964: *Cambridge Circus*

Michael Davidson

Throughout the 1960s Michael C. Davidson was an active lighting designer. In addition to designing a production on Broadway in 1969, he lit off-Broadway productions such as *Adaptation-Next, Get Thee to Canterbury* and *3 from Column A*. He designed lights for the Berkshire Theatre Festival in 1967 and 1968. As a technical and lighting consultant, he also lit displays, industrial promotions, residences, building interiors, and sculptures.

Lighting Designs:
1969: *No Place to Be Somebody*
Scenic Designs:
1969: *No Place to Be Somebody*

Charles Davis

Mr. Charles Davis created lights for a Broadway production in 1921.

Lighting Designs:
1921: *In the Night Watch*

Jeff Davis

Born on April 14, 1950 in Philadelphia, Jeff Davis received a Bachelor of Arts in 1972 from Northwestern University. He worked as an associate designer to Jo Mielziner and as an assistant to Tharon Musser, both of whom he credits with influencing his career (along with Delbort Unruh). In 1975 he designed *Ride the Winds*, his New York debut. With extensive credits in regional theatres, national tours, industrial shows and television, Jeff Davis is principally a lighting designer but he also occasionally designs settings.

Lighting Designs:
1980: *Man Who Came to Dinner, The* **1983:** *Man Who Had Three Arms, The* **1987:** *Musical Comedy Murders, The* **1989:** *Born Yesterday* **1990:** *Change in the Heir*

Joe Davis

A British lighting designer, Joe Davis was born in London on December 19, 1912. He became associated with H.M. Tennent, Ltd. when the production company was formed in 1936, and as their lighting designer created lighting effects for over five hundred productions during a career lasting fifty years. Earlier he had worked for Strand Electric (beginning in 1926), and as production electrician for Charles B. Cochran and Julian Wylie. As lighting designer for Marlene Dietrich for twenty-two years he worked in the United States, Vienna and Moscow. A founding member of the Society of British Theatre Lighting Designers, he also served that organization as President and Life President. He died at age 72 on July 5, 1984.

Lighting Designs:
1960: *Irma La Douce*

John Davis

John William Davis worked for the Shubert Organization and Sidney Kingsley as head of light crews. He won a Tony Award in the "Stage Technician Category" for *Picnic* in 1954. John Davis was probably responsible for the lighting design for many more productions than those for which he received credit, because he worked at a time when lighting designers were regarded primarily as electricians. At the time of his death on May 27, 1950 in Westport, Connecticut, he was an electrician for NBC-TV.

Lighting Designs:
1945: *Wind is Ninety, The* 1954: *Burning Glass, The*

S.J. Dawkins

Steven J. Dawkins designed lighting for a 1916 Broadway production. An electrician, he resided at 408 West 19th Street, New York City.

Lighting Designs:
1916: *Six Who Passed While the Lentils Boiled; Trimplet, The*

John Michael Deegan

Born on June 12, 1951 in Ridgeway, Pennsylvania, John Michael Deegan earned a B.F.A. at Carnegie Mellon University. He credits his experience working with Helen Pond and Herbert Senn with his success as a lighting designer. He began designing while in high school, where he first created sets for *You Can't Take It with You*. His designs have been seen in productions by many organizations, including the Cape Playhouse, The Acting Company, Houston Ballet, and the opera companies of Boston, Atlanta, Columbus and Portland among others. He is married to Sarah G. Conley, a costume designer and scene painter with whom he often collaborates, especially on operas. He is also lighting designer for *Shadowlands*, which opened on Broadway in December 1990.

Lighting Designs:
1989: *Circle, The*

William DeForest

William DeForest was responsible for the design of the sets, lights and costumes for a play in 1948, and sets for an additional production in 1949.

Lighting Designs:
1948: *Rats of Norway, The*

Scenic Designs:
1948: *Rats of Norway, The* 1949: *Diamond Lil*

Costume Designs:
1948: *Rats of Norway, The*

Edward Demmler

Edward Demmler designed lights for a Broadway production in 1922. He later worked at Radio City Music Hall where he was responsible for the hydraulics.

Lighting Designs:
1922: *Better Times*

Paul de Pass

Born in New York City on May 22, 1950, Paul de Pass began designing at age sixteen. He studied at the High School of Music and Art, Cooper Union, and Sarah Lawrence College, and received a B.F.A. at Carnegie Mellon University in 1972. In 1973 he formed a design partnership, Associated Theatrical Designers, Ltd., with Michael J. Hotopp. Credits include over one hundred national television commercials and numerous industrial shows for major companies. In 1981 he received a Clio for the IBM commercial "Partners". Also a graphic designer, Paul de Pass created the show poster for *The 1940's Radio Hour*.

Lighting Designs:
1982: *Cleavage*

Scenic Designs:
1979: *Oklahoma!* **1980:** *Brigadoon* **1981:** *Oh, Brother* **1983:** *Tapdance Kid, The*

John De Santis

An art director, production manager, scenic and lighting designer, John De Santis has worked extensively on the West Coast. He was Production Manager from 1968 to 1978 at the Mark Taper Forum. In 1984 he was Production Manager of the Olympic Arts Festival.

Lighting Designs:
1978: *Broadway Musical, A*

Frank Detering

Frank Detering was a lighting designer in the late 1920s and early 1930s who had his own stage electrical business, where he created lights and mechanical effects. Prior to his death in March 1939 he worked on the stage crew of *The Boys from Syracuse* handling spotlights.

Lighting Designs:
1920: *What's in a Name* **1927:** *Romancing 'Round; Show Boat* **1931:** *Laugh Parade, The*

T.J. Digby

Thomas J. Digby was primarily known as an electrician and worked extensively in Great Britian. He received credit for lighting twenty-one productions in London between 1920 and 1929. One of the productions he designed in London was transferred to Broadway in the late 1920s.

Lighting Designs:
1927: *Wandering Jew, The*

Leon Di Leone

Leon Di Leone, a scenic and lighting designer, was resident designer for Playhouse on the Mall, Paramus, New Jersey from 1969 to 1972 and from 1974 to 1976. He also designed the first national tour of *Jesus Christ Superstar*.

Lighting Designs:
1975: *Angel Street* **1976:** *Wheelbarrow Closers*

John Dodd

John Dodd was a lighting designer with many credits for dance companies, rock bands and theatres. He designed for the Harkness Ballet Company, La Mama, Theatre Genesis and was lighting director of the Living Theatre in the 1980s. Founder and president of 14th Street Stage Lighting, Inc., in New York, his off-Broadway credits included *Buried Child* in 1979. John Dodd died on July 14, 1991 in New York City.

Lighting Designs:
1972: *Inner City*

Peter Dohanos

S. Peter Dohanos was a scenic designer for television, film, and theater and a watercolor painter. He was born in Cleveland, the son of the artist Steve Dohanos. He grew up in Westport, Connecticut and graduated from Dartmouth. He designed many films including *Diary of a Mad Housewife*, and was active in television, notably as art director for *The Kraft Television Theatre* and as production designer for the *Bell Telephone Hour*. He died on December 27, 1988.

Lighting Designs:
1980: *Tricks of the Trade*

Scenic Designs:
1959: *Kataki* **1980:** *Tricks of the Trade*

Mary Jo Dondlinger

Mary Jo Dondlinger created the lighting design for one show in 1989 on Broadway. In 1990 she designed *East Texas* for the York Theatre Company and One World Arts Foundation in New York City.

Lighting Designs:
1989: *Sweeney Todd*

Richard Dorfman

Richard Dorfman was born in Colorado Springs, Colorado on February 2, 1955. He received a Bachelor of Arts in theater arts at Drew University in 1978 and a Master of Fine Arts at New York University in 1981. Richard Dorfman's first professional design was for *'Cause Maggie's Afraid of the Dark*, written and directed by Howard Ashman for the WPA Theatre in New York City in February 1978. Off-Broadway credits include designs for the Irondale Ensemble project where he was Resident Designer from 1983 to 1986. From 1980 to 1986 he designed thirty one productions as Resident Lighting Designer for the New Jersey Shakespeare Festival. He was nominated for an American Theater Wing Design Award in 1987 for *The Life of the Land*, produced at the Pan Asian Repertory Theatre.

Lighting Designs:
1980: *Of the Fields, Lately*

Edward Duryea Dowling

Edward Duryea Dowling was a lighting, costume and scenic designer as well as a director and producer for the Shubert Organization. For the Federal Theatre Project he served for a short time as director of vaudeville, with headquarters in New York City and responsibility for touring companies of comedy, vaudeville and circus. During World War II he was a Sergeant Major in change of theater activities in London for the Special Services Division, and also directed a show for the United Service Organizations to entertain troops in Iceland. Prior to directing plays he was a dialogue director for Paramount Pictures in the early days of sound movies. He died on December 18, 1967 at age 63.

Lighting Designs:
1939: *Streets of Paris* 1941: *Sons O'Fun*

Henry Dreyfuss

Henry Dreyfuss was a set designer who also designed theatre interiors. Born in New York City in 1904 he designed numerous sets for plays on Broadway, occasionally also designing the costumes and lights as well as the interiors of theatres. He also worked as art director for companies which presented films. An industrial designer, he formed Henry Dreyfuss and Associates to manufacture and merchandise products. He died a suicide with his wife, Mrs. Doris Marks Dreyfuss, on October 5, 1972. He was 68.

Lighting Designs:
1931: *Shoot the Works*

Scenic Designs:
1924: *Two Strangers from Nowhere* 1926: *Beau Gallant*; *Beau-Strings* 1927: *Manhatters, The* 1928: *Hold Everything* 1929: *Remote Control* 1930: *Affair of State, An*; *Blind Mice*; *Boundary Line, The*; *Fine and Dandy*; *Kiss of Importance, A*; *Last Mile, The*; *Pagan Lady*; *Sweet Stranger*; *This Is New York* 1931: *Cat and the Fiddle, The*; *Gang's All Here, The*; *Man on Stilts, The*; *Philip Goes Forth*; *Shoot the Works* 1933: *Strike Me Pink* 1934: *Continental Varieties* 1935: *Continental Varieties*; *Paths of Glory*

Costume Designs:
1927: *Manhatters, The* 1928: *Merry Wives of Windsor, The* 1930: *Affair of State, An*

Raoul Pène Du Bois

Raoul Pène Du Bois launched his career on Broadway in 1930 with the design of one costume for *Garrick Gaieties*. This design was the beginning of fifty years creating creative and colorful costumes, imaginative sets, and occasional lighting designs. He trained briefly at the Grand Central Art School, but coming from a family rich in artistic heritage his natural talents found ready employment in theatre and films. His grandfather, Henri Pène Du Bois, was an art and music critic; his uncle, Guy Pène Du Bois, a painter; and cousin, William Pène Du Bois, a book illustrator. He received a Tony Award for the costumes for *No, No, Nanette* in 1973 and a Tony Award for set design in 1953 for *Wonderful Town*. In addition to his Broadway credits he designed in London and Paris. Raoul Pène Du Bois' costumes and scenery graced films, ice shows, ballets, night clubs, aquacades, the Rockettes, and commercial illustrations. He was born on Staten Island and died in New York on January 1, 1985 at age 72.

Lighting Designs:
1948: *Lend An Ear*

Scenic Designs:
1934: *Thumbs Up* 1939: *Du Barry Was a Lady*; *One for the Money* 1940: *Hold Onto Your*

Hats; Panama Hattie; Two for the Show 1941: *Liberty Jones; Sons O'Fun* 1948: *Heaven on Earth; Lend An Ear* 1950: *Alive and Kicking; Call Me Madam* 1951: *Make a Wish* 1952: *In Any Language; New Faces of 1952* 1953: *John Murray Anderson's Almanac; Maggie; Wonderful Town* 1954: *Mrs. Patterson* 1955: *Plain and Fancy; Vamp, The* 1956: *Bells Are Ringing* 1957: *Ziegfeld Follies* 1963: *Student Gypsy, or The Prince of Liederkrantz* 1964: *P.S. I Love You* 1971: *No, No, Nanette* 1973: *Irene* 1975: *Doctor Jazz* 1979: *Sugar Babies*

Costume Designs:
1930: *Garrick Gaieties* 1934: *Keep Moving; Life Begins At 8:40; Ziegfeld Follies: 1934* 1935: *Jumbo* 1936: *Ziegfeld Follies: 1936* 1937: *Hooray for What!* 1938: *Leave It to Me!* 1939: *Du Barry Was a Lady; Leave It to Me!; One for the Money; Too Many Girls* 1940: *Hold Onto Your Hats; Panama Hattie; Two for the Show* 1941: *Liberty Jones; Sons O'Fun* 1943: *Carmen Jones* 1945: *Are You with It?; Firebrand of Florence, the* 1948: *Heaven on Earth; Lend An Ear* 1950: *Alive and Kicking; Call Me Madam* 1951: *Make a Wish* 1952: *In Any Language* 1953: *Maggie; Wonderful Town* 1954: *Mrs. Patterson* 1955: *Plain and Fancy; Vamp, The* 1956: *Bells Are Ringing* 1957: *Music Man, The; Ziegfeld Follies* 1959: *Gypsy* 1963: *Student Gypsy, or The Prince of Liederkrantz* 1964: *P.S. I Love You* 1968: *Darling of the Day* 1971: *No, No, Nanette* 1973: *Irene* 1974: *Gypsy* 1975: *Doctor Jazz* 1979: *Sugar Babies* 1980: *Reggae*

Clarke Dunham

Clarke Dunham is a prolific designer of both sets and lighting, with more than three hundred productions to his credit. He received a Marharam Award for *The Me Nobody Knows*, Tony nominations for the settings for *End of the World* and *Grind* and has worked often in collaboration with Harold Prince. He designs extensively in regional theatres such as the Goodman. Awards include a Jefferson Award for *Twentieth Century*. Additional credits include numerous operas, such as the New York City Opera production of *Candide*, *Madame Butterfly* at the Lyric Opera of Chicago, and design and direction of *Das Liebesverbot* at the 1983 Waterloo Festival. Raised on Philadelphia's Main Line, he is married to the poet, playwright, and lyricist Barbara Tumarkin Dunham.

Lighting Designs:
1967: *Girl in the Freudian Slip, The; Ninety-day Mistress, The* 1970: *Me Nobody Knows, The; Place for Polly, A* 1977: *Something Old, Something New*

Scenic Designs:
1970: *Me Nobody Knows, The; Place for Polly, A* 1973: *Iceman Cometh, The; Waltz of the Toreadors, The* 1976: *Bubbling Brown Sugar* 1984: *End of the World; Play Memory* 1985: *Grind* 1987: *Late Nite Comic*

Paul du Pont

Paul du Pont was born in Bradford, Pennsylvania, the son of an opera singer and a chemist. Originally trained to be a singer, he changed to painting and then to ballet. A serious fall through an open trap door while on tour with a ballet troupe cut short his dancing career. His first costume designs were for ballet, after which he designed for the Group Theatre and the Theatre Guild. In addition to his designs of scenery, costumes and lighting for the theatre, he designed extensively for television, including the Sid Caesar–Imogene Coca Variety series. Mr. du Pont died at age 51 on April 20, 1957.

Lighting Designs:
1951: *Diamond Lil*

Scenic Designs:
1951: *Diamond Lil*

Costume Designs:
1936: *Johnny Johnson* 1939: *Time of Your Life, The* 1940: *Another Sun; Fifth Column, The; Retreat to Pleasure; Time of Your Life, The* 1942: *All Comforts of Home; Chocolate Soldier, The; Kiss for Cinderella, A; Let Freedom Sing; Porgy and Bess; Strings, My Lord, Are False, The; Time, the Place, and the Girl, The* 1943: *First Million, The; One Touch of Venus; Porgy and Bess* 1944: *Anna Lucasta; Porgy and Bess; Pretty Little Parlor* 1949: *Diamond Lil* 1950: *All You Need Is One Good Break* 1951: *Diamond Lil* 1953: *Oh, Men! Oh, Women!*

DuWico

DuWico Lighting Equipment Company was formed by Gus Durkin and Harol Williams and operated at 313 West 41st Street. The name DuWico was prevalent in hundreds of Broadway playbills and is included in this volume as an example of suppliers of equipment also supplying aesthetic values. For additional information on lighting equipment companies, see "Acknowledgements Only."

Lighting Designs:
1919: *Penny Wise* 1923: *How Come?* 1925: *Don't Bother Mother; Easy Terms; Fool's Bells; Kosher Kitty Kelly* 1926: *Castles in the Air; Chicago; Half-Caste, The; Head Or Tail; Matinee Girl, The; Old Bill, M.P.; Sunshine; Wooden Kimono* 1927: *10 Per Cent; Excess Baggage; Judy; Madame X; Off-Key; Spider, The; Talk About Girls* 1928: *Clutching Claw, The; Divorce a La Carte; Present Arms; Skidding; Spider, The; Spring 3100; Street Wolf, The; Veils* 1929: *Dinner Is Served; Messin' 'Round; Silver Swan, The* 1930: *Light Wines and Beer; So Was Napoleon* 1931: *Here Goes the Bride* 1933: *Humming Sam; Lady Refuses, The; World Waits, The* 1936: *All Editions; Victoria Regina; Women, The* 1938: *Spring Thaw* 1939: *George White's Scandals* 1940: *Separate Rooms* 1942: *Janie; Kiss for Cinderella, A; You'll See the Stars* 1943: *Try and Get It* 1947: *For Love Or Money; I Gotta Get Out; Magic Touch, The* 1948: *Don't Listen Ladies; Hallams, The* 1949: *Diamond Lil; Gayden; Ivy Green, The; Love Me Long; Metropole*

Howard Eaton

Howard Eaton is a lighting designer whose work appeared on Broadway in 1979.

Lighting Designs:
1979: *Dogg's Hamlet, Cahoot's Macbeth*

Arthur Ebbetts

Arthur Ebbetts designed lighting on Broadway between 1917 and 1918 and sets on Broadway in 1924. He worked as a stage director in the late teens, and in the early 1930s worked as a stage manager, residing at 4611 Spuyten, Duyvil Parkway in New York City.

Lighting Designs:
1917: *Why Marry?* 1918: *Why Marry?*
Scenic Designs:
1924: *Main Line, The*

William and Jean Eckart

Beginning with sets and lights for *Glad Tidings* and *To Dorothy a Son* in 1951, William and Jean Eckart have provided designs for some of Broadway's most popular shows. William Eckart was born in 1920 in New Iberia, Louisiana and received a B.S. in architecture from Tulane University in 1942 and an M.F.A. in stage design at Yale in 1949. He married Jean Levy in 1943 and they have two children. Jean Eckart was born in Chicago on August 18, 1921 and received a B.F.A. at Newcomb College and an M.F.A. at Yale. Most of their design work has been done jointly and includes theatre, film, television and industrial productions. Their design credits are generally for scenery and lighting, but occasionally they also contribute costumes to a production. In 1954 they received the Donaldson Award for *The Golden Apple* for their scenery. In 1976 Jean Eckart returned to school, receiving a M.S.W.S. from the University of Texas at Arlington, and from 1978 to 1986 worked in the mental health field at the Community Psychotherapy Center in Dallas, as well as in private practice. She also continues to lecture on theatrical design, teaching recently on costume design. William continues to design, including a summer 1990 production for the Colorado Shakespeare Festival.

Lighting Designs:
1954: *Portrait of a Lady; Wedding Breakfast* 1956: *Li'l Abner* 1957: *Copper and Brass* 1958: *Body Beautiful, The* 1959: *Fiorello* 1960: *Viva Madison Avenue* 1961: *Happiest Girl in the World, The; Let It Ride!; Take Her, She's Mine* 1962: *Never Too Late* 1963: *She Loves Me* 1964: *Fade Out-Fade In* 1965: *Fade Out-Fade In; Zulu and the Zayda, The* 1966: *Agatha Sue, I Love You* 1974: *Of Mice and Men*
Scenic Designs:
1951: *Glad Tidings; To Dorothy, a Son* 1952: *Gertie* 1953: *Dead Pigeon; Oh, Men! Oh, Women!* 1954: *Golden Apple, The; Portrait of a Lady; Wedding Breakfast* 1955: *Damn Yankees* 1956: *Li'l Abner; Mister Johnson* 1957: *Copper and Brass* 1958: *Body Beautiful, The* 1959: *Fiorello* 1960: *Viva Madison Avenue* 1961: *Happiest Girl in the World, The; Let It Ride!; Take Her, She's Mine* 1962: *Never Too Late* 1963: *Here's Love; Oh Dad, Poor Dad, Mamma's Hung You...; She Loves Me* 1964:

Anyone Can Whistle; Fade Out-Fade In 1965:
Fade Out-Fade In; Flora, the Red Menace; Zulu
and the Zayda, The 1966: Agatha Sue, I Love
You; Mame 1967: Hallelujah, Baby! 1968:
Education of H.Y.M.A.N. K.A.P.L.A.N., The;
Maggie Flynn 1969: Fig Leaves Are Falling,
The 1970: Norman, Is That You? 1974: Of
Mice and Men

Costume Designs:

1955: Damn Yankees 1956: Mister Johnson
1959: Fiorello 1974: Of Mice and Men

Ben Edwards

Ben Edwards, born George Benjamin Edwards
in Union Springs, Alabama on July 5, 1916,
studied in New York City at the Feagin School
of Dramatic Arts, the Kane School of Art, and
through association with Gordon Craig, Robert
Edmond Jones and Jo Mielziner. He first designed sets and lights at the Barter Theater in
Abingdon, Virginia and first designed on Broadway in 1938. His credits for settings and lighting
design are extensive both in the theatre and for
television. Mr. Edwards also produces plays.
He is married to costume designer Jane Greenwood.

Lighting Designs:

1950: Captain Brassbound's Conversion 1952:
Time of the Cuckoo, The 1954: Anastasia; Lul-
laby; Travelling Lady, The 1955: Tonight on
Samarkind 1956: Ponder Heart, The; Someone Waiting 1957: Waltz of the Toreadors, The
1958: Ages of Man; Touch of the Poet, A;
Waltz of the Toreadors, The 1959: God and
Kate Murphy; Heartbreak House 1960: Face of
a Hero; Second String, A 1961: Aspern Papers,
The; Big Fish, Little Fish; Midgie Purvis; Purlie
Victorious; Shot in the Dark, A 1962: Harold
1965: Family Way, The; Race of Hairy Men, A
1966: How's the World Treating You?; Nathan
Weinstein, Mystic, Connecticut; Where's Daddy
1969: Mother Lover, The 1970: Hay Fever
1973: Finishing Touches; Moon for the Misbegotten, A 1976: Texas Trilogy, A 1977: Almost
Perfect Person, An; Anna Christie; Touch of the
Poet, A

Scenic Designs:

1938: Cap't Jinks of the Horse Marines; Coriolanus; Diff'rent; No More Peace; Pygmalion
1940: Another Sun 1947: Medea 1948: Sundown Beach 1949: Diamond Lil 1950: Cap-

tain Brassbound's Conversion 1952: Sunday
Breakfast; Time of the Cuckoo, The 1953: Re-
markable Mr. Pennypacker,the 1954: Anastasia; Lullaby; Travelling Lady, The 1955: Hon-
eys, The; Tonight on Samarkind 1956: Pon-
der Heart, The; Someone Waiting 1957: Dark
At the Top of the Stairs, The; Waltz of the
Toreadors, The 1958: Disenchanted, The; Jane
Eyre; Touch of the Poet, A; Waltz of the Tore-
adors, The 1959: God and Kate Murphy; Heart-
break House 1960: Face of a Hero; Second
String, A 1961: Aspern Papers, The; Big Fish,
Little Fish; Midgie Purvis; Purlie Victorious;
Shot in the Dark, A 1962: Harold 1963: Bal-
lad of the Sad Cafe, The 1964: Hamlet 1965:
Family Way, The; Race of Hairy Men, A 1966:
How's the World Treating You?; Nathan We-
instein, Mystic, Connecticut; Where's Daddy
1967: More Stately Mansions 1969: Mother
Lover, The 1970: Hay Fever; Purlie 1972:
Purlie 1973: Finishing Touches; Moon for the
Misbegotten, A 1976: Matter of Gravity, A;
Texas Trilogy, A 1977: Almost Perfect Per-
son, An; Anna Christie; Touch of the Poet, A
1981: To Grandmother's House We Go; West
Side Waltz, The 1982: Medea 1984: Death of
a Salesman 1985: Iceman Cometh, The 1988:
Long Day's Journey Into Night 1989: Few Good
Men, A

Costume Designs:

1938: Cap't Jinks of the Horse Marines; Cori-
olanus; Diff'rent; No More Peace; Pygmalion
1950: Bird Cage, The; Legend of Sarah 1952:
Desire Under the Elms; Sunday Breakfast 1953:
Emperor's Clothes, The; Remarkable Mr. Pen-
nypacker,the 1954: Anastasia; Travelling Lady,
The 1957: Waltz of the Toreadors, The 1958:
Touch of the Poet, A; Waltz of the Toreadors,
The

Hilton Edwards

Hilton Edwards, actor and director, was born in
London on February 2, 1903 and is best known
for founding (with Michael MacLiammoir) the
Dublin Gate Theatre in 1928, where he produced and directed over three hundred plays.
His first stage appearance was with the Charles
Doran Shakespeare Company in 1920, after
which he joined the Old Vic in London. He came
to the United States in 1948 and designed lighting for two plays which he directed and in which

he also appeared. While in America he was involved in additional productions and worked in television. Hilton Edwards died on November 18, 1982 in Dublin.

Lighting Designs:
1948: *Old Lady Says "No", The*; *Where Stars Walk*

Peter M. Ehrhardt

Peter M. Ehrhardt has designed lights for numerous productions at the Goodspeed Opera House, including plays later transferred to Broadway. He was born in Elizabeth, New Jersey on February 21, 1950, the son of Peter L. and Ardel Leimbach Ehrhardt. Although he began designing in high school with *West Side Story*, he studied engineering in college. He received design training through courses at the Lester Polakov Studio and Forum of Stage Design, and by association with Jean Rosenthal and Thomas Skelton. He has also designed at the Juilliard School, the New Jersey Shakespeare Festival, the New Jersey Institute of Technology and at the Hartt School of Music. The recipient of the Carbonel Award from the Southern Florida Critics Association, he is a full-time electrician at NBC-TV as well as a freelance designer.

Lighting Designs:
1975: *Very Good, Eddie* **1976:** *Going Up* **1979:** *Whoopee* **1987:** *Sally*

Peggy Eisenhauer

Peggy Eisenhauer has designed lighting for many productions for Graciela Daniele, including *Blood Wedding*, *Tango Apasioanado* and *Caoa Noche...Tango*. She has designed tours for the Cars, Billy Ocean, Lisa Lisa and other performers; the *New Chita Rivera Cabaret-Revue*; and the concert films *Cyndi Lauper in Paris* for Home Box Office, *Hearts of Fire* starring Bob Dylan, and *Michael Jackson* for Pepsi-Cola. Born in New York City on April 24, 1962, the daughter of Ray and Bebe Eisenhauer, she has a sister, Lyn, who is an architect. She received a B.F.A. from Carnegie Mellon University in drama and counts Bob Olson, Jules Fisher and Stephen Bickford as mentors. She began designing at age fifteen with *American Hurrah* for the

Elmwood Playhouse in Nyack, New York. *Dangerous Games* was nominated for a Maharam Award for 1989-1990.

Lighting Designs:
1989: *Dangerous Games*

Vasser Elam

Vasser Elam created one lighting design on Broadway in 1929.

Lighting Designs:
1929: *White Flame*

Eldon Elder

Eldon Elder is a setting and lighting designer who occasionally contributes costumes to plays and operas. He was born on March 17, 1921 in Atchison, Kansas. He studied at Kansas State Teachers College (now Emporia State College) with Professor R. Russell Porter and at the University of Denver. After receiving an M.F.A. from Yale in 1950, he assisted one of his mentors in New Haven, Donald Oenslager, for a year. His first professional designs were for the Provincetown Playhouse in 1949 and he first designed on Broadway in 1951 for *The Long Days* (sets and lights.) He designed sets, costumes and lights for many of the New York Shakespeare Festival's productions in the Belvedere Lake Theatre in the late 1950s and early 1960s. A teacher of design and an author, Mr. Elder also consults on the design of theatres. At the invitation of the Chinese Stage Decoration Institute he toured China and lectured while on a Guggenheim Foundation grant. Mr. Elder is the author of *Will It Make a Theatre?* and *Eldon Elder: Designs for the Theatre*.

Lighting Designs:
1951: *Long Days, The* **1952:** *Grey Eyed People, The*; *Time Out for Ginger* **1953:** *Take a Giant Step* **1954:** *Girl in Pink Tights, The*; *One Eye Closed* **1955:** *All in One, Trouble in Tahiti*; *Heavenly Twins, The*; *Twenty Seven Wagons Full of Cotton* **1956:** *Fallen Angels* **1962:** *Affair, The*; *Fun Couple, The* **1967:** *Of Love Remembered* **1974:** *James Whitmore in Will Rogers' U.S.A.*

Scenic Designs:
1951: *Legend of Lovers*; *Long Days, The* **1952:** *Grey Eyed People, The*; *Hook 'n Ladder*; *Time*

Out for Ginger 1953: *Take a Giant Step* 1954: *Girl in Pink Tights, The; One Eye Closed* 1955: *All in One, Trouble in Tahiti; Heavenly Twins, The; Phoenix '55; Twenty Seven Wagons Full of Cotton; Young and Beautiful, The* 1956: *Fallen Angels* 1957: *Shinbone Alley* 1962: *Affair, The; Fun Couple, The* 1965: *Mating Dance* 1967: *Of Love Remembered* 1974: *James Whitmore in Will Rogers' U.S.A.* 1976: *Music Is* 1989: *Hizzoner*

Costume Designs:
1974: *James Whitmore in Will Rogers' U.S.A.*

Chris Ellis

Chris Ellis, a British designer, has long been associated with the Leicester Theatre Trust as lighting designer and production manager. He designed lights on Broadway for a production in 1986. He has lit many productions in the West End, for the Royal Shakespeare Company, the National Theatre, the Hong Kong Arts Festival and the Welsh National Opera. A member of the Society of British Designers, he designed the lighting installation for the new Haymarket Theatre.

Lighting Designs:
1986: *Me and My Girl*

Todd Elmer

Todd Elmer was born in Staten Island, New York on November 21, 1956 and received a M.F.A. at Boston University in 1978. He spent several years in New York as a lighting designer working off-Broadway at the Juilliard School, the Manhattan School of Music, the School of American Ballet, the Harold Clurman Theatre and the Astor Place Theatre, among others. He assisted designers such as Thomas Skelton, Craig Miller, Richard Nelson, and Paul Gallo on Broadway shows. After touring with various productions he became lighting supervisor for the American Ballet Theatre in 1988. He also spent three years a production stage manager for an ice skating company and designed lights for the 1983 Bermuda Festival.

Lighting Designs:
1979: *Price, The*

Joseph Elsner

Joseph Elsner (a.k.a. Ellsner) was active on Broadway in the teens and twenties.

Lighting Designs:
1915: *Hip-Hip-Hooray* 1918: *Everything* 1920: *Good Times*

Charles Elson

Charles Elson was born on September 5, 1909 in Chicago and received degrees at the University of Illinois, the University of Chicago, and Yale University. He designed numerous settings, often designing the lighting for those same productions and occasionally contributing costume designs as well. He worked regularly as an assistant to Donald Oenslager. An author as well as a committed educator, Mr. Elson taught at Hunter College of the City University of New York from 1948 to 1974, when he became Professor Emertius. While on the Hunter College faculty he designed forty-eight productions for their theatre. He also served on the design faculties of the University of Iowa, Yale, and the University of Oklahoma.

Lighting Designs:
1945: *Pygmalion* 1946: *Born Yesterday; Hidden Horizon; Land's End; Loco; Present Laughter; Three to Make Ready; Years Ago* 1947: *As You Like It; Duet for Two Hands; First Mrs. Fraser, The; Message for Margaret* 1948: *Cup of Trembling; Kathleen; Power Without Glory; Private Lives* 1949: *Regina* 1950: *Enemy of the People, An; Lady's Not for Burning, The; Out of This World* 1951: *Borscht Capades; Nina; Rose Tattoo, The* 1952: *Collector's Item; Deep Blue Sea, The* 1953: *Little Hut, The* 1954: *His and Hers* 1955: *Champagne Complex* 1956: *Lovers, The* 1957: *Compulsion* 1958: *Blue Denim; Maria Golovin* 1959: *First Impressions* 1960: *Wildcat* 1962: *Perfect Setup, The* 1963: *Photo Finish* 1967: *Mother Courage*

Scenic Designs:
1946: *Hidden Horizon* 1947: *Duet for Two Hands; First Mrs. Fraser, The* 1948: *Cup of Trembling; Kathleen; Power Without Glory; Private Lives* 1950: *Enemy of the People, An* 1951: *Borscht Capades; Nina* 1952: *Collector's Item; Deep Blue Sea, The* 1954: *His and Hers* 1955: *Champagne Complex* 1956: *Lovers, The*

Costume Designs:
1951: *Nina* 1955: *Champagne Complex*

Beverly Emmons

Lighting designer Beverly Emmons was born on December 12, 1943. She studied dance at Sarah Lawrence College where she received a B.A. degree. As an apprentice at the American Dance Festival at Connecticut College she was influenced by the creative work of Jean Rosenthal and Thomas Skelton. This introduction to lighting design led to study with Tom Skelton at Lester Polalov's Studio and Forum of Stage Design and a career in lighting. On Broadway her designs have been honored with three Tony nominations and an Obie Award in 1980 for distinguished lighting design. Beverly Emmons has also designed for dance including works by Meredith Monk and the Martha Graham Dance Company. In collaboration with Robert Wilson she has lit *Einstein on the Beach* at the Metropolitan Opera and the Brooklyn Academy of Music, and also *CIVIL waRs*.

Lighting Designs:
1975: *Bette Midler's Clams on the Half Shell Revue*; *Letter for Queen Victoria, A* **1979:** *Elephant Man, The* **1980:** *Amadeus*; *Day in Hollywood, A/A Night in the Ukraine*; *Heartaches of a Pussycat*; *Reggae* **1981:** *Dresser, The*; *Piaf* **1982:** *Good*; *Is There Life After High School*; *Little Me* **1983:** *All's Well That Ends Well*; *Doonesbury*; *Total Abandon* **1986:** *Mummenschanz* **1987:** *Stepping Out* **1988:** *Michael Feinstein in Concert*

Victor En-Yu Tan

Victor En-Yu Tan has designed lights in regional theatres around the country, from Syracuse Stage and GEVA on the East Coast to the Cincinnati Playhouse and Milwaukee Repertory Theatre in the Midwest and the Alaska Repertory Theatre in Anchorage. He received an Obie Award for sustained excellence for his designs at the New York Shakespeare Festival, the Opera at 92nd Street, the Pan Asian Repertory and the New Federal Theatre. Recent productions include *Lucky Come Hawaii* for the Pan Asian Repertory Theatre.

Lighting Designs:
1986: *Shakespeare on Broadway for the Schools*

Eleanor Farrington

Eleanor Farrington, known primarily as a set designer, created sets, costumes and lights for a Broadway show in 1945, a remarkable accomplishment for a woman at that time. She made her Broadway debut in 1938.

Lighting Designs:
1945: *Deep Mrs. Sykes, The*

Scenic Designs:
1938: *Michael Drops In* **1945:** *Deep Mrs. Sykes, The*

Costume Designs:
1945: *Deep Mrs. Sykes, The*

A. H. Feder

A. H. (Abe) Feder has been well-known as a lighting and scenery designer throughout a career which began in 1932 with the lighting design for *Trick or Trick*. He was born in Milwaukee, Wisconsin on June 27, 1909 and studied at the Carnegie Institute of Technology with Woodman Thompson and Alexander Wykcoff. Mr. Feder has designed the lighting for plays, ballets and operas throughout the United States and lectures extensively. He has been consultant for the lighting of interiors of theatres, museums, galleries, and buildings, including the Kennedy Center in Washington, D.C., the Israel National Museum in Jerusalem and Rockefeller Plaza in New York City. He was instrumental in the development of the profession of lighting design as it progressed from relying on electricians for the presence of light on stage to relying on designers for the quality of light on stage.

Lighting Designs:
1934: *Calling All Stars*; *Four Saints in Three Acts* **1935:** *Ghosts*; *Hook-Up, The* **1936:** *Conjur Man Dies, The*; *Hedda Gabler*; *Macbeth*; *New Faces of 1936* **1937:** *Native Ground*; *Without Warning* **1938:** *Androcles and the Lion*; *Big Blow, The*; *Cap't Jinks of the Horse Marines*; *Coriolanus*; *Cradle Will Rock, The*; *Diff'rent*; *Here Come the Clowns*; *No More Peace*; *Prologue to Glory*; *Pygmalion*; *Sing for Your Supper* **1940:** *Hold Onto Your Hats*; *Johnny Belinda*; *Passenger to Bali, A* **1941:** *Angel Street* **1942:** *Autumn Hill*; *Magic/Hello, Out There*; *Walking Gentleman* **1943:** *Winged Victory* **1950:** *Gioconda Smile, The* **1951:** *Sleep of Prisoners, A* **1952:** *Three Wishes for Jamie* **1953:** *Pin to See the Peepshow, A* **1954:** *Boyfriend, The*; *Flowering Peach, The*; *Immoralist, The* **1955:**

Inherit the Wind; Seventh Heaven; Skin of Our Teeth, The; Young and Beautiful, The 1956: *My Fair Lady* 1957: *Clearing in the Woods, A*; *Orpheus Descending; Time Remembered; Visit to a Small Planet, A* 1958: *Cold Wind and the Warm, The; Goldilocks* 1959: *Loss of Roses, A* 1960: *Camelot; Greenwillow* 1962: *Tiger Tiger Burning Bright* 1963: *Once for the Asking* 1964: *Blues for Mr. Charley; Three Sisters, The* 1965: *On a Clear Day You Can See Forever* 1971: *Scratch* 1975: *Doctor Jazz; Goodtime Charley* 1979: *Carmelina*

Scenic Designs:
1950: *Gioconda Smile, The* 1963: *Once for the Asking* 1964: *Blues for Mr. Charley*

Costume Designs:
1964: *Blues for Mr. Charley*

Gerald Feil

Gerald Feil, who designed lights on Broadway in the mid-1960s, works primarily in the film industry. His assignments as a photographer, cameraman, and producer have taken him on location to several continents. Perhaps best known for his camera work and editing for *Lord of the Flies*, Gerald Feil was also director of photography for *He Knows You're Alone* and *Friday the 13th, Part III*.

Lighting Designs:
1964: *Traveller Without Luggage*

Arden Fingerhut

Arden Fingerhut, one of the foremost contemporary lighting designers, studied chemistry at New York University and received a graduate degree in scene design from Columbia University before turning her attention and talents to lighting design. She worked for several years honing her skills at the O'Neill Theatre Center under the tutelage of John Gleason, who encouraged her innovative and abstract approach to lighting. Her early association with Joseph Chaikin at the Open Theatre has continued to influence her style, as has her long term relationship with Elizabeth Swados. She taught lighting design for twelve years at New York University and in 1987 was named chair of the theatre department at Williams College in Williamstown, Massachusetts. She has designed lights in most

of the regional theatres in the United States, on and off-Broadway, and for dance and opera.

Lighting Designs:
1978: *Da* 1979: *Bent* 1980: *Hide and Seek* 1981: *Einstein and the Polar Bear; Father, The* 1983: *Plenty; Slab Boys; Teaneck Tanzi: The Venus Flytrap* 1984: *Alone Together* 1985: *Hay Fever*

Imero Fiorentino

Born on July 12, 1928 in New York City, Imero Ovidio Fiorentino has been instrumental in developing the art of lighting design for television, elevating design for the small screen from its origins in engineering. After graduating with a Bachelor of Fine Arts from Carnegie Mellon University in 1950, he served as lighting director for ABC-TV from 1950 to 1960. In 1960 he formed Imero Fiorentino Associates, a consulting company specializing in lighting for sepcial events and television. His credits on television range from Miss Piggy to Miss America, and since 1960 (when he first lit the Nixon-Kennedy debates) he has been lighting political conventions, including the 1988 Republican National Convention in the Louisiana Superdome. He has been honored with a Merit Award from his alma mater in 1974 and nominations for Emmy Awards in lighting and scenic design, and has received an Excellence in Design Award and an Award of Excellence from the Illuminating Engineering Society.

Lighting Designs:
1975: *Night That Made America Famous, The*

Jules Fisher

Jules Fisher is a lighting designer of considerable reknown with design experience dating back to his high school days when he designed *January Thaw*. He was born in Norristown, Pennsylvania on November 12, 1937 and attended Pennsylvania State University before receiving a B.F.A. from the Carnegie Institute of Technology. After working as a carpenter, stage manager and lighting designer in Pennsylvania, he arrived in New York in October 1959 to become lighting director at the 74th Street Theater, and has been designing lights in New York City steadily ever since. He has received several Tony Awards:

for *Pippin* (1972), *Ulysses in Nighttown* (1974), *Dancin'* and *Grand Hotel* in (1990). Not only an active designer, Mr. Fisher is also involved with consulting as a principal in Jules Fisher Associates, Inc., (a theatre consulting group), Jules Fisher Enterprises, Inc., (a production company) and Jules Fisher & Paul Marantz Inc. (architectural lighting design specialists).

Lighting Designs:
1964: *Anyone Can Whistle*; *Girl Could Get Lucky, A*; *High Spirits*; *P.S. I Love You*; *Sign in Sidney Brustein's Window, The*; *Subject Was Roses, The*; *White House, The* **1965:** *And Things That Go Bump in the Night*; *Devils, The*; *Do I Hear a Waltz?*; *Half a Sixpence*; *Pickwick*; *Yearling, The* **1966:** *Hail Scrawdyke!* **1967:** *Black Comedy*; *Little Murders*; *Minor Adjustment, A*; *Natural Look, The*; *Trial of Lee Harvey Oswald, The*; *You Know I Can't Hear You When the Water's* **1968:** *Before You Go*; *Cuban Thing, The*; *Grand Music Hall of Israel, The*; *Hair*; *Here's Where I Belong*; *Man in the Glass Booth, The*; *Only Game in Town, The* **1969:** *But, Seriously*; *Butterflies Are Free*; *Canterbury Tales*; *Trumpets of the Lord*; *Watering Place, The* **1970:** *Engagement Baby, The*; *Gantry*; *Home*; *Inquest*; *Minnie's Boys*; *Sheep of the Runway* **1971:** *Jesus Christ Superstar*; *Lenny*; *No, No, Nanette*; *You're a Good Man, Charlie Brown* **1972:** *Fun City*; *Lysistrata*; *Mourning Becomes Electra*; *Pippin* **1973:** *Full Circle*; *Iceman Cometh, The*; *Molly*; *Seesaw*; *Uncle Vanya* **1974:** *Thieves*; *Ulysses in Nighttown* **1975:** *Chicago* **1976:** *Rockabye Hamlet* **1977:** *American Buffalo*; *Golda*; *Hair* **1978:** *Dancin'* **1981:** *Frankenstein* **1982:** *Rock 'n Roll! The First 5,000 years* **1983:** *La Cage Aux Folles* **1985:** *Song & Dance* **1986:** *Big Deal*; *Rags* **1988:** *Legs Diamond* **1989:** *Grand Hotel, The Musical*

Rick Fisher

Rick Fisher was born in Philadelphia on October 19, 1954. He received a B.A. from Dickenson College in Carlisle, Pennsylvania in 1976 where he learned the art and craft of theatre. He also served as an apprentice at the Viking Theatre in Atlantic City and as an apprentice and later master carpenter at the Playhouse in the Park in Philadelphia. His lighting designs have been seen almost exclusively throughout the United

Kingdom and London, where he has lived since 1976. His design has been influenced by associations in London with Tom Donnellan and Steve Whitson. Design credits include the lighting for numerous fringe shows, regional theatres, productions for the Royal Shakespeare Company, and recently *Peer Gynt* for the National Theatre. Shows in London's West End include *Serious Money*, *J.J. Farr*, *A Walk in the Woods*, *Marya* and *Hidden Laughter*.

Lighting Designs:
1988: *Serious Money* **1990:** *Some Americans Abroad*

Edward Fitzpatrick

As a lighting designer Edward Fitzpatrick created effects for one production in 1939.

Lighting Designs:
1939: *Steel*

Frederick Fox

Frederick Fox is a scenic and lighting designer who occasionally contributes costume designs to a production as well. Born in 1910 in New York City, he studied at Yale and worked initially as an architect. Before his New York debut, *Farewell Summer* in 1937, he designed many summer stock productions. A prolific designer of plays and operas, Mr. Fox now concentrates on creating designs for television. He designed numerous films between 1936 and 1961 as a scenic designer and lighting director, and received additional credits as a producer and costume designer. The setting for *Darkness At Noon* won him a Donaldson Award in 1951.

Lighting Designs:
1943: *Men in Shadow* **1944:** *Career Angel* **1945:** *Alice in Arms*; *Good Night Ladies*; *Secret Room, The* **1946:** *Little Brown Jug* **1947:** *John Loves Mary* **1950:** *Southern Exposure* **1951:** *Angels Kiss Me*; *Darkness At Noon* **1952:** *Seven Year Itch, The* **1953:** *Room Service* **1954:** *Anniversary Waltz*; *King of Hearts*; *Lunatics and Lovers*; *Reclining Figure* **1955:** *Wayward Saint, The* **1956:** *Speaking of Murder* **1957:** *Greatest Man Alive, The* **1958:** *Howie* **1959:** *Golden Fleecing*; *Warm Peninsula, The* **1960:** *Hostage, The*; *Mighty Man Is He, A*; *Send Me No Flowers* **1961:** *From the Second City*; *Mandingo*

Scenic Designs:

1937: *Bat, The; Farewell Summer; Orchids Preferred* **1938:** *Man from Cairo, The; There's Always a Breeze* **1940:** *Blind Alley; Johnny Belinda; Strangler Fig, The* **1941:** *All Men Are True; Brooklyn Biarritz; Good Neighbor; Junior Miss; Snookie* **1942:** *Doughgirls, The; Johnny on a Spot; Magic/ Hello, Out There; Wine, Women and Song; Yankee Point* **1943:** *Lady, Behave; Land of Fame; Men in Shadow; Naked Genius, The; Snark Was a Boojum, The; Those Endearing Young Charms; Two Mrs. Carrolls, The* **1944:** *Anna Lucasta; Day Will Come, The; Dear Ruth; Decision; Hickory Stick; Man Who Had All the Luck, The; Odds on Mrs. Oakley, The; Only the Heart; Ramshackle Inn* **1945:** *Alice in Arms; Calico Wedding; Good Night Ladies; Goose for the Gander, A; Kiss Them for Me; Marriage is for Single People; Wind is Ninety, The* **1946:** *Little Brown Jug; Mr. Peebles and Mr. Hooker* **1947:** *John Loves Mary* **1948:** *Light Up the Sky; Make Mine Manhattan* **1949:** *They Knew What They Wanted* **1950:** *Southern Exposure* **1951:** *Angels Kiss Me; Darkness At Noon; Never Say Never* **1952:** *Climate of Eden, The; Seven Year Itch, The* **1953:** *Room Service* **1954:** *Anniversary Waltz; King of Hearts; Lunatics and Lovers; Reclining Figure* **1955:** *Wayward Saint, The* **1956:** *Speaking of Murder* **1957:** *Fair Game; Greatest Man Alive, The* **1958:** *Howie* **1959:** *Golden Fleecing; Warm Peninsula, The* **1960:** *Hostage, The; Mighty Man Is He, A; Send Me No Flowers* **1961:** *From the Second City; Mandingo*

Costume Designs:

1942: *Johnny on a Spot* **1944:** *Only the Heart* **1945:** *Alice in Arms* **1949:** *They Knew What They Wanted* **1952:** *Seven Year Itch, The* **1954:** *King of Hearts; Lunatics and Lovers; Reclining Figure* **1957:** *Greatest Man Alive, The* **1959:** *Golden Fleecing* **1960:** *Send Me No Flowers* **1961:** *Mandingo* **1965:** *La Grasse Valise*

Wesley France

Wesley France is a lighting designer who currently works as production manager for the Market Theatre Company of Johannesburg, South Africa. His first production was *Sweeney Todd* in the Laager. Additional credits in New York include lighting supervision of *Woza Africa!* at Lincoln Center.

Lighting Designs:

1987: *Asinamali!*

Beulah Frankel

Beulah Frankel received her first credit on Broadway as technical director for *Me, the Sleeper* in 1949. A native of New York City, she studied at Carnegie Tech and the New School for Social Research. As a child she took dance and acting classes at the Neighborhood Playhouse but began her professional career in lighting assisting Bill Richardson. Her first designs in New York were costumes for *Show-Off* and *Julius Caesar* at the Arena Theatre in the Edison Hotel in New York City. She became an independent producer after initially working in New York and Hollywood as a scenic designer and art director. The first woman member of the Motion Picture Art Directors Society, her designs for commercials have been awarded fifteen Clios. She is associated with the following companies: Beulah Frankel Productions, Inc., Los Angeles (producing plays, films and television); Eastern Scenic Backdrops, Inc. (renting painted backdrops); and D'Arcy Design, Ltd. (designing restaurant interiors). She is married to William Stokes Tillisch.

Lighting Designs:

1950: *Show-Off, The*

Costume Designs:

1950: *Julius Caesar; Show-Off, The*

Charles Friedman

Born in Russia on September 20, 1902, Charles Friedman was raised on the Lower East Side of New York City, where he died on July 18, 1984. He directed plays wherever he found the opportunity, in settlement houses and small theatres. Representative productions include *Pins and Needles, Carmen Jones, Street Scene* and the Federal Theatre production of *Sing for Your Supper* in 1939. He wrote the script and lyrics for *My Darlin' Aida*. Charles Friedman was also a director, producer and writer for television.

Lighting Designs:

1935: *Mother*

Scenic Designs:
1927: *Rutherford and Son* **1928:** *Waltz of the Dogs* **1929:** *Silver Tassie, The*

V.C. Fuqua

In addition to his credits as a lighting designer on Broadway in the mid-1960s, V.C. Fuqua has designed in regional theatres including the Cape Playhouse, Playhouse-in-the-Park in Philadelphia, the McCarter Theatre and off-Broadway. He received a B.A. in Technical Writing at the Massachusetts Institute of Technology and an M.A. from the University of Texas in lighting design.

Lighting Designs:
1965: *Glass Menagerie, The*; *Me and Thee* **1966:** *Pousse-Cafe*

David S. Gaither

David S. Gaither was principally a set designer who also created lights and costumes on Broadway between 1924 and 1933. He served as President of United Scenic Artists in the late 1930s. He was also a painter and in 1932 resided at 29 Perry Street in New York City.

Lighting Designs:
1927: *Ghosts*

Scenic Designs:
1923: *Rivals, The* **1924:** *Wonderful Visit, The* **1925:** *Episode*; *Nocturne* **1926:** *Ghosts*; *Old Bill, M.P.* **1927:** *Ghosts* **1929:** *Queen Bee* **1930:** *Gold Braid* **1932:** *Riddle Me This* **1933:** *Foolscap*; *Riddle Me This*; *Two Strange Women*

Costume Designs:
1927: *Ghosts* **1930:** *Gold Braid*

Paul Gallo

Paul Gallo's collaborations with Martha Clarke include *Vienna: Lusthaus, The Garden of Earthly Delights* (for which he received the 1984 Marharam Award), and *The Hunger Artist*. In 1986 his lighting designs were honored with an Obie Award for sustained excellence for work that season: *The House of Blue Leaves, Smile, The Front Page* (which also received a Tony nomination), and *Drood* (which also won the 1986 Outer Critics Circle Award). Since 1984

he has been associate lighting designer at Arena Stage, Washington, D.C. He first studied music, art, and dance at Ithaca College, but became interested in stage design, changing his major to theatre and art. He studied at Yale University with Ming Cho Lee and received an M.F.A. there in 1977. From 1979 to 1981 he was resident designer at Juilliard and from 1981 to 1983 resident designer at the American Repertory Theatre. He has also designed at Playwrights Horizon and the New York Shakespeare Festival. Recent designs include the settings for *Machinal*, which was written by Sophie Treadwell and directed by Michael Greif.

Lighting Designs:
1980: *John Gabriel Borkman*; *Passione*; *Tintypes* **1981:** *Candida*; *Grown-ups*; *Kingdoms*; *Little Foxes, The* **1982:** *Beyond Therapy*; *Come Back to the 5 & Dime, Jimmy Dean, Jimmy Dean* **1983:** *Heartbreak House* **1985:** *Mystery of Edwin Drood, The* **1986:** *House of Blue Leaves, The*; *Smile* **1987:** *Front Page, The* **1988:** *Spoils of War* **1989:** *City of Angels*; *Lend Me A Tenor*

Leo Gambacorta

Leo Gambacorta was scenic, costume and lighting designer for one show on Broadway in 1980.

Lighting Designs:
1980: *Black Broadway*

Scenic Designs:
1980: *Black Broadway*

Costume Designs:
1980: *Black Broadway*

Barry Garlinger

On Broadway, Barry Garlinger was lighting designer for one show in 1964.

Lighting Designs:
1964: *Conversation At Midnight*

Henry L. Gebhardt

Henry L. Gebhardt, a theatrical properties maker in New York City, also designed one set on Broadway in 1918. He supplied "theatrical properties, papier maché and advertising novelties" from 433-5 West 42nd Street, and "theatrical supplies and equipment" from 523 West

45th Street in New York City through the 1920s and 1930s. He was born in Germany and moved to the United States as a young man. He served two terms on the Board of Education in Cliffside Park, New Jersey, where he resided at the time of his death on September 29, 1942 at the age of seventy-six.

Lighting Designs:
1918: *Garden of Allah, The*

Larry Gebhardt

Larry Gebhardt created one lighting design on Broadway in 1949.

Lighting Designs:
1949: *All for Love*

Peter Gennaro

Peter Gennaro is well-known as a dancer and choreographer. He was born in 1924 in Metairie, Louisiana (a suburb of New Orleans). After studying dance with Katherine Dunham and José Limon he joined the ballet company of the San Carlo Opera. He danced on Broadway in musicals including *Make Mine Manhattan* and *Kiss Me, Kate*, and choreographed *Fiorello!*, *Irene* (for which he received a Tony nomination for choreography) and *The Unsinkable Molly Brown*. In 1948 he married Jean Kinsella, a former ballet dancer. His credits as a dancer and choreographer also extend to films and television. In 1962 he not only choreographed the Broadway production *Mr. President*, but also designed the scenery and lighting. In 1964 Peter Gennaro received an award from *Dance Magazine*.

Lighting Designs:
1962: *Mr. President*

Scenic Designs:
1962: *Mr. President*

Zvi Geyra

Zvi Geyra was born in Jerusalem and studied art at Bezalel in Israel. He moved to New York City in 1950 to study design at the Dramatic Workshop. After completing service in the Israeli Army he designed in Tel Aviv, but later returned to the Dramatic Workshop to teach.

Off-Broadway credits include *Uncle Vanya* and plays at Equity Library Theatre. He has also designed for television, and in the late 1950s was in residence at La Jolla Playhouse for a summer season.

Lighting Designs:
1958: *Edwin Booth*

Scenic Designs:
1958: *Edwin Booth* 1960: *Long Dream, The*

Michael Giannitti

Michael Giannitti was born in Stamford, Connecticut on July 27, 1962, the son of Joseph and Marie Giannitti. He attended Bates College, where he began designing and received a Bachelor of Arts in 1984. After attending the Yale University School of Drama, where he received an M.F.A. in 1987, he assisted Jennifer Tipton. His first professional design in New York City was *Soft Sell* at La Mama E.T.C. in 1986, which was choreographed by Marta Renzi.

Lighting Designs:
1988: *Joe Turner's Come and Gone*

Enid Gilbert

Enid Gilbert designed scenery, costumes and lights for plays on Broadway in the mid-1940s.

Lighting Designs:
1946: *Bees and the Flowers, The*

Scenic Designs:
1946: *Bees and the Flowers, The*

Costume Designs:
1945: *Assassin, The* 1946: *Bees and the Flowers, The*

John J. Gleason

John J. Gleason was born on April 10, 1941 in Brooklyn, New York, and attended Hunter College where he received a Bachelor of Arts degree. He was the resident lighting designer from 1967 to 1972 for the Repertory Theatre of Lincoln Center, where he designed twenty-one productions. His first professional design was *Tartuffe* in January, 1965 at the ANTA Washington Square Theatre. Influenced by his mentor, Charles Elson, he is not only a designer of lights but also a master teacher on the faculty of the Tisch School of the Arts at New York University. With over ninety shows on Broadway to his credit including Nicol Williamson's *Hamlet*, *The Great White Hope*, *My Fair Lady*, and *The Royal Family*, he has also designed off-Broadway including *Small Craft Warnings*, in regional theatres, at the National Theatre of the Deaf, and for opera, including *Live from Lincoln Center*. A man of diverse talents, he has also written screenplays and contributed articles on lighting design to *Lighting Dimensions*. In 1973 he received the Maharam Award for Lighting, and in 1975 a Los Angeles Drama Critics Circle Award for *Savages*.

Lighting Designs:
1965: *La Grasse Valise* **1968:** *Cry of Players, A*; *Great White Hope, The*; *Lovers and Other Strangers*; *We Bombed in New Haven* **1969:** *Hamlet (Starring Nichol Williamson)*; *Home Fires/ Cop Out*; *National Theatre of the Deaf, The* **1970:** *Brightower*; *Candida*; *Othello*; *Sganarelle*; *Songs from Milkwood*; *Two By Two* **1971:** *Frank Merriwell (or Honor Changed)* **1972:** *Love Suicide At Schofield Barracks, The*; *Tough to Get Help* **1973:** *Pajama Game, The*; *Streetcar Named Desire, A*; *Veronica's Room*; *Women, The* **1974:** *All Over Town*; *Flowers*; *Lorelei or Gentlemen Still Prefer Blondes*; *Over Here*; *Who's Who in Hell* **1975:** *Don't Call Back*; *Hello, Dolly (Starring Pearl Bailey)*; *Royal Family, The* **1976:** *Herzl*; *My Fair Lady* **1978:** *Angel*; *Platinum* **1980:** *Philadelphia Story, The* **1981:** *Macbeth*; *Survivor, The* **1983:** *Guys in the Truck, The*

Michael Gordon

Michael Gordon, a lighting designer, director, and actor, was born on September 6, 1909 in Baltimore. He attended the John Hopkins University and received a Bachelor of Arts degree in 1929. He also attended Yale University, where he studied under George Pierce Baker and received a Master's of Fine Arts degree in 1932. He directed many films including *Cyrano de Bergerac*, *For Love of Money*, *Another Part of the Forest*, and *Pillow Talk*. In the latter he pioneered the split screen technique. On television he directed *Room 222* (among other series) and various special programs. He has also taught at the University of California, Los Angeles. As a lighting designer he is also credited with *Casey*

Jones and *Rocket to the Moon* (1938), *Gentle People* and *My Heart's in the Highlands* (1939), and *Thunder Rock*, *Night Music* and *Heavenly Express* (1940).

Lighting Designs:
1939: *Thunder Rock* **1940:** *Night Music*

Mordecai Gorelik

Mordecai (Max) Gorelik, a scenic designer, director, author and educator, also occasionally designed costumes and lights during his long, distinguished career. He attended the Pratt Institute and studied with Norman Bel Geddes, Robert Edmond Jones and Serge Soudeikine. He was born on August 25, 1899 in Shchedrin, Russia. His family emigrated to New York in 1905 and as a youth Max worked in his father's newsstand. His first professional production was *King Hunger* at the Hedgerow Theatre in Moylan, Pennsylvania in 1924. He made his Broadway debut with scenic designs for *Processional* in 1925, after working at the Neighborhood Playhouse as a scene painter and technician and at the Provincetown Playhouse. He served as principal designer for The Group Theatre from 1937 to 1940. The author of over one hundred articles and the books *New Theaters for Old* and *Toward a Larger Theatre*, he taught design and lectured widely. From 1960 to 1972 he was on the faculty of Southern Illinois University, which awarded him an honorary degree in 1988. Mordecai Gorelik died on March 23, 1990 at age 90.

Lighting Designs:
1947: *All My Sons* **1955:** *Hatful of Rain, A*

Scenic Designs:
1925: *Processional* **1926:** *Moon Is a Gong, The* **1927:** *Loud Speaker* **1928:** *Final Balance, The* **1931:** *1931–* **1932:** *Success Story* **1933:** *All Good Americans*; *Big Night*; *Little Ol' Boy*; *Men in White* **1934:** *Gentlewoman*; *Sailors of Cattaro* **1935:** *Let Freedom Ring*; *Mother*; *Young Go First, The* **1938:** *Casey Jones*; *Rocket to the Moon*; *Tortilla Flat* **1939:** *Thunder Rock* **1940:** *Night Music* **1947:** *All My Sons* **1952:** *Desire Under the Elms* **1954:** *Flowering Peach, The* **1955:** *Hatful of Rain, A* **1957:** *Sin of Pat Muldoon, The* **1960:** *Distant Bell, A*

Costume Designs:
1925: *Processional* **1929:** *Fiesta* **1955:** *Hatful of Rain, A*

Anthony Greshoff

Anthony Greshoff (a.k.a. Tony Greshoff, A. Greshoff) was active on Broadway from 1915 to 1931 as a lighting designer. No clues to his background are available in any of the standard (or unusual) sources. He also had some early credits, including the 1902 production of *A Modern Magdalen* which lists the following technical or design elements in the playbill: "Set Painted by Joseph Physioc, Electrical Effects by A. Greshoff."

Lighting Designs:
1915: *Fads and Fancies* 1919: *Angel Face; Clarence; On the Hiring Line* 1920: *Bab; Girl in the Spotlight, The; Poldekin* 1921: *Alias Jimmy Valentine; Dulcy; Golden Days; Intimate Strangers, The; Perfect Fool, The; Two Little Girls; Wren, The; Ziegfeld Midnight Follies* 1922: *Drums of Jeopardy, The; Listening In* 1923: *Adrienne; Rivals, The* 1924: *Chocolate Dandies, The* 1927: *Adventurous Age, The; Behold This Dreamer; Spellbound* 1928: *Diplomacy; Sherlock Holmes* 1929: *Houseparty; Sherlock Holmes; Your Uncle Dudley* 1930: *It's a Grand Life; Mr. Samuel; Rivals, The* 1931: *Admirable Crichton, The*

Jerry Grollnek

Jerry Grollnek, a lighting designer, did one show in 1976 on Broadway.

Lighting Designs:
1976: *Debbie Reynolds Show*

Moe Hack

Moe Hack (a.k.a. Monroe B. Hack, Mac Hack) was a driector and lighting specialist. His parents were co-owners and managers of the Thalia and Atlantic Theatres in the Bowery in New York City, and although they encouraged their son to study law he pursued a career in theatre. David Belasco arranged for a scholarship for Hack to attend Carnegie Technical College. After service in World War II he returned to New York and in 1945 he directed *Winterset* at Equity Library Theatre. He gradually specialized in lights and became known as a lighting technical director around the country. He served as a design and lighting expert on the staff of the Federal Theatre where he worked with Howard Bay and others to develop *The Living Newspaper, One Third of A Nation, Power,* and *Pinnochio*. He toured with Gertrude Lawrence providing technical support for *Pygmalion*. However, he never entirely gave up directing and directed plays including *Phamtoms* (1930, *Blue Holiday* (1945) and *E=MC2* (1948) on Broadway. He also produced *Seeds in the Wind* (1948), the Old Vic tour to New York City in 1948 (with Howard Newman), and *Talent '49* in 1949. In 1956 he produced *Fat Tuesday* at the Tamiment (Pennsylvania) Playhouse.

Lighting Designs:
1937: *One Third of a Nation* 1938: *Life and Death of An American; Pinocchio* 1941: *Brooklyn, U.S.A.* 1942: *Eve of Saint Mark, The; Proof Through the Night* 1943: *Family, The; Patriots, The* 1944: *Storm Operation; Thank You, Svoboda* 1945: *Tempest, The* 1948: *Gone Tomorrow/Home Life of a Buffalo/Hope is the Thing*

Jeanne Hackett

Jeanne (Janette, Jeanette) Hackett, an actress and dancer in musical revues, was born in 1898 in New York City and died there on August 16, 1979. She first performed in vaudeville in 1907, touring until her eighteenth birthday when she could legally perform in New York, and remained active until the 1940s. She initially performed with her brother Albert before forming her own company, the Jeannette Hackett Chorus, performing, choreographing and also designing settings, lights and costumes. She later teamed up with Harry Delmar whom she subsequently married. They separated both professionally and personally in the late 1920s. In 1930 she married the singer John Steel and staged productions for her husband while continuing to perform and choreograph.

Lighting Designs:
1943: *Hairpin Harmony*

Costume Designs:
1927: *Delmar's Revels*

James Hamilton

James Hamilton designed lighting and settings for a Broadway show in 1969, and designed a set for an additional production in 1979.

Lighting Designs:
1969: *New Music Hall of Israel, The*
Scenic Designs:
1969: *New Music Hall of Israel, The* 1979: *Got Tu Go Disco*

Terry Hands

Terrence David Hands started his career in theatre as founder/director of the Everyman Theatre in Liverpool, England where he worked from 1964 to 1966. He is known in the United States primarily for his association with the Royal Shakespeare Company which he joined in 1966 as artistic director of Theatre-Go-Round (for touring productions). From 1967 to 1977 he was Associate Director of the Royal Shakespeare Company, and in 1978 became Co-Artistic Director with Trevor Nunn. From 1986 until 1989 he was Artistic Director of RSC. From 1975 to 1977 he was also Consultant Director of the Comédie Française in Paris. His directorial debut on Broadway was *All's Well That Ends Well* in 1984. He was born on January 9, 1941 in Aldershot, Hampshire, England and attended Birmingham University (Bachelor of Arts, English language and literature with honors) and the Royal Academy of Dramatic Art.

Lighting Designs:
1984: *Cyrano De Bergerac*; *Much Ado About Nothing* 1988: *Carrie*

Roy Hargrave

Roy Hargrave was the lighting designer for a Broadway production in 1944 which he also directed. He first appeared on stage as Alexander in a 1927 production of *The Spider* in New Haven which subsequently moved into New York City. He worked steadily thereafter, acting, writing and directing plays into the late 1940s. Roy Hargrave was born in New York City in 1908 and was educated at the Barnard and McKenzie Schools.

Lighting Designs:
1944: *Pick-Up Girl*

Edward Hartford

Edward Hartford, an actor, stage manager, and lighting designer, began professional life as stage manager for the Theatre Guild's production of *The Guardsman*, followed by *Porgy* in New York and London. He has also toured throughout the Orient as a stage mangaer. He performed in *The Second Man* with Lynn Fontanne and Alfred Lunt. His father, Michael Hartford, helped build the Boston Opera House. Edward Hartford, who originated a method to handle film in early movies, died on May 29, 1942 at age 53 in New York City.

Lighting Designs:
1925: *Love's Call*

Louis Hartmann

Louis Hartmann (a.k.a. Hartman) started in theatre in the 1890s as a prop boy at Hammerstein's Harlem Opera House. He became David Belasco's chief electrician in 1901 and worked with him until Belasco's death in 1931. An innovative stage electrician, he was one of the first lighting designers and readily transferred his expertise from gas lighting systems to electrical systems. He developed many techniques including the first incandescent spotlights, indirect overhead lighting, and silvered reflectors. Together Belasco and Hartmann banished footlights for the 1915 production of *The Return of Peter Grimm*. At the time of his death at age 64 on February 9, 1941, Hartmann was on the sound staff at Radio City Music Hall. He was the author of *Theatre Lighting: A Manual of the Stage Switchboard*, a work which documented some of the developments he pioneered.

Lighting Designs:
1918: *Auctioneer, The* 1919: *Son-Daughter, The* 1920: *Deburau* 1921: *Easiest Way, The*; *Return of Peter Grimm, The* 1923: *Mary, Mary, Quite Contrary* 1924: *Ladies of the Evening*; *Tiger Cats* 1925: *Accused*; *Canary Dutch*; *Dove, The* 1926: *What Never Dies* 1928: *Bachelor Father, The* 1929: *It's a Wise Child* 1930: *Dancing Partner*

John Harvey

John Harvey was active as a Broadway lighting designer between 1961 and 1973. A native of Philadelphia, he founded the Philadelphia Opera Company and headed the production departments for seven years. He worked as an assistant to Jo Mielziner for sixteen years on more than forty Broadway productions and on the design of the Vivian Beaumont Theatre. He also designed lights for the Opera Company of Boston.

Lighting Designs:
1961: *Kean* 1962: *Come On Strong; Passage to India, A* 1963: *110 Degrees in the Shade; Tovarich* 1964: *Deputy, The* 1965: *Mating Dance; Very Rich Woman, A* 1967: *More Stately Mansions* 1968: *Happiness Is Just a Little Thing Called a Rolls Royce* 1969: *My Daughter, Your Son* 1973: *No Sex Please, We're British*

David Hays

David Arthur Hays, a scenic and lighting designer and producer, was born on June 2, 1930 in New York City. During his career he has worked with many great designers, actors and directors, including Roger Furse, Leslie Hurry, Oliver Gielgud and Peter Brook. He received a Bachelor of Arts at Harvard University in 1952 and began a Fulbright Fellowship to the Old Vic in the same year. He attended the Yale University School of Drama from 1953 to 1954 and then Boston University, where he earned an M.F.A. in 1955 under Raymond Sovey and Horace Armistead. He was an apprentice at the Brattle Theatre in Cambridge, Massachusetts from 1949 to 1952 where he worked with Robert O'Hearn. His first design, *Hay Fever* in 1951, was at the Brattle Theatre. His inspiration has come from Jo Mielziner, George Balanchine and Tyrone Guthrie. With fifty Broadway plays and thirty ballets for George Balanchine to his credit, it is little wonder he has received two Obie Awards (for *The Quare Fellow* and *The Balcony*), several Tony nominations, two honorary doctorates, and the New York Drama Critics Award for *No Strings*. His book, *Light on the Subject*, was published by Limelight Editions in 1990.

Lighting Designs:
1956: *Innkeeper, The* 1959: *Tenth Man, The; Triple Play* 1960: *All the Way Home; Love and Libel; Roman Candle* 1961: *Gideon; Look: We've Come Through; No Strings; Sunday in New York* 1962: *Family Affair, A; In the Counting House* 1963: *Lorenzo; Strange Interlude* 1964: *Baby Wants a Kiss; Hughie; Last Analysis, The; Marco Millions; Murderer Among Us, A* 1965: *Diamond Orchid; Drat! the Cat!; Mrs. Dally; Peterpat* 1966: *Dinner At Eight; We Have Always Lived in the Castle* 1967: *Dr. Cook's Garden* 1968: *Goodbye People, The* 1981: *Bring Back Birdie*

Scenic Designs:
1956: *Innkeeper, The; Long Day's Journey Into Night* 1958: *Night Circus, The* 1959: *Rivalry, The; Tenth Man, The; Triple Play* 1960: *All the Way Home; Love and Libel; Roman Candle* 1961: *Gideon; Look: We've Come Through; No Strings; Sunday in New York* 1962: *Family Affair, A; In the Counting House* 1963: *Lorenzo; Strange Interlude* 1964: *Hughie; Last Analysis, The; Marco Millions; Murderer Among Us, A* 1965: *Diamond Orchid; Drat! the Cat!; Mrs. Dally; Peterpat* 1966: *Dinner At Eight; We Have Always Lived in the Castle* 1967: *Dr. Cook's Garden* 1968: *Cry of Players, A; Goodbye People, The* 1969: *National Theatre of the Deaf, The* 1970: *Gingerbread Lady, The; Songs from Milkwood; Two By Two* 1978: *Platinum*

Timothy Heale

Timothy Heale was lighting designer on Broadway in 1977 for one production.

Lighting Designs:
1977: *Ipi Tombi*

Gilbert V. Hemsley, Jr.

Gilbert V. Hemsley, Jr., was born in Bridgeport, Connecticut in 1936. He debuted in New York with the lighting designs at the New York City Opera in 1978 for *Andrea Chenier*. This production was the first of thirty-five operas for the New York City Opera and the Metropolitan Opera, with many other productions for major opera companies. In addition, he designed numerous productions for dance companies such as the American Ballet Company, Alvin Alley, Martha Graham, and the Bolshoi Opera and Ballet. He was also a noted production manager who managed the opening of the Kennedy Center for the Performing Arts in Washington, D.C., and national tours of European and Asian companies around the United States. He did his undergraduate and graduate work at Yale University, completing an M.F.A. in 1960, after which he joined the faculty at Princeton. Later he became an assistant to Jean Rosenthal. After several very busy seasons, he looked for a respite and joined the faculty at the University of Wisconsin, where his "retirement" lasted only a brief time. Using his students as assistants he resumed an active career, teaching students in the same way he had learned from Jean Rosenthal. When he died on September 5, 1983 his family, friends, colleagues and students established a lighting internship in his honor at the New York City Opera.

Lighting Designs:
1966: *Right You Are...*; *School for Scandal, The*; *We, Comrades Three* **1967:** *War and Peace*; *Wild Duck, The*; *You Can't Take It with You* **1973:** *Cyrano* **1974:** *Jumpers* **1976:** *Porgy and Bess*; *Your Arms Too Short to Box with God* **1977:** *I Love My Wife* **1978:** *Mighty Gents, The* **1979:** *Comin' Uptown*; *Monteith and Rand*; *Most Happy Fella, The*; *Sugar Babies* **1983:** *Porgy and Bess*

Mark Henderson

Mark Henderson is a British lighting designer. He has designed operas throughout Europe and the United Kingdom, dance for Sadler's Wells Ballet and Ballet Rambert, fashion shows for Zandra Rhodes and Laura Ashley, and numerous plays for the Royal Shakespeare Festival. In the West End he has designed *Caine Mutiny Court Martial*, *A Patriot for Me* with Alan Bates (both in London and Los Angeles), *Figaro*, *Pump Boys and Dinettes*, and *Scarlet Pimpernel* among others. He has also been lighting designer for Rowan Atkinson in New York, Australia, and New Zealand.

Lighting Designs:
1986: *Rowan Atkinson at The Atkinson* **1990:** *Cat on a Hot Tin Roof*

Jocelyn Herbert

Jocelyn Herbert, a British designer of sets and costumes, was born on February 22, 1917. She studied in England and France with George Devine and Michel St. Denis, who have been influential during her career. She did not begin to design until the age of forty, with *The Chairs* for the English Stage Company at the Royal Court Theatre. Since that time she has designed countless productions, working extensively in theatre and opera. Companies for which she has designed include the National Theatre, Royal Shakespeare Company, Metropolitan Opera, Paris Opera, and Sadler's Wells in addition to productions in London's West End and on Broadway. While Jocelyn Herbert's film designs have been few they have been notable, including *Tom Jones, Hamlet, If...* and *The Hotel New Hampshire*.

Lighting Designs:
1963: *Chips with Everything*; *Luther*

Scenic Designs:
1963: *Chips with Everything*; *Luther* **1965:** *Inadmissable Evidence* **1969:** *Hamlet (Starring Nichol Williamson)* **1970:** *Home* **1977:** *Merchant, The* **1989:** *3Penny Opera*

Costume Designs:
1963: *Chips with Everything*; *Luther* **1965:** *Inadmissable Evidence* **1969:** *Hamlet (Starring Nichol Williamson)* **1970:** *Home* **1977:** *Merchant, The* **1989:** *3Penny Opera*

Leo Herbert

Leo Herbert, an actor and occasional lighting designer, designed lights on Broadway in 1944 for a production in which he also appeared. In 1945 he performed in *Seven Mirrors* and was also on the stage crew.

Lighting Designs:
1944: *Earth Journey*

David Hersey

Although David Hersey began his career in theatre as an actor, he promptly became one of Europe's leading lighting designers upon moving to London in 1968. His work in opera, ballet and with major theatre companies comprise over two hundred productions. The list of his awards is almost as long as the list of his credits: three Tony Awards, for *Evita, Les Miserables* and *Cats*; a Maharam Award for *Nicholas Nickleby*; a Dora Mavor Moore Award for *Les Miserables* and *Cats*; and also Drama Logue Critic's Awards, Los Angeles Drama Critics Awards, Civil Trust Awards, and Drama Desk Awards. He was born in Rochester, New York on November 30, 1939 and was educated at Oberlin College. In 1971 he founded David Hersey Associates, Limited which specializes in the design and manufacture of specialist lighting equipment and effects for theatre and also architectural lighting. Recent credits include the 1991 Broadway production of *Miss Saigon*.

Lighting Designs:

1981: *Life and Adventures of Nicholas Nickleby, The*; *Merrily We Roll Along* **1982:** *Cats* **1986:** *Life and Adventures of Nicholas Nickleby, The* **1987:** *Les Miserables*; *Starlight Express* **1988:** *Chess*

Girvan Higginson

Girvan Higginson was a lighting designer, scenic designer and director who was active on Broadway in the 1940s. He graduated from Yale University where he specialized in stage lighting. His father was the architect Augustus Higginson, who worked in Chicago and Santa Barbara, California. He was the nephew of John Higginson, founder of the Boston Symphony. Girvan Higginson also directed *Speak of the Devil* and produced *Eye on the Sparrow* and *The Nightingale* in New York City, and appeared in *1776* and *Gentlemen, the Queen* in the mid-1920s.

Lighting Designs:

1942: *Willow and I, The* **1947:** *Story of Mary Surratt, The*

Scenic Designs:

1942: *Willow and I, The*

Charles E. Hoefler

Charles E. Hoefler, who has designed sets on and off-Broadway and for stock companies, makes his living designing industrial promotions. He was born on May 25, 1930 in Detroit and attended the University of Michigan, where he received a B.A. in 1952 and an M.F.A. in 1953. He served an apprenticeship with Tobins Lake Studios, South Lyon, Michigan when it was a design and construction shop. His first Broadway experience was with projections for the Oliver Smith design for *Jimmy* in 1970. His designs have been honored with the Drama Critics Award and Bronze, Silver and Gold Awards at the New York International Film and Television Festival.

Lighting Designs:

1980: *It's So Nice to Be Civilized*

Scenic Designs:

1980: *It's So Nice to Be Civilized*

Donald Holder

Donald Holder, a native of New York City, was born on May 12, 1958 and received a B.S. degree in forestry at the University of Maine in 1980, and an M.F.A. in Technical Design at Yale in 1986, where he received the Edward C. Cole Award for Excellence. His career has been influenced by the lighting designs of Jennifer Tipton. His first professional design, *The Water Engine*, was performed at the Muhlenberg Theatre Program in 1981. He is resident designer for the SoHo Repertory Theatre, the George Street Playhouse and Ballet Hispanico of New York, and is a facilities design consultant with Imero Fiorentino Associates. Donald Holder is married to director Evan Yinoulis. Recent credits include *Caucasian Chalk Circle* for the New York Shakespeare Festival, directed by George C. Wolfe.

Lighting Designs:

1989: *Eastern Standard*

Klaus Holm

Klaus Holm is both a scenic and lighting designer, although the majority of his Broadway credits are for lighting. He was born Klaus Kuntze in Dresden, Germany on June 27, 1920, the son of sculptor and painter Martin Kuntze and dancer and choreographer Hanya Holm. He attended New York University, receiving a B.S. in 1948, and earned an M.F.A. at Yale in 1951. He designed as well as acted in college and stock productions. He has designed scenery for many productions off-Broadway at the Phoenix Theatre and Circle in the Square, New York City Center, Goodspeed Opera House, and New York City Opera among others. Between 1961 and 1962 he was lighting design consultant at the New York State Theatre and at Lincoln Philharmonic Hall at Lincoln Center. His designs for television include the set for *The Kate Smith Show* in 1951 for NBC. He shared the 1956 Obie Award for design and lighting with Alvin Colt.

Lighting Designs:

1954: *Girl on the Via Flamina, The*; *Golden Apple, The* **1955:** *Phoenix '55* **1960:** *Advise and Consent*; *Semi-Detached* **1961:** *Donnybrook!*; *Once There Was a Russian* **1962:** *Private Ear, The/ The Public Eye*; *Something About a Soldier* **1963:** *Heroine, The*

Scenic Designs:
1962: *Moby Dick*; *Private Ear, The/ The Public Eye*

Ralph Holmes

Ralph Holmes is a lighting designer who works in theatre, opera, ballet and modern dance. He also has extensive credits for television design and has been associated with CBS-TV since 1949.. He has served as lighting and art director for *Dance in America* on P.B.S. and is lighting designer for the daytime television series *The Guiding Light*.

Lighting Designs:
1961: *General Seeger*

Roy Holmes

Roy Holmes designed lighting for one show in 1940 on Broadway.

Lighting Designs:
1940: *Meet the People*

Harry Horner

Harry Horner worked as an architect before devoting his talents to the theatre. Known primarily as a scenic designer and director, he was born on July 24, 1912 in Holic, Czechoslovakia and studied acting and directing with Max Reinhardt. In the early 1930s he acted, directed and occasionally designed settings, lighting and costumes. After coming to the United States in 1935 he assisted Max Reinhardt and Norman Bel Geddes in New York. His credits for set design in theatre and opera are numerous and he has also continued to direct for theatre and television. His film designs have garnered him Academy Awards for the art direction of *The Hustler*, *The Heiress* and *They Shoot Horses, Don't They?*

Lighting Designs:
1942: *Lily of the Valley* 1946: *Christopher Blake* 1953: *Hazel Flagg* 1961: *How to Make a Man*

Scenic Designs:
1938: *All the Living*; *Escape This Night* 1939: *Family Portrait*; *Jeremiah*; *World We Make, The* 1940: *Burning Deck, The*; *Reunion in New York*; *Weak Link, The* 1941: *Banjo Eyes*; *Five Alarm Waltz*; *In Time to Come*; *Lady in the Dark*; *Let's Face It* 1942: *Kiss for Cinderella, A*; *Let's Face It*; *Lily of the Valley*; *Star and Garter*; *Under This Roof*; *Walking Gentleman* 1943: *Lady in the Dark*; *Winged Victory* 1946: *Christopher Blake* 1948: *Joy to the World*; *Me and Molly* 1953: *Hazel Flagg* 1961: *How to Make a Man*

Costume Designs:
1939: *Family Portrait*; *Jeremiah*

Michael J. Hotopp

Michael J. Hotopp works primarily in association with fellow designer Paul de Pass. They have extensive credits for productions on and off-Broadway, fashion shows, industrial promotions and television commercials through their company "Associated Theatrical Designs, Limited". Michael Hotopp studied at Carnegie Mellon and New York Universities. The national tours of *Evita* and *Annie* are also among their credits, as well as designs in regional theatres such as the Goodspeed Opera House, the Baltimore Opera, and Pittsburgh Playhouse. Michael Hotopp created the environment for *CBS This Morning* and has designed music videos. Awards include a Clio for an IBM commercial. For additional information see "Paul de Pass".

Lighting Designs:
1982: *Cleavage*

Scenic Designs:
1979: *Oklahoma!* 1980: *Brigadoon* 1981: *Oh, Brother* 1983: *Tapdance Kid, The*

Allen Lee Hughes

Lighting designer Allen Lee Hughes is a native of Washington, D.C. who began designing in high school while working with the Garrick Players in Middleton, Virginia and as a lighting assistant at Arena Stage. He received a B.A. from Catholic University in 1972 and an M.F.A. from New York University in 1979, where he studied with John Gleason. His first main stage design at Arena Stage was *Once In A Lifetime* in 1976. He debuted off-Broadway in 1979 with *Bebop the Hip Musical*. From 1979 to 1981 he assisted Jennifer Tipton and Arden Fingerhut, while continuing to design at Arena Stage and for small opera and dance companies. He became resident lighting designer for Eliot Feld in 1985. His designs have been honored many times and include nominations for Tony awards for *K-2* and *Strange Interlude*, a Maharam and an Outer Circle Critics Award for *K-2*, a Hollywood Drama Logue Critics Award for *Quilters*, and a Boston Theatre Critics Circle Award for *A Solider's Story*. Several designs at Arena Stage have been nominated for the Helen Hayes Award which he won for *Six Characters in Search of an Author* in the 1988-89 season.

Lighting Designs:
1983: *K-2* **1984:** *Accidental Death of An Anarchist*; *Quilters* **1985:** *Strange Interlude*

Peter Hunt

Peter Hunt, a director and lighting designer, was active on Broadway between 1963 and 1977. He was born in Pasadena, California on December 16, 1938. He attended The Hotchkiss School, where he first designed lights, and Yale University where he received both a B.A and an M.F.A. His first production in New York was in 1961 off- Broadway, *The Sap Of Life*. From 1964 to 1968 he designed for Richard Rogers at Lincoln Center and at the New York State Theatre. He directed his first play for the Williamstown Theatre, where he also designed lighting, beginning in 1957. His directorial debut in New York City was *Book* in 1968. He has also designed in London and for the film *1776*.

Lighting Designs:
1963: *Tambourines to Glory* **1966:** *Annie Get Your Gun*; *Wayward Stork* **1968:** *Noel Coward's Sweet Potato* **1977:** *Bully*

James F. Ingalls

James F. Ingalls studied at the University of North Carolina at Chapel Hill, received his undergraduate degree from the University of Connecticut, and took his M.F.A. from the Yale University School of Drama in stage management. He served as stage manager at Yale for three seasons prior to moving to New York City and spending two years as production stage manager for Twyla Tharp. His first New York production as lighting designer was *96A* for Eccentric Circles Theatre at St. Malachy's Church. When Paul Gallo left Amen Repertory Theatre, Jim Ingalls was named lighting designer and spent three years with the company. He has also been principal lighting designer for the American Repertory Theatre. His credits include numerous productions in regional theatres and collaborations with Peter Sellars, Adrianne Lobel, George Tsypin, and Stanley Wojewodski. Jennifer Tipton has been instrumental in shaping his career, in part because he studied her original designs for Twyla Tharp while re-creating them on the road. He also has been influenced by Thomas Skelton, with whom he worked while a stage manager at Yale. In 1985 Ingalls received the Helen Hayes Award in Washington D.C. for *The Count of Monte Cristo*. He has also received an Obie Award for sustained excellence in lighting. Recent productions includes *Passageio* and *Il Combatimento di Tancredi e Clorinda* in Aix-en-Provence, and *Lohengrin* for the Brussels National Opera.

Lighting Designs:
1983: *'Night Mother* **1984:** *Human Comedy, The*

Edward Jacobi

Edward J. Jacobi designed lighting for one production on Broadway in 1927. An electrician, he resided at 317 West 58th Street in New York City in 1925.

Lighting Designs:
1927: *Love in the Tropics*

Finlay James

Finlay James gave up a career in law to design for the theatre. He was born in Angus, Scotland and received a Diploma of Art in Dundee, Scotland. He has designed sets and costumes in Glasgow, Rome, Amsterdam, London (including the Old Vic and in the West End), and in Edinburgh among many other locations. His first designs on Broadway were seen in 1971. A teacher as well as a designer, he spent fourteen years as head of the School of Design in the College of Art and Design in Birmingham, England and has also been head of design at the City of Birmingham Polytechnic. In 1974 his costume designs for *Crown Matrimonial* were nominated for a Tony Award.

Lighting Designs:

1970: *Conduct Unbecoming*

Scenic Designs:

1970: *Conduct Unbecoming* 1973: *Crown Matrimonial* 1985: *Aren't We All?* 1987: *Blithe Spirit*

Costume Designs:

1970: *Conduct Unbecoming* 1973: *Crown Matrimonial*

Neil Peter Jampolis

Neil Peter Jampolis has numerous credits for designing lighting and sets on Broadway and for opera companies in the United States. He was born in Brooklyn on March 14, 1943 and received a B.F.A. from the Art Institute of Chicago in 1971. He occasionally also designs costumes for plays and operas. Mr. Jampolis received a Tony award for the lighting design for *Sherlock Holmes* in 1975. Recent designs include sets and lights for *Jackie Mason*, which opened on Broadway in October 1990.

Lighting Designs:

1970: *Borstal Boy*; *Les Blancs* 1971: *Earl of Ruston*; *To Live Another Summer* 1972: *Butley*; *Wild and Wonderful*; *Wise Child* 1973: *Crown Matrimonial*; *Emperor Henry IV*; *Let Me Hear You Smile* 1974: *Sherlock Holmes* 1976: *Innocents, The* 1977: *Otherwise Engaged* 1979: *Knockout*; *Night and Day* 1980: *American Clock, The*; *Harold and Maude* 1984: *Kipling* 1985: *Search for Signs/Intellegent Life...* 1986: *Into The Light*; *World According to Me, The* 1988: *World According to Me, The* 1989: *Black and Blue*; *Merchant of Venice, The*; *Orpheus Descending*; *Sid Caesar and Company*

Scenic Designs:

1970: *Borstal Boy* 1971: *Earl of Ruston*; *To Live Another Summer* 1985: *Search for Signs/Intellegent Life...* 1986: *World According to Me, The* 1988: *World According to Me, The* 1989: *Sid Caesar and Company*

Costume Designs:

1971: *Earl of Ruston* 1972: *Butley* 1986: *Into The Light*

George Clarke Jenkins

George Clarke Jenkins is a well-known scenery and lighting designer and art director for films.

Occasionally during his career he has also contributed costume designs to a production. He was born in Baltimore on November 19, 1911 and studied architecture at the University of Pennsylvania. He worked as an architect and interior designer before assisting Jo Mielziner from 1937 to 1941. His first Broadway show was *Early to Bed* in 1943, for which he designed the sets and lights. This production was followed by many others in New York City and throughout the country, including designs for the San Francisco Opera Association. He is also an art director for films known for his detail and realistic sets, as evidenced in movies such as *All the President's Men* (Academy Award), *The Miracle Worker*, *The China Syndrome*, *The Subject Was Roses*, *Sophie's Choice*, *The Dollmaker* and *Presumed Innocent*. He received the Donaldson Award for his settings for *I Remember Mama* in 1945. From 1985 to 1988 he was Professor of Motion Picture Design at the University of California at Los Angeles.

Lighting Designs:

1943: *Early to Bed* 1944: *Allah Be Praised*; *I Remember Mama* 1945: *Are You with It?*; *Common Ground*; *Dark of the Moon*; *French Touch, The*; *Memphis Bound*; *Strange Fruit* 1950: *Bell, Book and Candle*; *Curious Savage, The* 1953: *Gently Does It*; *Touchstone* 1954: *Bad Seed, The* 1955: *Ankles Aweigh*; *Desk Set, The* 1956: *Happiest Millionaire, The*; *Too Late the Phalarope* 1957: *Rumple* 1958: *Cue for Passion*; *Once More, with Feeling*; *Two for the Seesaw* 1959: *Miracle Worker, The*; *Tall Story* 1960: *Critics Choice*; *One More River* 1961: *Thirteen Daughters* 1962: *Step on a Crack*; *Thousand Clowns, A* 1965: *Catch Me If You Can*; *Generation* 1966: *Wait Until Dark* 1976: *Sly Fox*

Scenic Designs:

1943: *Early to Bed* 1944: *Allah Be Praised*; *I Remember Mama*; *Mexican Hayride* 1945: *Are You with It?*; *Common Ground*; *Dark of the Moon*; *French Touch, The*; *Memphis Bound*; *Strange Fruit* 1948: *Time for Elizabeth*; *Tonight At 8:30* 1949: *Lost in the Stars* 1950: *Bell, Book and Candle*; *Curious Savage, The*; *Curious Savage, The* 1952: *Three Wishes for Jamie* 1953: *Gently Does It*; *Touchstone* 1954: *Bad Seed, The*; *Immoralist, The* 1955: *Ankles Aweigh*; *Desk Set, The* 1956: *Happiest Millionaire, The*; *Too Late the Phalarope*

1957: *Rumple* 1958: *Cue for Passion; Once More, with Feeling; Two for the Seesaw* 1959: *Jolly's Progress; Miracle Worker, The; Tall Story* 1960: *Critics Choice; One More River* 1961: *Thirteen Daughters* 1962: *Step on a Crack; Thousand Clowns, A* 1963: *Jennie* 1965: *Catch Me If You Can; Generation* 1966: *Wait Until Dark* 1968: *Only Game in Town, The* 1972: *Night Watch* 1976: *Sly Fox*

Costume Designs:

1930: *So Was Napoleon* 1934: *Anything Goes* 1945: *Common Ground; French Touch, The* 1950: *Curious Savage, The* 1955: *Desk Set, The*

Donald Jensen

Donald F. Jensen, the son of Ernest and Margaret O'Conner Jensen, was born in Emporia, Kansas on October 2, 1931. He received a B.F.A. in the School of Drawing and Painting at the University of Kansas in 1953, and studied scenic design with Milton Smith at Columbia University and with Lester Polakov. Principally a costume designer, his first costume designs were for the opera *Gallantry* at Columbia and in 1957 he designed *Winkelburg* at the Renata Theatre in New York. He has assisted both Desmond Heeley and Theoni Aldredge in addition to his own designing. Other costume designs include the New York premiere of *Cock-a-Doodle Dandy* by Lucile Lortel. He was art director for the 1989 films *Dad* and *In Country*.

Lighting Designs:
1964: *Sunday Man, The*

Scenic Designs:
1964: *Sunday Man, The*

Costume Designs:
1964: *Sunday Man, The*

Albert R. Johnson

Albert Richard Johnson was primarily a set designer who also occasionally designed lights. He began designing in 1929 and his final production opened in October 1967, just prior to his death on December 21, 1967. He was born in La Crosse, Wisconsin on February 1, 1910 and first worked in theatre at the age of fifteen as a scene painter for the Farmington, Long Island Opera House. His first New York design

was *The Criminal Code* in 1929 at the age of nineteen, after which he studied with Norman Bel Geddes. During his busy career he was a consultant on productions and designs for the New York World's Fair, Radio City Music Hall, Ringling Brothers & Barnum and Bailey Circus, and Jones Beach. He also directed and designed lights for industrial promotions.

Lighting Designs:

1932: *Americana* 1941: *Crazy with the Heat* 1945: *Girl from Nantucket, The; Live Life Again* 1947: *Dear Judas* 1958: *Cloud 7* 1962: *Night Life*

Scenic Designs:

1929: *Criminal Code, The; Half Gods* 1930: *Three's a Crowd* 1931: *Band Wagon, The* 1932: *Americana; Face the Music; Foreign Affairs; Mad Hopes, The* 1933: *As Thousands Cheer; Face the Music; Let 'em Eat Cake* 1934: *Great Waltz, The; Life Begins At 8:40; Revenge with Music; Union Pacific; Ziegfeld Follies: 1934* 1935: *Great Waltz, The; Jumbo* 1937: *Betweeen the Devil* 1938: *Great Lady; Leave It to Me!; You Never Know* 1939: *George White's Scandals; Leave It to Me!* 1940: *John Henry* 1941: *Crazy with the Heat* 1942: *Proof Through the Night; Skin of Our Teeth, The* 1943: *My Dear Public* 1944: *Sing Out, Sweet Land* 1945: *Girl from Nantucket, The; Live Life Again* 1947: *Dear Judas* 1949: *Two Blind Mice* 1950: *Pardon Our French* 1952: *Chase, The; Fancy Meeting You Again; Of Thee I Sing; Shuffle Along* 1958: *Cloud 7* 1962: *Night Life* 1967: *What Did We Do Wrong?*

Alfred Cheney Johnston

As a lighting designer, Alfred Cheney Johnston was active on Broadway in the late 1930s. He was the official photographer for Florenz Ziegfeld Jr. from 1917 to 1931 and is best known for his photos of various editions of *Ziegfeld Follies*, especially studio shots of showgirls. He also photographed advertising and industrial layouts and published *Enchanting Beauty*, a 1937 photographic study of the human figure, issued by Swan Publications in New York. Alfred Cheney Johnston, Inc., a commercial photography studio, was located at 114 E. 47th Street City. Mr. Johnston also had a studio at his home in Oxford, Connecticut. He died in Ansonia, Connecticut on April 19, 1971 at age 87.

Lighting Designs:

1937: *Sea Legs*

Bassett Jones

Bassett Jones was born in New Brighton, Staten Island on February 6, 1877 and died at the age of 82 on January 25, 1960. He studied engineering at the Stevens Institute of Technology and the Massachusetts Institute of Technology and spent his life principally designing elevators and architectural lighting systems. He designed lights for the New York World's Fair, the Empire State Building, the Chrysler Building, and the Irving Trust Company. Bassett Jones also made several contributions to stage lighting, creating the first floodlight units and also devising other special equipment. He supervised stage lighting for Maude Adams' plays and was consultant for *Peter Pan* in 1912.

Lighting Designs:

1925: *Cain*

Scenic Designs:

1925: *Cain*

Costume Designs:

1925: *Cain*

Robert Edmond Jones

Robert Edmond Jones, designer and producer, was born in Milton, New Hampshire on December 12, 1887 and began designing for the theatre in 1911. He studied at Harvard and brought great originality of design and color to the theatre, perhaps influenced by his admiration of Max Reinhardt. While working on a pageant in Madison Square Garden he became acquainted with one of Reinhardt's artists, who invited him to Germany to see the producer's methods. The outbreak of war forced his return to America in 1915. Jones' designs for *The Man Who Married A Dumb Wife*, included at the last moment as a curtain raiser for *Androcles and the Lion*, are generally regarded as marking the beginning of the "New American Stagecraft." He was associated with Kenneth MacGowan and Eugene O'Neill in the production of many plays at the Greenwich Village Playhouse, where he directed and designed many of O'Neill's plays. A prolific designer, he had many productions to his credit, well beyond the list included here. He

was art director for the opening production at Radio City Music Hall. His book, *The Dramatic Imagination*, is a classic. Robert Edmond Jones died on November 26, 1954.

Lighting Designs:

1933: *Mary of Scotland* 1938: *Devil and Daniel Webster, The*; *Susanna, Don't You Cry* 1939: *Summer Night* 1940: *Romeo and Juliet* 1942: *Without Love* 1943: *Othello* 1944: *Helen Goes to Troy* 1946: *Iceman Cometh, The*; *Lute Song*

Scenic Designs:

1915: *Devil's Garden, The*; *Man Who Married a Dumb Wife, The*; *Trilby* 1916: *Caliban By the Yellow Sands*; *Good Gracious, Annabelle*; *Happy Ending, The* 1917: *Deluge, The*; *Rescuing Angel, The*; *Rider of Dreams, The/ Granny Maumee/ Simon*; *Successful Calamity, A* 1918: *Be Calm, Camilla*; *Gentile Wife, The*; *Hedda Gabler*; *Redemption*; *Wild Duck, The* 1919: *Jest, The* 1920: *George Washington*; *Samson and Delilah*; *Tragedy of Richard III, The* 1921: *Anna Christie*; *Claw, The*; *Daddy's Gone A-Hunting*; *Idle Inn, The*; *Macbeth*; *Mountain Man, The*; *Swords* 1922: *Deluge, The*; *Hairy Ape, The*; *Hamlet*; *Romeo and Juliet*; *Rose Bernd*; *S.S. Tenacity, The*; *Voltaire* 1923: *Hamlet*; *Laughing Lady, The*; *Launzi*; *Royal Fandango, A* 1924: *Desire Under the Elms*; *Fashion*; *George Dandin, Or the Husband Confounded*; *Living Mask, The*; *Saint, The*; *Spook Sonata, The*; *Welded* 1925: *Beyond*; *Buccaneer, The*; *Fountain, The*; *In a Garden*; *Love for Love*; *Michel Auclair*; *Trelawney of the Wells* 1926: *Great God Brown, The*; *Jest, The*; *Love 'em and Leave 'em* 1927: *Claw, The*; *House of Women, The*; *Paris Bound*; *Trelawney of the Wells* 1928: *Holiday*; *Machinal*; *Martine*; *Money Lender, The*; *Mr. Moneypenny*; *Salvation*; *These Days* 1929: *Becky Sharpe*; *Channel Road, The*; *Commodore Marries, The*; *Cross Roads*; *Ladies Leave*; *See Naples and Die*; *Serena Blandish*; *Week-End* 1930: *Children of Darkness*; *Green Pastures, The*; *Rebound*; *Roadside* 1931: *Camille*; *Lady with a Lamp, The*; *Mourning Becomes Electra*; *Passing Present, The* 1932: *Camille*; *Lucrece*; *Mourning Becomes Electra*; *Night Over Taos* 1933: *Ah, Wilderness*; *Green Bay Tree, The*; *Mary of Scotland*; *Nine Pine Street* 1934: *Dark Victory*; *Joyous Season* 1935: *Green Pastures* 1937: *Othello* 1938: *Devil and Daniel Webster, The*; *Everywhere I Roam*; *Seagull, The*; *Susanna, Don't*

You Cry 1939: *Kindred*; *Philadelphia Story, The*; *Summer Night* 1940: *Juno and the Paycock*; *Love for Love* 1942: *Without Love* 1943: *Othello* 1944: *Helen Goes to Troy*; *Jackpot* 1946: *Iceman Cometh, The*; *Lute Song* 1950: *Enchanted, The* 1951: *Green Pastures*

Costume Designs:

1915: *Devil's Garden, The*; *Man Who Married a Dumb Wife, The* 1916: *Caliban By the Yellow Sands* 1917: *Rider of Dreams, The/ Granny Maumee/ Simon* 1920: *George Washington*; *Tragedy of Richard III, The* 1921: *Macbeth*; *Swords* 1922: *Hamlet*; *Romeo and Juliet*; *Voltaire* 1923: *Hamlet*; *Launzi* 1924: *Fashion*; *George Dandin, Or the Husband Confounded*; *Living Mask, The*; *Spook Sonata, The*; *Welded* 1925: *Beyond*; *Buccaneer, The*; *Fountain, The*; *Love for Love*; *Trelawney of the Wells* 1926: *Great God Brown, The*; *Jest, The*; *Little Eyolf* 1927: *House of Women, The* 1928: *Martine*; *Mr. Moneypenny* 1929: *Becky Sharpe*; *Channel Road, The*; *See Naples and Die* 1930: *Children of Darkness* 1931: *Camille*; *Mourning Becomes Electra*; *Passing Present, The* 1932: *Lucrece*; *Mourning Becomes Electra*; *Night Over Taos* 1933: *Mary of Scotland*; *Nine Pine Street* 1935: *Green Pastures* 1937: *Othello* 1938: *Devil and Daniel Webster, The*; *Everywhere I Roam*; *Seagull, The*; *Susanna, Don't You Cry* 1939: *Summer Night* 1942: *Without Love* 1943: *Othello* 1946: *Iceman Cometh, The*; *Lute Song* 1950: *Enchanted, The* 1951: *Green Pastures*

Jason Kantrowitz

Jason Kantrowitz made his New York debut as a lighting designer with the opening of *Irene Worth: Letters of Love* at the Roundabout Theatre in 1979. He attended Carnegie Mellon University and held an apprenticeship at the National Opera Institute from 1979 to 1980. He was born on May 31, 1957 in Glens Falls, New York and has accumulated many off-Broadway credits, including *The Doctor Dilemma* at the Roundabout, productions at the Westside Arts Theatre, the Equity Library Theatre, the American Ballet Company, in regional theatres and for national tours. Since 1980 he has been associated with lighting designer Ken Billington.

Lighting Designs:

1989: *Starmites*; *Tru*

Nat Karson

Nat Karson, a scenic designer and television producer, was Art Director at Radio City Music Hall from 1936 to 1943. He was born in Zurich, Switzerland, the son of an architect who was a refugee from Russia. At a young age he moved with his family to Chicago where he won an art prize in high school and a scholarship to the Art Institute of Chicago. His debut in the theatre as a designer occurred with *Hamlet* as conceived by John Houseman and Orson Welles. In addition he designed the so-called "voodoo" *Macbeth* for Houseman and Welles for the Federal Theatre Project. He considered his design for the *Hamlet* produced in Elsinore, Denmark in 1949 a great personal success. His credits as a set designer were numerous and he occasionally contributed costumes and lighting as well. Mr. Karson also spent several years designing in London. He died at age 46 on September 29, 1954.

Lighting Designs:

1943: *Connecticut Yankee, A* 1946: *Nellie Bly* 1948: *Ballet Ballads*

Scenic Designs:

1934: *Calling All Stars* 1935: *Hook-Up, The* 1936: *Macbeth*; *White Man* 1937: *Arms for Venus* 1938: *Journeyman*; *Right This Way*; *Roosty* 1939: *Hot Mikado, The* 1940: *Keep Off the Grass*; *Liliom* 1941: *High Kickers* 1943: *Connecticut Yankee, A* 1946: *Front Page, The*; *Nellie Bly* 1948: *Ballet Ballads*

Costume Designs:

1936: *Macbeth*; *White Man* 1939: *Hot Mikado, The* 1940: *Keep Off the Grass*; *Liliom* 1946: *Nellie Bly* 1948: *Ballet Ballads*

Natasha Katz

Natasha Katz was born in New York and attended Oberlin College. At Oberlin she studied set and lighting design and held an internship with Roger Morgan. While there she began designing lights, starting with *Otherwise Engaged*, and later spent two summer seasons as the resident lighting designer for the Pittsburgh Civic Light Opera. She was associate to Jules Fisher for the national and world tours of *La Cage aux Folles* and has also assisted Marcia Madeira, Ken Billington, and David Segal. She has designed in regional theatres such as the Mark Taper Forum, the Great Lakes Shakespeare Festival, the Dallas Theatre Center, Trinity Rep, and the Spoleto Festival, as well as in Australia and Europe. Off-Broadway productions include *Oil City Symphony, The Normal Heart, The Widow Claire, Urban Blight, Zero Positive* and *Closer than Ever.* Additional credits include Tommy Tune's nightclub and concert act and the 1988 *Tommy Tune and the Manhattan Rhythm Kings* tour of Russia. Natasha Katz's most recent credits include the 1990-91 Broadway productions *Shogun, The Musical* and *Cemetery Club.*

Lighting Designs:
1985: *Aren't We All?*; *Pack of Lies* 1986: *Honky Tonk Nights* 1987: *Breaking the Code* 1989: *Gypsy*

Robert Kellogg

Robert Kellogg designed the lighting for a Broadway production in 1973. In the early 1970s he worked as an assistant to Martin Aronstein at the New York Shakespeare Festival and has also worked as an actor.

Lighting Designs:
1973: *Here Are Ladies*

Lloyd Kelly

Lloyd Kelly created lighting designs for a Broadway production in the mid-1920s.

Lighting Designs:
1925: *Princess Ida*

Kennel and Entwistle

Louis Kennel and Robert C. Entwistle designed settings for productions on Broadway between 1919 and 1931. Robert Entwistle worked primarily as an electrician and Louis Kennel as a scenic designer and builder. For additional information and individual credits see the entries under their names.

Lighting Designs:
1920: *Skin Game, The* 1922: *Nest, The* 1927: *Lady Do*

Scenic Designs:
1919: *Phantom Legion, The* 1920: *Skin Game, The* 1922: *Nest, The*; *Swifty* 1927: *Lady Do* 1931: *Savage Rhythm*

Louis Kennel

Louis Kennel had Broadway credits as a costume and lighting designer, but his major activity in the theatre was as a scenic designer. He was born in North Bergen, New Jersey on May 7, 1886 and studied painting with George Bridgman, Charles Graham, Ernest Gros, and William Lippincott. In 1940 he brought together theatre technicians and director Royce Emerson into Louis Kennel, Inc. to produce and support play production by other producers. His primary business, however, was Louis Kennel Scenic Studios, 1427 44th Street in North Bergen, New Jersey, specializing in "Designing, Building and Painting for Theatre and T.V." His solo credits range from the twenties through the fifties. He also designed in collaboration with Robert C. Entwistle through "Kennel and Entwistle" from 1919 to 1931, and in collaboration with Rollo Peters through "Peters and Kennel" in 1918.

Lighting Designs:
1949: *Anybody Home*

Scenic Designs:
1924: *Leah Kleschna* 1926: *Hangman's House*; *One Man's Woman* 1928: *Falstaff* 1930: *Apron Strings*; *Plutocrat, The*; *That's Gratitude*; *Those We Love* 1932: *Little Black Book, The* 1934: *Moor Born*; *Order Please*; *Re-Echo* 1935: *Moon Over Mulberry Street* 1936: *Black Widow*; *Halloween* 1937: *London Assurance* 1938: *Day in the Sun*; *Don't Throw Glass Houses* 1940: *Horse Fever* 1941: *Brother Cain*; *First Stop to Heaven* 1947: *Magic Touch, The* 1949: *Anybody Home*; *Twelfth Night* 1951: *Springtime Folly*; *Springtime for Henry* 1957: *Waiting for Godot*

Costume Designs:
1934: *Re-Echo* 1949: *Anybody Home*; *Twelfth Night*

Sean Kenny

Sean Kenny was an Irish designer and architect. He was born in Portoe, Tipperary, Ireland on December 23, 1932 and studied architecture in Dublin and with Frank Lloyd Wright. He designed settings for the first time in Hammersmith, England, but it was *The Hostage* in London which gave him his real entrance into the theatre--thanks to the offer of work from an old

Irish friend, Brendan Behan. His credits for settings, and occasionally costumes, were extensive in England. He also designed for film, television and night clubs. He continued to practice as an architect when his schedule allowed, especially for new theatres and theatre renovations. Mr. Kenny, who received a Tony Award for the sets for *Oliver!* in 1963, died on June 11, 1973.

Lighting Designs:

1962: *Stop the World, I Want to Get Off* **1965:** *Roar of the Greasepaint – The Smell of the Crowd* **1973:** *Here Are Ladies*

Scenic Designs:

1962: *Stop the World, I Want to Get Off* **1963:** *Oliver!* **1965:** *Oliver!*; *Pickwick*; *Roar of the Greasepaint – The Smell of the Crowd* **1973:** *Here Are Ladies* **1984:** *Oliver!*

Costume Designs:

1963: *Oliver!* **1965:** *Oliver!* **1973:** *Here Are Ladies* **1984:** *Oliver!*

Carl Kent

Carl Kent, a set, lighting and costume designer and a native of New York City, was born on January 28, 1918. He studied at the Art Students League and the National Academy of Design. Also well known as a jazz pianist, he entered theatre as a technical supervisor and assistant to scenic designer Harry Horner. His credits for sets on Broadway were numerous and he occasionally designed costumes as well. Mr. Kent also designed sets for NBC-TV and CBS-TV. In addition to the theatre he designed for ballet, including *The New Yorker* for Ballet Russe in 1940. Mr. Kent died in New York City on December 13, 1959.

Lighting Designs:

1944: *Peepshow*

Scenic Designs:

1940: *'Tis of Thee* **1944:** *Career Angel* **1945:** *Concert Varieties* **1949:** *Leaf and Bough*

Costume Designs:

1945: *Concert Varieties*

Leo Kerz

Leo Kerz was a scenic, lighting, and costume designer, as well as a producer and director. He was born on November 1, 1912 in Berlin, and studied there with Bertolt Brecht, Erwin Piscator and Laszlo Moholy-Nagy. His first settings were produced in Berlin in 1932, after which he designed throughout Europe and in South Africa. He came to the United States in 1942 and assisted Jo Mielziner, Watson Barratt and Stewart Chaney. He also designed sets for numerous operas, including *The Magic Flute* and *Parsifal* for the Metropolitan Opera, and the premieres of *The Moon* by Carl Orff and *The Tempest* by Frank Marin at New York City Opera in collaboration with Erich Leinsdorf. He also designed for films and television, including a stint as a CBS-TV staff designer between 1949 and 1954. Mr. Kerz, who lectured widely and wrote on trends in design, died on November 4, 1976 in New York City.

Lighting Designs:

1944: *According to Law*; *Strange Play, A* **1946:** *Christopher Blake*; *Flamingo Road* **1947:** *Heads Or Tails*; *Little A*; *Louisiana Lady*; *Open House* **1948:** *For Heaven's Sake, Mother*; *Me and Molly* **1949:** *Biggest Thief in Town, The* **1950:** *Edwina Black* **1951:** *Ti-Coq* **1952:** *Sacred Flame, The*; *Whistler's Grandmother* **1954:** *Hit the Trail* **1959:** *Moonbirds* **1961:** *Rhinoceros* **1973:** *Children of the Wind*

Scenic Designs:

1947: *Anthony and Cleopatra*; *Open House* **1948:** *Bravo*; *For Heaven's Sake, Mother* **1949:** *Biggest Thief in Town, The* **1950:** *Edwina Black* **1952:** *Sacred Flame, The*; *Whistler's Grandmother* **1954:** *Hit the Trail* **1959:** *Moonbirds* **1961:** *Rhinoceros* **1973:** *Children of the Wind*

Costume Designs:

1947: *Open House*

Frederick J. Kiesler

Frederick John Kiesler lived from September 22, 1892 to December 27, 1965 and worked as an architect and scenic designer. He was born in Vienna and came to the United States in 1926. He was head of set design at the Juilliard School of Music from 1933 to 1957 and director of the Laboratory at the Columbia University School of Architecture. His first set was for *R.U.R.* in 1922 in Berlin. He received credit for numerous designs at Juilliard, exhibited architectural and theatrical designs, and influenced the emerging environmental theatre with plans and design for

"Endless Theatre." He also designed the first projected scenery at the Metropolitan Opera, for *In the Pasha's Garden* in 1935. He was a member of United Scenic Artists from 1934 to 1965.

Lighting Designs:
1946: *No Exit*

Scenic Designs:
1946: *No Exit*

Debra Kletter

Debra Kletter has designed lighting for many off-Broadway theatres including Playwrights Horizons, Manhattan Theatre Club, WPA, and Circle Rep. She has also designed for numerous regional theatres including Berkeley Repertory, the Long Wharf Theatre, South Coast Rep and Hartford Stage. She received a Drama-Logue Award for lighting design for work at South Coast Rep and has more than forty productions to her credit as resident designer for the Production Company. Her Broadway debut, *Prelude to a Kiss*, was designed for playwright Craig Lucas and director Norman René, a team with whom she has also designed *Reckless, Three Postcards, Missing Persons,* and *Marry Me a Little.*

Lighting Designs:
1990: *Prelude to a Kiss*

Kliegl Brothers

Kliegl Brothers Universal Electric Stage Lighting Company, Inc., founded in 1896, was the first American company to specialize in manufacturing equipment for stage lighting. Brothers John H. Kliegl and Anton T. Kliegl devised a light which projected a powerful beam by means of carbons, making indoor motion pictures more practical. That light became known as the "Klieg light." In 1903 Kliegl Brothers installed the first incandescent lighting system at the Metropolitan Opera House. They also supplied lighting equipment and effects to producers including David Belasco, George M. Cohan, Charles Frohman and William A. Brady. John and Anton Kliegl were born in Bad Kissingen, Bavaria, Germany and attended school in Munich. They emigrated to the United States in 1918, arriving during the blizzard of that year. John Kliegl died at age 89 on September 30,

1959. (Anton Kliegl had died earlier.) John's son, Herbert A. (Henry) Kliegl, joined his father in the business and continued to respond to the requirements of theatre, television and film lighting. While the company continues its speciality in theatrical lighting, it has also pioneered electric lighting systems in schools, museums, golf driving ranges, auditoriums, arenas and offices. Devices developed by the company included footlights with special features, remote systems, pinhole dimlights, and projection equipment. Kliegl Brothers has supplied lighting instruments for thousands of productions on the Broadway stage, but Kliegl Brothers and Henry Kliegl received design credit for only a few.

Lighting Designs:
1917: *Eileen; Seremonda* 1921: *Wandering Jew, The* 1923: *Exile, The* 1926: *Half-Caste, The*

Herbert A. Kliegl

Herbert A. (Henry) Kliegl was the son of John H. Kliegl who founded Kliegl Brothers with his brother Anton. Henry joined his father in the theatrical lighting business and also designed the lighting for a Broadway production in 1919, although as a member of Kliegl Brothers he was certainly responsible for additional productions in the format generally followed before lighting designers emerged in their own right. Herbert Kliegl died at age 64 on October 3, 1968.

Lighting Designs:
1919: *Aphrodite*

Fred Kolo

Fred Kolo was born on September 27, 1942 in Columbus, Nebraska, the son of Fred T. and Helen Paulson Kolouch. He received a B.A. at Dartmouth College and attended the Yale University School of Drama, Lester Polakov's Studio and Forum of Stage Design and the Art Students League. He worked as an assistant at the Metropolitan Opera for Raoul Pène Du Bois and made his New York debut with Robert Sealy's *Meat and Potatoes* at Cafe La Mama. He has received two Joseph Jefferson Award nominations in Chicago for productions at the Academy Festival Theatre and three Carbonell

Awards in Miami. A designer of scenery, costumes and lights for theatre, television, industrial promotions and film, he also directs, produces and writes. Fred Kolo is also known for his collaborations with Robert Wilson: *The Life and Times of Sigmund Freud* at the Brooklyn Academy of Music; *Deafman Glance* at the Brooklyn Academy of Music, the University of Iowa, the Nancy Festival, Holland Festival and in Paris; and scenery for *The Life and Times of Joseph Stalin* at the Brooklyn Academy of Music and the Teatro Municipal, São Paulo, Brazil.

Lighting Designs:
1990: *Truly Blessed*

Scenic Designs:
1990: *Truly Blessed*

Ralph Koltai

Ralph Koltai, a designer of Hungarian-German descent, was born in Berlin on July 31, 1924 and studied there and at London's Central School of Arts and Crafts, where he was head of theatre design from 1965 to 1973. His first design assignment was the opera *Angelique* in 1950 and since that time he has designed sets and costumes for nearly two hundred plays, operas and ballets around the world. An Associate of the Royal Shakespeare Company from 1963 to 1966 and since 1975, he has also designed for the National Theatre, Royal Opera House, and English National Opera. He directed and designed *The Flying Dutchman* in Hong Kong in 1987 and *Metropolis* in 1988. The recipient of numerous awards, he was co-winner of an Individual Gold Medal for Stage Design and co-winner of the Golden Troika National Award at the 1975 Prague Quadriennale. He was recipient of the 1979 Designer of the Year Award from the Society of the West End Theatres for *Brand*.

Lighting Designs:
1968: *Soldiers*

Scenic Designs:
1968: *Soldiers* 1974: *As You Like It* 1984: *Cyrano De Bergerac*; *Much Ado About Nothing* 1985: *Pack of Lies* 1988: *Carrie*

Costume Designs:
1968: *Soldiers* 1974: *As You Like It* 1985: *Pack of Lies*

Jay Krause

Jay Krause designed sets, lights and costumes for a production on Broadway in 1955.

Lighting Designs:
1955: *Day By the Sea, A*

Scenic Designs:
1955: *Day By the Sea, A*

Costume Designs:
1955: *Day By the Sea, A*

Nick Kronyack

Nick Kronyack, who was responsible for one lighting design on Broadway in 1915, spent two years as head electrician of the Winter Garden Theatre beginning at its founding. For nineteen years he was Chief of Electrical Maintenance at Radio City Music Hall. Nick Kronyack, who resided at 987 2nd Avenue in New York City, died at the age of 74 on May 12, 1952.

Lighting Designs:
1915: *Maid in America*

Félix Labisse

Félix Louis Victor Léon Labisse was a painter and scenic designer who founded the Club du Cinema in Ostend, Belgium. He served as editor-in-chief for *Tribord* in Ostend from 1927 to 1931 after which he settled in Paris. Born in Marchiennes, France on March 9, 1905, he exhibited paintings widely in Europe, South America, the Far East and the United States. His works are in the permanent collections of New York City's Museum of Modern Art, Paris' Musée d'Art Moderne, and the Musée de Lille. In addition to scenic design on Broadway he has created theatrical settings for the Comédie Française, the Ballets de Monte-Carlo, and for theatre companies in Lyon, Geneva and Lausanne. He began designing in Paris in 1935 and designed numerous productions through the thirties, forties and fifties.

Lighting Designs:
1952: *Le Process*

Scenic Designs:
1952: *Le Process*; *Occupe Toi d'Amelie*

Jack Landau

Jack Landau, a director and producer, was born on January 5, 1925 in Braddock, Pennsylvania and studied in the United States and England, including a year at the Old Vic in London. During the 1940s and 1950s while designing sets, costumes, and occasionally lights for plays, he gradually began directing. In 1956 he joined the American Shakespeare Festival Theatre and Academy as associate director and directed numerous plays for the company. He has also designed, produced and directed for television. Mr. Landau died on March 16, 1967 in Boston at 42 years of age.

Lighting Designs:
1944: *War President*

Scenic Designs:
1950: *Phoenix Too Frequent, A* 1951: *Buy Me Blue Ribbons* 1952: *Dear Barbarians*

Costume Designs:
1950: *Phoenix Too Frequent, A* 1951: *Buy Me Blue Ribbons* 1952: *Dear Barbarians*

Peter Larkin

Peter Larkin, a designer of sets, lights and sometimes costumes, was born in Boston on August 25, 1926. He studied at Yale University and with Oliver Larkin. His Broadway debut as a scenic designer was in 1952 but he made his New York debut a year earlier with *The Wild Duck* at City Center. He has been honored for outstanding set design with Tony Awards for *Teahouse of the August Moon* and *Ondine* in 1954, and *Inherit the Wind* and *No Time for Sergeants* in 1956, as well as a Maharam Award for *Les Blancs* (1970). Additional credits include production design for the films *Tootsie, Compromising Positions* and *Three Men and a Baby*, and art direction for *Reuben, Reuben* among others.

Lighting Designs:
1952: *Dial M for Murder* 1953: *Teahouse of the August Moon, The* 1955: *Damn Yankees* 1956: *Shangri-La*

Scenic Designs:
1952: *Dial M for Murder* 1953: *Teahouse of the August Moon, The* 1954: *Ondine; Peter Pan* 1955: *Inherit the Wind; No Time for Sergeants* 1956: *New Faces of '56; Protective Custody; Shangri-La* 1957: *Compulsion; Good As Gold; Miss Isobel* 1958: *Blue Denim; Goldilocks; Shadow of a Gunman, The* 1959: *First Impressions; Only in America* 1960: *Greenwillow; Wildcat* 1962: *Giants, Sons of Giants; Nowhere To Go But Up* 1963: *Marathon '33* 1964: *Crucible, The; Seagull, The* 1966: *Great Indoors, The; Hail Scrawdyke!* 1970: *Les Blancs; Sheep of the Runway* 1971: *Twigs* 1972: *Wise Child* 1973: *Let Me Hear You Smile* 1974: *Thieves* 1977: *Ladies At the Alamo* 1978: *Dancin'* 1979: *Break a Leg* 1981: *Broadway Follies* 1983: *Doonesbury* 1984: *Rink, The* 1986: *Big Deal*

Costume Designs:
1956: *Protective Custody*

Robert Larkin

In 1917 Robert Larkin designed lights for a production on Broadway.

Lighting Designs:
1917: *Maytime*

Johannes Larsen

A scenic and lighting designer, Johannes Larsen designed one Broadway show in 1940. He designed the scenery for four additional shows between 1939 and 1942. He worked in the construction trade in the early 1930s and resided at 636 West 138th Street in New York City.

Lighting Designs:
1940: *Boyd's Daughter*

Scenic Designs:
1939: *Three Sisters, The* 1940: *Boyd's Daughter; Return Engagement* 1942: *First Crocus, The*

Eugene Lee

Eugene Lee has many recent design credits for television including *Night Music, Kids in the Hall,* and *House Party.* He is a proponent of real items instead of façades and of environmental settings which encompass not only the stage but the entire theatre space, including the relationship between actor and audience. Eugene Lee is well known as the designer of *Saturday Night Live,* which he initially designed in collaboration with his former wife, Franne Lee. He has been principal designer at Trinity Square since 1968 and with David Rotundo is co-owner of Scenic Services, a lighting and design company located in Providence, Rhode Island. His first professional designs were *A Dream of Love* and *Belch* at the Theatre of the Living Arts in Philadelphia in 1966. Eugene and Franne Lee received the "most promising designers" Drama Desk Award in 1970-71 and each recieved a Tony, Marharam and Drama Desk Award for *Candide*. Their scenic design for *Sweeney Todd* also garnered a Tony Award. Born on March 9, 1939, he studied at Carnegie-Mellon and Yale and has been married to Brooke Lutz since 1981.

Lighting Designs:
1982: *Hothouse, The*

Scenic Designs:
1970: *Wilson in the Promise Land* 1972: *Dude* 1974: *Candide* 1975: *Skin of Our Teeth, The* 1977: *Some of My Best Friends* 1979: *Gilda Radner Live from N.Y.*; *Sweeney Todd* 1981: *Merrily We Roll Along* 1982: *Agnes of God*; *Hothouse, The*

Ming Cho Lee

Ming Cho Lee began designing in New York City in 1958 with *The Infernal Machine* at the Phoenix Theatre. He was born in Shanghai on October 3, 1930 and received a B.A. at Occidental College. He attended the University of California at Los Angeles from 1953 to 1954. He studied with Chinese watercolorist Kuo-Nyen Chang and spent five years working as assistant to Jo Mielziner. Ming Cho Lee's productions on Broadway are barely representative of his design work which has been seen for opera, dance and theatre in major companies around the country. His originality is remarkable and he has influenced countless students at New York University and at the Yale University School of Drama, where he is now Co-Chair of Design. He likes to work with students that he has trained and regularly hires them as assistants. His list of awards is also long and includes a 1990 Distinguished Career Achievement Award from the National Endowment for the Arts, the Peter Zeisler Award at Arena Stage in 1987, Maharam Awards for *Electra* in 1965 and *Ergo* in 1968, a Tony Award for *K-2* in 1983, a Guggenheim in 1988, and a Los Angeles Drama Critics and Hollywood Drama Logue Critics Awards for *Traveller in the Dark* in 1985. His wife, the former

Betsy Rapport, works as his assistant and they have three sons.

Lighting Designs:
1962: *Moon Beseiged, The*

Scenic Designs:
1962: *Moon Beseiged, The* 1963: *Mother Courage and Her Children* 1966: *Slapstick Tragedy*; *Time for Singing, A* 1967: *Little Murders* 1968: *Here's Where I Belong* 1969: *Billy*; *La Strada* 1972: *Much Ado About Nothing*; *Two Gentlemen of Verona* 1975: *All God's Chillun Got Wings*; *Glass Menagerie, The* 1976: *For Colored Girls Who Have Considered Suicide When...* 1977: *Caesar and Cleopatra*; *Romeo and Juliet*; *Shadow Box, The* 1978: *Angel* 1979: *Grand Tour, The* 1983: *Glass Menagerie, The*; *K2* 1986: *Execution of Justice,*

Benjamin Leffler

Ben Leffler spent eighteen years as master electrician at the Hudson Theatre, 141 West 44th Street in New York City. He designed lighting for many productions on Broadway in the 1920s, and as staff electrician was certainly responsible for additional productions during those years when lighting designers were seldom credited. He died at age 76 in 1949.

Lighting Designs:
1922: *Last Warning, The* 1924: *Flossie* 1926: *Climax, The*; *Man from Toronto, The* 1927: *Banshee, The*; *Lady Screams, The*; *Love Thief, The* 1928: *Gods of the Lightening* 1929: *Octoroon, The*; *Pansy*

Hugh Lester

Hugh Lester designed the lighting for a Broadway production in 1980. He has worked as lighting consultant for the National Air and Space Museum in Washington, D.C. and designed the lighting for an exhibition hall at the Folger Shakespeare Library. As lighting designer at Arena Stage in the late 1960s and early 1970s he designed many productions. He was also tour director for *Gin Game* starring Jessica Tandy and Hume Cronyn.

Lighting Designs:
1980: *Charlie and Algernon*

Samuel Leve

Samuel Leve, a scenic designer who has also occasionally designed costumes and lighting, was born on December 7, 1910 near Pinsk, Russia. He came to the United States in 1920 and studied at Yale University and art schools in New York before beginning his career in theatre designing summer stock. He has designed sets for over one hundred productions on Broadway and at the Metropolitan Opera, the Mercury Theatre, and the Theatre Guild, among others. He has designed throughout the world as well, including productions in Rio de Janeiro, Canada, Israel, and London. He has also designed spectacles and two synagogues; lectured at Yale, New York University, and Florida State University, and written books, including *On Jewish Art*. Samuel Leve's many awards include the 1985 Goldie, named for Abraham Goldfadn, the father of Yiddish Theatre.

Lighting Designs:

1937: *Julius Caesar* 1938: *Shoemaker's Holiday, The* 1940: *Medicine Show* 1943: *Apology* 1944: *Hand in Glove* 1948: *Madwoman of Chaillot* 1951: *Dinosaur Wharf* 1952: *Buttrio Square* 1963: *Have I Got a Girl for You*; *Cafe Crown* 1982: *Dybbuck, The*

Scenic Designs:

1937: *The Miser/ The Great Cat/ Snickering Horses*; *Cherokee Night*; *Julius Caesar*; *Tobias and the Angel* 1938: *Big Blow, The*; *Shoemaker's Holiday, The* 1940: *Medicine Show* 1941: *Beautiful People, The*; *Distant City, The*; *Macbeth* 1942: *All in Favor*, *Beat the Band*; *Life of Reilly, The*; *Mr. Sycamore*; *They Should Have Stood in Bed* 1943: *Apology* 1944: *Dark Hammock*; *Hand in Glove*; *Last Stop*; *Sophie*; *Thank You, Svoboda*; *Wallflower* 1945: *It's a Gift*; *Oh, Brother*; *Round Trip*; *Sound of Hunting, A* 1946: *Family Affair, A* 1947: *Story of Mary Surratt, The* 1949: *Clutterbuck* 1950: *All You Need Is One Good Break* 1951: *Dinosaur Wharf*; *Lace on Her Petticoat* 1952: *Buttrio Square* 1953: *Fifth Season, The* 1955: *Hear! Hear!* 1956: *Double in Hearts*; *Goodbye Again* 1963: *Have I Got a Girl for You* 1964: *Cafe Crown* 1982: *Dybbuck, The*

Costume Designs:

1951: *Dinosaur Wharf*

Ted Levy

Irving (Ted) Levy designed lights for a production on Broadway in 1928. He is known primarily as a partner with Ed Kook in Century Lighting Company, founded in 1929. The "leko", a compact ellipsoidal spotlight, was developed by and named after Levy and Kook. Century Lighting has supplied lighting equipment for thousands of Broadway shows and other productions.

Lighting Designs:

1928: *Wrecker, The*

Todd Lichtenstein

Todd Lichtenstein designed lighting for one production on Broadway in 1983. He has designed in numerous regional theatres, including the Capital Repertory Company, Albany, New York and the Pennsylvania Stage Company. Credits in off-Broadway theatres include productions at the Equity Library Theatre, Phoenix Theatre, La Mama, and Playwright's Horizons. He has also assisted lighting designer Dennis Parichy. Television experience includes lighting design for the ABC-TV program *Daytime*.

Lighting Designs:

1983: *Ritz, The*

Edward Clarke Lilley

Edward Clarke Lilley was an actor and director. He began his career in Salt Lake City, Utah with the Leighton Players Stock Company before moving on to form his own company as actor, director and manager. He debuted as a Broadway director with *Ziegfeld Follies* in 1931, which was followed by editions of *Ziegfeld Follies* in 1934 and 1935, *Hot Cha*, *The Show Is On* and others. He also directed for films and musical stock companies. Edward Lilley died at age 86 on April 3, 1974.

Lighting Designs:

1939: *One for the Money*

D. Scott Linder

D. Scott Linder was born on August 6, 1948 in Tulsa, Oklahoma. He attended the University of Texas and began designing for opera, theatre, and ballet groups in Tulsa. He spent six years as lighting director for *Holiday on Ice*, and five years as technical director for Madison Square Garden. He also served as master electrician and assistant designer for over thirty road companies, ballets and Broadway plays. His career has been influenced by Gilbert Hemsley whom he assisted on a couple of productions. Currently Scott Linder is working as a theatre, broadcast and media designer/consultant.

Lighting Designs:
1977: *Toller Cranston's Ice Show*

Charles Lisanby

Charles Lisanby has created lighting and scenic designs on Broadway since 1955. His television credits are extensive and include *The Garry Moore, Red Skelton,* and *Jack Benny* shows and more than one hundred specials. He has been nominated for nine Emmy Awards and won two, including one for *Baryshnikov on Broadway.* He has designed productions at Radio City Music Hall (including the 1984 *MTV Awards), Night of 100 Stars,* television commercials, and the *Folies Bergère* in Las Vegas. He also designed a Hilton Hotel in Australia.

Lighting Designs:
1955: *Little Glass Clock, The* **1956:** *Glass Clock, The*

Scenic Designs:
1957: *Hotel Paradiso* **1979:** *Magnificent Christmas Spectacular, The* **1980:** *Magnificent Christmas Spectacular, The* **1988:** *Christmas Spectacular*

John Robert Lloyd

John Robert Lloyd, a scenic and sometimes costume and lighting designer, began his career in the theatre as an actor performing in Italian productions. Born in St. Louis on August 4, 1920, he studied at the Art Students League, the Hadley Art School, Washington University and the University of Missouri. He assisted Robert Edmond Jones, Lemuel Ayers and Nat Karson and developed an early specialization in masks, make-up and sculptural stage elements. After working as a designer in summer stock he made his New York debut in 1948 off-Broadway with *The Duenna* at the Greenwich Mews Theatre.

His Broadway debut was in 1949. Since that time he has designed numerous industrials, exhibits, films and television shows, both freelance and as staff designer for NBC-TV. John Robert Lloyd has served as production designer for the films *The Boys in the Band, The Owl and the Pussycat,* and *The Exorcist.*

Lighting Designs:
1951: *Stalag 17* **1952:** *Bernadine* **1955:** *Almost Crazy* **1957:** *Holiday for Lovers* **1958:** *Drink to Me Only* **1960:** *Laughs and Other Events*

Scenic Designs:
1949: *Touch and Go* **1951:** *Stalag 17* **1952:** *Bernadine* **1955:** *Almost Crazy* **1957:** *Holiday for Lovers; Monique* **1958:** *Drink to Me Only* **1960:** *Laughs and Other Events*

Costume Designs:
1949: *Mrs. Gibbon's Boys; Touch and Go* **1960:** *Laughs and Other Events*

Milton Lowe

Milton Lowe, who designed lighting for a Broadway production in 1946, worked for the Shubert Producing Organization as an electrician. He died at age 59 on March 8, 1947 in New York City.

Lighting Designs:
1946: *Yours Is My Heart*

Kert Lundell

Kert Lundell was born in Malmö, Sweden on June 17, 1936. Mr. Lundell, who studied at Yale, came to New York after study at the Goodman School of Drama. He is a scenic designer who occasionally also contributes costume and lighting designs to productions. His sets for theatre have been seen throughout the United States and in Europe. He served as consultant to the American Place Theatre in 1971 when its new space was built. He has also taught, designed films (including *They All Laughed* in 1981) and designed for television.

Lighting Designs:
1968: *Carry Me Back to Morningside Heights*

Scenic Designs:
1966: *Investigation, The; Under the Weather* **1968:** *Carry Me Back to Morningside Heights*

1971: *Ain't Supposed to Die a Natural Death*; *Solitaire/ Double Solitaire* 1972: *Don't Play Us Cheap*; *Lincoln Mask, The*; *Sunshine Boys, The* 1975: *Hughey/ Duet*; *Night That Made America Famous, The* 1976: *1600 Pennsylvania Avenue*; *Rockabye Hamlet* 1978: *November People, The* 1982: *Waltz of the Stork* 1989: *Shenandoah*

Costume Designs:
1966: *Under the Weather* 1968: *Carry Me Back to Morningside Heights*

Jack Maclennan

Jack Maclennan designed sets and lights for one play in 1935. An electrician, he resided at 4523 Barnes Avenue in New York City with his wife Mary in 1932.

Lighting Designs:
1935: *Something More Important/The Old Woman/etc.*

Scenic Designs:
1935: *Something More Important/The Old Woman/etc.*

Marcia Madeira

Marcia Madeira won a Drama Desk Award and a Tony nomination for the lighting design for *NINE*. She was born in Boston on January 25, 1945 and graduated from Bradford College in 1965. She studied for two years at Yale and received a B.F.A. from Carnegie Mellon University in 1969. Her design debut was at the Kennebunkport Playhouse with a production of *My Fair Lady* in 1964. She has been a member of United Scenic Artists since 1972. Additional credits off-Broadway include *Cloud Nine* and *Privates on Parade*. She has also designed lights in regional theatres, for opera, and for national tours.

Lighting Designs:
1980: *Music Man, The* 1982: *Nine* 1983: *Marilyn*; *My One and Only*

Bruno Maine

Bruno Jalmar Manninen was born in Finland and came to the United States at age thirteen, changing his name when he became a citizen in 1923. He apprenticed at a scenic studio and subsequently designed for John Murray Anderson.

In 1933 he succeeded Vincent Minnelli as Art Director at Radio City Music Hall, where he remained for eighteen years. His Christmas and Easter Pageants were well known, as were the ice shows he designed for Sonja Henie and the inaugural balls he created for Dwight D. Eisenhower in 1953 and 1957. Bruno Maine died at age 65 on July 30, 1962.

Lighting Designs:
1951: *Bagels and Yox*

Scenic Designs:
1942: *Stars on Ice* 1944: *Hats Off to Ice* 1947: *Icetime of 1948* 1948: *Howdy, Mr Ice* 1949: *Howdy Mr. Ice of 1950*

Rouben Mamoulian

Rouben Mamoulian, an innovative director of theatre and films, was a founding member of the Directors' Guild of America. He was born on October 8, 1897 in Tiflis, Georgia, Russia and studied law at the University of Moscow and then theatre at the Vakhtangov Studio of the Moscow Art Theatre. He began directing in London in 1922 and came to New York in 1923 to direct several landmark musicals, including *Oklahoma!* and *Carousel*. A versatile and creative figure, he won numerous prizes throughout his distinguished career. The awards included the Donaldson Award in 1945 for *Carousel*. He also received first prize at the Venice International Film Festival in 1931 for *Dr. Jekyll and Mr. Hyde* and for *Queen Christina* in 1934 for film direction. Occasionally Mr. Mamoulian designed scenery, lights and/or costumes for productions which he directed. Rouben Mamoulian died on December 4, 1987 in Los Angeles.

Lighting Designs:
1949: *Leaf and Bough*

Costume Designs:
1927: *Porgy*

Mannie Manim

Mannie Manim was born on July 10, 1941 in South Africa. Over the past thirty years he has designed, directed and/or produced over three hundred productions in South Africa and abroad. He is producing director of the Market Theatre Company and Managing Trustee of the Market Theatre Foundation. His designs have been influenced by Frank Staff, Meshak Mosia, and Jean Rosenthal and been informed by practical experience. He is the recipient of several awards: AA Life Vita Awards for Best Original Lighting Design (1985 through 1988); The Shirley Moss Award for Greatest Practical and Technical Contribution to Theatre in South Africa (1980); the South African Institute for Theatre Technology Award for Outstanding Achievement as a Theatre Technician, Administrator and Lighting Designer (1981); and the AA Life Award for Most Enterprising Producer (1984).

Lighting Designs:
1988: *Sarafina!*

Peter Maradudin

Peter Maradudin, a lighting designer, was born on February 16, 1959 in Washington, D.C. to Alexi and Margaret Maradudin. He did his undergraduate work at Stanford University and received his M.F.A. from the Yale University School of Drama. Jennifer Tipton has been a major career influence and mentor. His first professional job after school was also his first Broadway production, *Ma Rainey's Black Bottom*. It opened in October of 1984 at the Cort Theatre after a trial run in Philadelphia. Since that time he has designed over ninety shows around the country, primarily on the West Coast in regional theatres such as the South Coast Repertory. He has won several awards including two Los Angeles Drama Critics Circle Awards, Theatre Critics Awards in San Diego and Portland, and fourteen Drama Logue Awards.

Lighting Designs:
1984: *Ma Rainey's Black Bottom*

Marvin March

Marvin March designed sets and lights for one production on Broadway in 1964. He is known primarily as an art director for films, with *Lethal Weapon 2, Skin Deep, Ghostbusters, Flashdance, The Toy, Fletch* and *Tango & Cash* among his many credits. He began his career in television, specializing in properities and lighting. In the early 1960s he sailed across the Atlantic Ocean with scenic designer David Hayes and Eddie Biegelow, at the time the assistant manager of the New York City Ballet Company.

Lighting Designs:
1964: *Caretaker, The*

Gregg Marriner

Gregg Marriner has designed lights for regional theatres such as the Indiana Repertory Theatre, the Portland Stage Company, Paper Mill Playhouse, Ogunquit Playhouse and the Poinciana Playhouse. He has also designed off-Broadway productions at the Equity Library Theatre and the Actor's Studio. He assisted Tharon Musser for *42nd Street* and *Dreamgirls* and has designed club acts for performers Tammy Grimes and Lee Roy Reams.

Lighting Designs:
1980: *Canterbury Tales*

Mr. Maxwell

Mr. Maxwell designed lighting for one play on Broadway in 1914. He also designed costumes for the 1923 London production of *If Winter Comes* by A.S.M. Hutchinson and B. Macdonald Hastings.

Lighting Designs:
1914: *Silent Voice, The*

Duane F. Mazey

Duane F. Mazey designed scenes and lighting for one play in 1976.

Lighting Designs:
1976: *Let My People Come*

Scenic Designs:
1976: *Let My People Come*

Stanley McCandless

Stanley McCandless, co-founder of the graduate theatre program at Yale University, spent forty years teaching lighting design at Yale. He was born on May 9, 1897 in Chicago and received a B.A. from the University of Wisconsin in 1920 and an M.A. in architecture from Harvard University in 1923. In addition to teaching at Yale he was associated with Century Lighting from 1944 to 1964, and was a consultant for Radio City Music Hall, the United Nations Assembly Hall, and the National Gallery of Art. He wrote

Methods of Lighting the Stage, Syllabus of Stage Lighting and many articles. His few credits on the Broadway stage do not begin to measure the influence he had on generations of students and colleagues. He devoted his ingenuity and technical skills to developing the field of lighting design. Stanley McCandless died in 1967.

Lighting Designs:
1937: *Lady Has a Heart, The*; *Many Mansions* **1944:** *Rhapsody*

Langdon McCormick

Playwright Langdon McCormick was born in Port Huron, Michigan and studied at Albion College. An actor, he appeared with Otis Skinner in the late 1890s and in his own plays. He designed sets and lights for a 1919 Broadway production which he also wrote and in 1926 repeated the feat. His many plays included *How Hearts Are Broken, The Life of an Actress, Wanted by the Police* and *Toll Gate Inn*. Langdon McCormick died in June 1954.

Lighting Designs:
1919: *Storm, The* **1926:** *Ghost Train, The*

Scenic Designs:
1919: *Storm, The*

Michael McGiveney

Michael McGiveney has designed lights and worked as a production manager for performers Vikki Carr and Johnny Mathis, as well as for the productions *Ice Follies* and *Concert on Ice* with Peggy Fleming. He was born in 1941 and raised in Los Angeles, the son of Owen McGiveney (1884-1967), a British vaudeville performer who brought the "Bill Sikes Act" to the United States. He succeeded his father as a fast change artist in *Quick Change*, a 90-minute stage show which features one actor, fifty-seven costume changes and twenty-four characters.

Lighting Designs:
1984: *Doug Henning and His World of Magic*

John McLain

John McLain attended the College of William and Mary and Carnegie Mellon University. He has designed lights throughout the United States and Europe for most major regional theatres and many opera companies. Designs include: *Peter Allen and the Rockettes*, the international tour of *Porgy and Bess*, *The Golden Land* off-Broadway, and *Falstaff* to open the new Opera House in Amsterdam. He has also designed lights for television and film.

Lighting Designs:
1969: *Flea in Her Ear, A*; *Three Sisters, The*; *Tiny Alice* **1974:** *Leaf People* **1977:** *Importance of Being Earnest, The*; *Night of the Tribades, The*; *Saint Joan*; *Tartuffe* **1978:** *13 Rue De l'Amour* **1979:** *Spokesong* **1980:** *Major Barbara*; *Past Tense* **1982:** *Queen and the Rebels, The* **1983:** *On Your Toes* **1989:** *Hizzoner*

Roi Cooper Megrue

Roi Cooper Megrue was a playwright who had several hits on Broadway. His plays, *Potash and Perlmutter, Under Cover* and *It Pays to Advertise* among others were popular light comedies produced in the teens and twenties. He was born on June 12, 1883 in New York City and graduated from Columbia University in 1903. He worked for Elizabeth Marbury brokering plays and while on her staff began to write his own. Roi Megrue died in New York City on February 27, 1927.

Lighting Designs:
1917: *Why Marry?* **1918:** *Why Marry?*

Joseph Menchen, Jr.

Joseph Menchen, Jr. designed lights for a Broadway play in 1921. In collaboration with T. Digby he was electrician for the 1913 London production of *Brewster's Millions*. He worked as a consulting engineer in New York in the 1920s, at 701 7th Avenue.

Lighting Designs:
1921: *Nobody's Money*

Chester Menzer

Chester Menzer designed lighting for one production on Broadway in 1947.

Lighting Designs:
1947: *Trial Honeymoon*

Lawrence Metzler

Lawrence Metzler was born in Montclair, New Jersey on February 6, 1937, the son of Pauline Wells and Fred Metzler. His New York debut was *The Bold and the Beautiful* at the off-Broadway Theatre East. He worked at the New York Shakespeare Fesitval as an electrician during the 1960s, designing *Electra* in 1969 among other productions. He has also worked in theatres throughout the country in various aspects of technical theatre. Chair of the Western Region of United Scenic Artists, he is currently working in broadcasting at KFI in Los Angeles.

Lighting Designs:
1972: *Two Gentlemen of Verona*

Leo B. Meyer

Leo B. Meyer has designed scenery and lights, taught design, painted scenery, and produced plays during his thirty-five years in the theatre. He has worked throughout the United States and designed hundreds of plays. As president and owner/operator of Atlas Scenic Studios, Ltd. in Bridgeport, Connecticut he has supervised the construction of productions which have collectively won seven Tony Awards, five Pulitzer Prizes and one Emmy. He was born on July 10, 1934, was graduated in 1955 from Carnegie Mellon, and also studied at the Pratt Institute. The son of a textile designer, he began designing in 1953 at the White Barn Theatre with *The Moon is Blue*.

Lighting Designs:
1963: *Pajama Tops* 1967: *What Did We Do Wrong?* 1972: *All the Girls Come Out to Play*

Scenic Designs:
1963: *Pajama Tops* 1967: *Girl in the Freudian Slip, The; Minor Adjustment, A* 1972: *All the Girls Come Out to Play*

Keith Michael

Keith Michael received credit for one lighting design in 1970. He has also designed for the New York Ballet Theatre, Balletforte and Toni Smith and Dancers.

Lighting Designs:
1970: *Gloria and Esperanza*

Jo Mielziner

Jo Mielziner, known primarily as a scenic designer, created numerous costume and lighting designs as well, a common occurrence for designers of his generation. He was born on March 19, 1901 in Paris and attended art schools, including the Art Students League. His father, Leo Mielziner, was a portrait painter and his mother a journalist. He began his career in the theatre as an actor, stage manager and scene designer, first in stock and then for the Theatre Guild. His collaborations with Elia Kazan for plays by modern American playwrights are examples of his enormous influence on theatre and the quality of design. He received many awards including five Tonys for set design, Drama Desk awards, Critics Awards, Maharam Awards, Donaldson Awards, and a number of honorary degrees, all for his outstanding contributions to the theatre. Mr. Mielziner, who died on March 15, 1976, has also received posthumous credit for designs including the revival of *Slaughter on Tenth Avenue* at the New York City Ballet during the 1985-86 season.

Lighting Designs:
1934: *Romeo and Juliet* 1935: *Panic* 1937: *Too Many Heroes* 1938: *Boys from Syracuse, The* 1939: *Too Many Girls* 1940: *Journey to Jerusalem; Pal Joey; Two on An Island* 1941: *Best Foot Forward; Candle in the Wind; Land Is Bright, The; Pal Joey; Seventh Trumpet, The* 1942: *By Jupiter* 1945: *Beggars Are Coming to Town; Carib Song; Dream Girl; Firebrand of Florence, The; Foolish Notion; Glass Menagerie, The; Hollywood Pinafore; Rugged Path, The* 1946: *Annie Get Your Gun; Another Part of the Forest; Happy Birthday; Jeb* 1947: *Allegro; Barefoot Boy with Cheek; Chocolate Soldier, The; Command Decision; Finian's Rainbow; Street Scene; Streetcar Named Desire, A* 1948: *Anne of 1000 Days; Mr. Roberts; Sleepy Hollow* 1949: *Death of a Salesman; South Pacific* 1950: *Burning Bright; Guys and Dolls; Man from Mel Dinelli, The* 1951: *King and I, The; Tree Grows in Brooklyn, A* 1952: *Gambler, The; Wish You Were Here* 1953: *Can-Can; Kind Sir; Me and Juliet; Picnic; Tea and Sympathy* 1954: *All Summer Long; By the Beautiful Sea; Fanny* 1955: *Cat on a Hot Tin Roof; Island of Goats; Lark, The; Pipe Dream; Silk Stockings* 1956: *Happy Hunting; Middle of the Night; Most Happy Fella, The* 1957: *Look Homeward,*

Angel; Miss Lonely Hearts; Square Root of Wonderful, The **1958:** *Day the Money Stopped, The; Gazebo, The; Handful of Fire; Oh Captain!; Whoop-Up; World of Suzie Wong, The* **1959:** *Gang's All Here, The; Gypsy; Rashomon; Silent Night, Lonely Night; Sweet Bird of Youth* **1960:** *Best Man, The; Christine; Little Moon of Alban; Period of Adjustment; There Was a Little Girl* **1961:** *All American; Everybody Loves Opal* **1963:** *Milk Train Doesn't Stop Here Anymore, The* **1964:** *Owl and the Pussycat, The* **1965:** *Playroom, The* **1966:** *Don't Drink the Water; My Sweet Charley* **1967:** *Daphne in Cottage D; Paisley Convertible, The; That Summer-That Fall* **1968:** *I Never Sang for My Father; Prime of Miss Jean Brodie, The; Seven Descents of Myrtle, The* **1969:** *1776* **1970:** *Child's Play; Georgy; Look to the Lilies* **1971:** *Father's Day* **1972:** *Children! Children!; Voices* **1973:** *Out Cry* **1974:** *In Praise of Love*

Scenic Designs:

1924: *Guardsman, The; Nerves* **1925:** *Caught; First Flight; Lucky Sam McCarver; Wild Duck, The* **1926:** *Little Eyolf; Masque of Venice, The; Pygmalion; Seed of the Brute* **1927:** *Doctor's Dilemna, The; Fallen Angels; Mariners; Marquise, The; Right You Are If You Think You Are; Saturday's Children; Second Man, The* **1928:** *Cock Robin; Grey Fox, The; Jealous Moon, The; Lady Lies, The; Most Immoral Lady, A; Saturday's Children; Servant of Two Masters; Strange Interlude* **1929:** *Amorous Antic, The; First Mortgage; Jenny; Judas; Karl and Anna; Little Show, The; Meet the Prince; Skyrocket; Street Scene; Young Alexander* **1930:** *Mr. Gilhooley; Second Little Show, The; Solid South; Sweet and Low; Uncle Vanya* **1931:** *Anatol; Barretts of Wimpole Street, The; Brief Moment; House Beautiful, The; I Love An Actress; Of Thee I Sing; Third Little Show, The* **1932:** *Biography; Bloodstream; Bridal Wise; Distant Drums; Gay Divorce; Hey, Nonny Nonny; Never No More* **1933:** *Champagne Sec; Dark Tower, The; Divine Drudge, A; I Was Waiting for You; Lake, The; Of Thee I Sing* **1934:** *Accent on Youth; Biography; By Your Leave; Dodsworth; Merrily We Roll Along; Pure in Heart, The; Romeo and Juliet; Spring Song; Yellow Jack* **1935:** *Barretts of Wimpole Street, The; Deluxe; Flowers of the Forest; It's You I Want; Jubilee; Kind Lady; Panic; Pride and Prejudice; Romeo and Juliet; Winterset* **1936:** *Co-Respondent Unknown; Daughters of Atreus; Ethan Frome; Hamlet; On Your Toes; Postman Always Rings Twice, The; Room in Red and White, A; Saint Joan; St. Helena; Wingless Victory, The; Women, The* **1937:** *Barchester Towers; Father Malachy's Miracle; High Tor; Star Wagon, The; Susan and God; Too Many Heroes* **1938:** *Boys from Syracuse, The; I Married An Angel; Knickerbocker Holiday; No Time for Comedy; On Borrowed Time; Save Me the Waltz; Sing Out the News; Yr. Obedient Husband* **1939:** *Christmas Eve; Key Largo; Mornings At Seven; Mrs. O'Brien Entertains; Stars in Your Eyes; Too Many Girls* **1940:** *Flight to the West; Higher and Higher; Journey to Jerusalem; Pal Joey; Two on An Island* **1941:** *Best Foot Forward; Candle in the Wind; Cream in the Well; Land Is Bright, The; Mr. and Mrs. North; Pal Joey; Seventh Trumpet, The; Talley Method, The; Watch on the Rhine; Wookey, The* **1942:** *By Jupiter; Solitaire* **1943:** *Susan and God* **1945:** *Barretts of Wimpole Street, The; Beggars Are Coming to Town; Carib Song; Carousel; Dream Girl; Firebrand of Florence, The; Foolish Notion; Glass Menagerie, The; Hollywood Pinafore; Rugged Path, The* **1946:** *Annie Get Your Gun; Another Part of the Forest; Happy Birthday; Jeb* **1947:** *Allegro; Barefoot Boy with Cheek; Chocolate Soldier, The; Command Decision; Finian's Rainbow; Street Scene; Streetcar Named Desire, A* **1948:** *Anne of 1000 Days; Mr. Roberts; Sleepy Hollow; Summer and Smoke; Summer and Smoke* **1949:** *Death of a Salesman; South Pacific* **1950:** *Burning Bright; Dance Me a Song; Guys and Dolls; Innocents, The; Man from Mel Dinelli, The; Wisteria Trees, The* **1951:** *King and I, The; Point of No Return; Top Banana; Tree Grows in Brooklyn, A* **1952:** *Flight Into Egypt; Gambler, The; Wish You Were Here* **1953:** *Can-Can; Kind Sir; Me and Juliet; Picnic; Tea and Sympathy* **1954:** *All Summer Long; By the Beautiful Sea; Fanny* **1955:** *Cat on a Hot Tin Roof; Island of Goats; Lark, The; Pipe Dream; Silk Stockings* **1956:** *Happy Hunting; Middle of the Night; Most Happy Fella, The* **1957:** *Look Homeward, Angel; Miss Lonely Hearts; Square Root of Wonderful, The* **1958:** *Day the Money Stopped, The; Gazebo, The; Handful of Fire; Oh Captain!; Whoop-Up; World of Suzie Wong, The* **1959:** *Gang's All Here, The; Gypsy; Silent Night, Lonely Night; Sweet Bird of Youth* **1960:**

Best Man, The; Christine; Little Moon of Alban;
Period of Adjustment; There Was a Little Girl
1961: *All American; Devil's Advocate, The; Ev-*
erybody Loves Opal 1963: *Milk Train Doesn't*
Stop Here Anymore, The 1964: *Owl and the*
Pussycat, The 1965: *Playroom, The* 1966:
Don't Drink the Water; My Sweet Charley 1967:
Daphne in Cottage D; Paisley Convertible, The;
That Summer-That Fall 1968: *I Never Sang*
for My Father; Prime of Miss Jean Brodie,
The; Seven Descents of Myrtle, The 1969: *1776*
1970: *Child's Play; Georgy; Look to the Lilies*
1971: *Father's Day* 1972: *Children! Children!;*
Voices 1973: *Out Cry* 1974: *In Praise of Love*

Costume Designs:
1924: *Guardsman, The* 1925: *Wild Duck, The*
1926: *Little Eyolf; Pygmalion* 1927: *Right You*
Are If You Think You Are 1929: *Karl and Anna*
1931: *Admirable Crichton, The; Anatol; Bar-*
retts of Wimpole Street, The; Brief Moment;
House Beautiful, The 1932: *Hey, Nonny Nonny*
1933: *Divine Drudge, A* 1934: *Romeo and*
Juliet 1935: *Barretts of Wimpole Street, The;*
Pride and Prejudice; Romeo and Juliet 1936:
Ethan Frome; Hamlet; Saint Joan; St. Helena;
Wingless Victory, The 1937: *Barchester Tow-*
ers; Father Malachy's Miracle; High Tor 1938:
Wild Duck, The; Yr. Obedient Husband 1939:
Christmas Eve; Mrs. O'Brien Entertains 1945:
Barretts of Wimpole Street, The; Dream Girl

Anne E. Militello

Anne E. Militello launched her lighting design
career with *Josephine the Mouse Singer* in 1980
at the Magic Theatre in San Francisco. Since
moving to New York City in 1981 she has
been working steadily. She was born on April
29, 1957 in Buffalo, New York, the daughter
of Emmanuella (Patricia) Pollina and Orazino
(George) Militello. She studied acting at SUNY-
Buffalo and design at Lester Polakov's Studio
and Forum of Stage Design. In 1984 she received
an Obie Award for sustained excellence in lighting design and has also been nominated for an
American Theatre Wing Award. Off-Broadway
she has designed *A Lie of the Mind*, productions
for Mabou Mines, La Mama, and Maria Irene
Fornes, among others.

Lighting Designs:
1986: *Cuba & His Teddy Bear*

Craig Miller

Craig Miller was born on August 7, 1950 in
Hugoton, Kansas. He majored in directing at
Northwestern University where he received a
B.S. in 1972. He has designed theatre, opera
and dance throughout the United States. Since
1979 he has been resident lighting designer at
the Santa Fe Opera. He has also been resident
designer since 1976 for the Lar Lubovitch Dance
Company, since 1983 for the Elisa Monte Dance
Company and since 1985 for the Laura Dean
Dance Company. He worked as an assistant to
Thomas Skelton and several other lighting designers at the beginning of his career and en-
courages his own assistants to gain experience
through this process.

Lighting Designs:
1979: *On Golden Pond* 1980: *Barnum* 1981:
Five O'clock Girl, The; I Won't Dance 1983:
Brothers 1985: *Doubles; Take Me Along; Wind*
in the Willows 1987: *Safe Sex* 1988: *Ro-*
mance/Romance

Joe Miller

Joe Miller had two lighting designs to his credit
on Broadway in the early 1930s. An electrician,
he resided at 2039 Creston Avenue in 1932. He
was associated, also as an electrician, with "Industrial Mexican Drawing Works" at 230 West
29th Street, New York City. Joe Miller appeared
in the film *Days of the Buffalo.*

Lighting Designs:
1932: *She Loves Me Not* 1934: *Distaff Side,*
The

William Mintzer

William Mintzer received a B.F.A. from Carnegie Institute of Technology in 1966 and an
M.F.A. from New York University in 1969. He
has designed lights for regional theatres around
the United States, including numerous productions for the Milwaukee Repertory Theatre,
Arena Stage, Seattle Repertory Theatre, and
the Goodman Theatre. He has also amassed numerous credits off-Broadway. He has supervised
scenery for American tours by the Royal Shakespeare Company, the Abbey Theatre of Dublin
and the Comédie Française. He is a member of
the faculty of the State University of New York

at Purchase, and has been visiting professor at the National Theatre School of Canada.

Lighting Designs:
1973: *Raisin* **1974:** *Yentl* **1977:** *Cold Storage* **1978:** *Eubie*; *History of the American Film, A*

Danianne Mizzy

Danianne Mizzy was born on November 8, 1960 in New York City into a family with many theatre associations. Her mother, a Broadway press agent, worked for producer/director Eddie Jaffe; her great-grandfather, Charles Louis LaMarche, ran the Empire Theatre in Cleveland; and her grandmother, Pauline O'Keefe LaMarche, acted in summer productions of Ohio's Kenley Players. She received an International Baccalaureate in 1978 from U.N.I.S.; an A.B. from Brown University in 1982, where she began designing with *Getting Out* in the Production Workshop; and an M.F.A. in design from the Yale University School of Drama in 1986. Career influences include Jennifer Tipton, Mark Stanley, Allen Lee Hughes and Mark Reiff.

Lighting Designs:
1987: *Fences*

Robert W. Mogel

Robert W. Mogel began designing lights in New York City for the Roundabout Theatre's production of *A Taste of Honey*. He has also designed sets and lights in regional theatres, taught design at Texas Tech University and received extensive credits for outdoor theatres and concerts.

Lighting Designs:
1981: *Taste of Honey, A*

Tanya Moiseiwitsch

Tanya Moiseiwitsch, a British scenic designer, theatre designer lighting designer and costume designer, was born in London on December 3, 1914. She attended the Central School of Arts and Crafts in London. Her first design assignment was *The Faithful* in London in 1934. A longtime colleague of Tyrone Guthrie, they often collaborated, notably to create the theatre for the Stratford (Ontario) Festival, The Guthrie Theatre and the Crucible Theatre in

Sheffield, England. Known for her designs for opera and theatre in Europe and North America, she served as Principal Designer at The Guthrie Theatre from 1963 to 1969. Other companies for which she has worked include the Royal Shakespeare Company, the Old Vic, the Metropolitan Opera and the Abbey Theatre. Other designs include the 1984 film *King Lear* with Laurence Olivier. In 1975 her costume designs for *The Misanthrope* were nominated for a Tony Award. She was honored with a Commander of the British Empire in 1974 and a Distinguished Service Award from the United States Institute of Theatre Technology for fifty years of design in 1987.

Lighting Designs:
1955: *Matchmaker, The* **1968:** *House of Atreus, The*

Scenic Designs:
1946: *Critic, The*; *Uncle Vanya* **1955:** *Matchmaker, The* **1968:** *House of Atreus, The* **1975:** *Misanthrope, The*

Costume Designs:
1946: *Critic, The*; *Uncle Vanya* **1955:** *Matchmaker, The* **1968:** *House of Atreus, The* **1975:** *Misanthrope, The*

Robby Monk

Robby Monk designed lights on Broadway between 1979 and 1982. He was associate lighting designer for *Beatlemania* and assistant set designer for the Broadway and national tours of *Dracula*. He also has numerous credits for productions in regional theatres including *What I Did Last Summer*, *Cabaret* and *Terra Nova* for Studio Arena Theatre.

Lighting Designs:
1979: *Strider* **1981:** *Ned and Jack* **1982:** *World of Shalom Aleichem, The*

Yves Montand

Yves Montand, the popular French actor and singer, was born Yves Livi on October 13, 1921 in Monsummano, Italy and educated in Marseilles. His first film appearance was in 1946 in *Les Portes de la Nuit* and since then he has appeared in many French and American films, notably *On a Clear Day You Can See Forever*, *Is Paris Burning?*, and *Jean De Florette*. He was married to Simone Signoret from 1951 until her death in 1985. He contributed scene and lighting designs to a concert appearance he made on Broadway in 1961.

Lighting Designs:
1961: *An Evening with Yves Montand*

Scenic Designs:
1961: *An Evening with Yves Montand*

Beni Montresor

Beni Montresor was born on March 31, 1926 near Verona, Italy and reared in Venice. He studied at the Academy of Art in Venice. He designs extensively for opera companies around the world, specializing in opulence and fantasy, and occasionally directs. He has also designed films, including the autobiographical *Pilgrimage* shown at the Cannes Film Festival in 1972. In 1962 he met Gian Carlo Menotti and subsequently designed Barber's *Vanessa*, his first opera, for the Spoleto Festival. His career was established with *Last Savage* by Menotti at the Metropolitan Opera in 1964 and was soon followed by numerous productions for the major opera companies around the world. His costume designs for *Marco Millions* were nominated for a Tony Award in 1964, as were his designs for *The Marriage of Figaro* in 1985.

Lighting Designs:
1985: *Marriage of Figaro, The*

Scenic Designs:
1965: *Do I Hear a Waltz?* 1985: *Marriage of Figaro, The* 1986: *Rags*

Costume Designs:
1964: *Marco Millions* 1965: *Do I Hear a Waltz?* 1985: *Marriage of Figaro, The*

John J. Moore

John Jay Moore received both a B.S. and an M.A. in drama from Syracuse University and has designed scenery and lighting on Broadway since 1967. He assisted Jo Mielziner and Robert Randolph and was scenic consultant for Disneyland and Disney World. He has also been Professor of Theatre at Ramapo College in New Jersey. Film credits include art direction for *Black Rain, Just Tell Me What You Want* and *Sea of Love*.

Lighting Designs:
1967: *How to Be a Jewish Mother* 1969: *Teaspoon Every Four Hours, A*

Scenic Designs:
1972: *Don Juan* 1976: *Pal Joey*

Robert Morgan

Robert Morgan is a costume designer, set designer, lighting designer and director. He was born in Ocala, Florida on June 15, 1944 and received a B.A. at Dartmouth (1966) and an M.F.A. at Stanford (1969) in costume design and stage direction. His first professional costume designs were for *The House of Blue Leaves* at the American Conservatory Theatre in San Francisco in 1972. He has won numerous awards for costume design, including the Los Angeles Drama Critics Circle, four Drama Logues, several San Diego Critics Association Awards and a Drama Desk nomination for *Loves of Anatol.* He currently works primarily as a stage director.

Lighting Designs:
1981: *Broadway Follies*

Costume Designs:
1985: *I'm Not Rappaport*; *Loves of Anatol, The* 1987: *Sherlock's Last Case*

Roger Morgan

Roger Morgan was born on December 19, 1938 in New Kensington, Pennsylvania and graduated from the Carnegie Mellon University Department of Drama in 1961. He has designed over two hundred productions on and off-Broadway and in regional theatres and received both Tony and Drama Desk Awards for *The Crucifer of Blood.* He worked for three years as assistant theatre designer to Jo Mielziner, assisting with the Vivian Beaumont Theatre at Lincoln Center and the Power Center for the Performing Arts at the University of Michigan. As principal owner of the firm Roger Morgan Studios, Inc. he has had several theatre projects honored with regional and national awards, including both the Indiana Repertory Theatre and the Circle Theatre in Indianapolis, the Playhouse Square in Cleveland, and the Grand Opera House in Wilmington, North Carolina. He is co-author of *Space for Dance* and a founding member of Ensemble Studio Theatre in New York City.

Lighting Designs:

1966: *Under the Weather* 1968: *Sudden and Accidental Reeducation of Horse Johnson, The* 1970: *Wilson in the Promise Land* 1971: *Unlikely Heroes* 1972: *Elizabeth I; Ring Round the Bathtub* 1974: *Saturday Sunday Monday* 1977: *Dracula* 1978: *Crucifer of Blood, The; First Monday in October; Gorey Stories* 1979: *Gilda Radner Live from N.Y.; I Remember Mama* 1980: *Nuts* 1981: *It Had to Be You* 1982: *Agnes of God; Almost An Eagle* 1985: *Octette Bridge Club, The* 1987: *Mort Sahl on Broadway!*

Scenic Designs:

1972: *Dude*

Carter Morningstar

Carter Morningstar, scenic designer for theatre and television, was born in Lanstown, Pennsylvania and studied at the Philadelphia Academy of Fine Arts and in Europe. He began his professional life as a graphic artist and illustrator, but after service in the Navy during World War II he moved to New York and became a scenic designer. He only rarely designed costumes and lighting. Carter Morningstar died in February 1964 at the age of 53.

Lighting Designs:

1960: *Beg, Borrow, Or Steal*

Scenic Designs:

1960: *Beg, Borrow, Or Steal*

Costume Designs:

1960: *Beg, Borrow, Or Steal*

Paul Morrison

Paul Morrison, a scenic, lighting and costume designer, was born in Altoona, Pennsylvania on July 9, 1906. He graduated from Lafayette College where he also taught. He began his theatre career as an actor and stage manager and first designed costumes in New York in 1939 for *Thunder Rock*. Beginning in 1941 he specialized in scenery and lighting and had numerous shows to his credit on Broadway and in other locations. Mr. Morrison served as Executive Director of the Neighborhood Playhouse beginning in 1963. He died in New York City on December 29, 1980.

Lighting Designs:

1941: *Walk into My Parlor* 1942: *Hedda Gabler* 1943: *I'll Take the High Road* 1944: *Mrs. January and Mr. X; That Old Devil* 1946: *John Gabriel Borkman; What Every Woman Knows* 1948: *Young and the Fair, The* 1949: *Closing Door, The* 1950: *Affairs of State; Arms and the Man* 1951: *Billy Budd; Faithfully Yours; Twilight Walk* 1952: *Four Saints in Three Acts; Golden Boy* 1953: *On Borrowed Time* 1954: *Abie's Irish Rose; Confidential Clerk, The; Tender Trap, The* 1955: *Bus Stop; Joyce Grenfell Requests the Pleasure; Once Upon a Tailor; Tiger At the Gate* 1956: *Candide; Cranks; Loud Red Patrick, The; Separate Tables; Sixth Finger in a Five Finger Glove; Tamburlaine the Great* 1957: *Sin of Pat Muldoon, The; Ziegfeld Follies* 1958: *Make a Million; Maybe Tuesday* 1959: *Flowering Cherry; Happy Town; Kataki; Masquerade; Much Ado About Nothing; Nervous Set, The* 1960: *Duel of Angels; Invitation to a March; Rape of the Belt; Thurber Carnival, A* 1961: *Complaisant Lover, The; Man for All Seasons, A* 1962: *Cantilevered Terrace* 1963: *Student Gypsy, or The Prince of Liederkrantz; Too True to Be Good* 1964: *Sponomo* 1968: *Price, The* 1973: *Jockey Club Stakes, The*

Scenic Designs:

1941: *Walk into My Parlor* 1942: *Hedda Gabler* 1943: *I'll Take the High Road* 1944: *Love on Leave; Mrs. January and Mr. X; That Old Devil* 1946: *John Gabriel Borkman; What Every Woman Knows* 1948: *Young and the Fair, The* 1949: *Closing Door, The* 1950: *Affairs of State; Arms and the Man* 1951: *Billy Budd; Faithfully Yours; Twilight Walk* 1952: *Four Saints in Three Acts; Golden Boy* 1953: *On Borrowed Time* 1954: *Abie's Irish Rose; Confidential Clerk, The; Tender Trap, The* 1955: *Joyce Grenfell Requests the Pleasure* 1956: *Loud Red Patrick, The; Sixth Finger in a Five Finger Glove* 1958: *Make a Million; Maybe Tuesday; Visit, The* 1959: *Masquerade; Nervous Set, The* 1960: *Rape of the Belt* 1962: *Cantilevered Terrace* 1963: *Too True to Be Good* 1973: *Jockey Club Stakes, The*

Costume Designs:

1939: *Thunder Rock* 1940: *Night Music* 1941: *Walk into My Parlor* 1943: *Apology* 1946: *John Gabriel Borkman* 1947: *All My Sons* 1950: *Arms and the Man* 1952: *Four Saints in Three Acts; Golden Boy* 1953: *On Borrowed Time* 1954: *Abie's Irish Rose; Confidential Clerk, The* 1955: *Bus Stop; Once Upon a Tailor* **1956:** *Loud Red Patrick, The* **1962:** *Cantilevered Terrace*

Spencer Mosse

Spencer Mosse was born in New York City on October 17, 1945. He attended the Rudolf Steiner School where he began designing with productions of *The Mikado* and *The Christmas Play*. He has designed lights extensively in regional theatres throughout the United States and off-Broadway since serving an apprenticeship at age fifteen with John Robertson and Martin Aronstein at the New York Shakespeare Festival. He attended Bard College where he designed over forty-five productions including dance pieces. At the Yale University School of Drama he designed the lighting for six productions and was the first student in the school's history to light a major production (*Coriolanus*) in his first year. He began his career as an assistant working and training with Gilbert Hemsley, Jean Rosenthal, Joan Larkey, H.R. Poindexter, Tharon Musser and John Gleason. Major influences include John Gleason, Martin Aronstein, Tharon Musser, and Jean Rosenthal.

Lighting Designs:
1974: *Lamppost Reunion; Mourning Pictures; Rainbow Jones* **1976:** *Godspell*

Motley

Motley is the trade name of three scenery and costume designers from Britain. The trio consisted of two sisters, Margaret Harris and (Audrey) Sophia Harris, who worked mainly in London, and Elizabeth Montgomery, who represented them in the United States. They first worked together to design a production of *Romeo and Juliet* for the Oxford University Dramatic Society in 1932, and from then until the early 1970s designed countless plays and operas in England and the United States. The three met in art school and entered a contest at the Old Vic's annual costume ball. They won half the prizes and a job offer from the judge, John Gielgud. Elizabeth Montgomery, who was responsible for most of the Broadway designs, was born on February 15, 1904 in Kidlington, Oxfordshire, England, and studied at the Westminster School of Art. Sophia Harris Devine was

born in 1901 and died in 1966. Margaret Harris, who resides in London and has had a long term relationship with Riverside Studios, was born in 1904. In 1987 she was head of the design course at Almeda Theatre in London. Motley's first Broadway design was *Romeo and Juliet* for Laurence Olivier and Vivian Leigh. Winners of numerous awards, their Tonys include *The First Gentlemen* (1958) and *Becket* (1961) and many additional nominations. Their name is taken from a line of Jacques in *As You Like It*, in which he says "Motley's the only wear." In 1981 a 5,500 item collection of the 300 productions designed by Motley between 1932 and 1976 was acquired by the University of Illinois at Urbana-Champaign.

Lighting Designs:
1959: *Requiem for a Nun*

Scenic Designs:
1940: *Romeo and Juliet* **1942:** *Three Sisters, The* **1943:** *Lovers and Friends; Richard III* **1944:** *Bell for Adano, A; Cherry Orchard, The* **1945:** *Hope for the Best; Skydrift; Tempest, The; You Touched Me* **1946:** *Dancer, The; He Who Gets Slapped; Second Best Boy* **1947:** *Importance of Being Earnest, The* **1950:** *Happy As Larry* **1957:** *Country Wife* **1959:** *Requiem for a Nun* **1961:** *Complaisant Lover, The; Man for All Seasons, A; Ross*

Costume Designs:
1934: *Richard of Bordeaux* **1940:** *Romeo and Juliet* **1941:** *Doctor's Dilemma* **1942:** *Three Sisters, The* **1943:** *Lovers and Friends* **1944:** *Bell for Adano, A; Cherry Orchard, The; Highland Fling, A; Sadie Thompson* **1945:** *Carib Song; Pygmalion; Skydrift; Tempest, The; You Touched Me* **1946:** *Dancer, The; He Who Gets Slapped; Second Best Boy* **1947:** *Importance of Being Earnest, The* **1948:** *Anne of 1000 Days* **1949:** *Miss Liberty; South Pacific* **1950:** *Happy As Larry; Innocents, The; Liar, The; Peter Pan* **1951:** *Grand Tour, The; Paint Your Wagon* **1952:** *Candida; To Be Continued* **1953:** *Can-Can; Mid-summer* **1954:** *Immoralist, The; Mademoiselle Colombe; Peter Pan* **1955:** *Honeys, The; Island of Goats; Young and Beautiful, The* **1956:** *Long Day's Journey Into Night; Middle of the Night; Most Happy Fella, The* **1957:** *Country Wife; First Gentleman, The; Look Homeward, Angel; Shinbone Alley* **1958:** *Cold Wind and the Warm, The; Jane Eyre; Love Me Little* **1959:** *Majority of One, A; Requiem*

for a Nun; *Rivalry, The* 1960: *Becket* 1961: *Kwamina*; *Man for All Seasons, A*; *Ross* 1963: *110 Degrees in the Shade*; *Lorenzo*; *Mother Courage and Her Children*; *Tovarich* 1964: *Ben Franklin in Paris* 1965: *Baker Street*; *Devils, The* 1966: *Don't Drink the Water*

Rob Munnik

Rob Munnik designed lights in 1982 for a Broadway production.

Lighting Designs:
1982: *Herman Van Veen: All of Him*

Rupert Murray

Rupert Murray was born in England and studied at Trinity College, Dublin. His debut as a lighting designer was *Savages* for the Dublin University Players. In addition to credits in the United Kingdom he has designed lights in France, Italy, Hong Kong and the United States. He founded Lighting Diemnsions in Ireland, a company specializing in theatrical lighting equipment. He has also designed fashion shows and commercial projects.

Lighting Designs:
1988: *Juno And The Paycock*

Tharon Musser

Tharon Musser was born on January 8, 1925 in Roanoke, Virginia. She received a B.A. in 1946 from Berea College in Kentucky and an M.F.A. from Yale in 1950. She worked at the Provincetown Playhouse, the YMHA and for José Limon as a stage manager and lighting designer, gaining background to launch her own prolific career and in the process helping to advance the field of lighting design to its present professional level. Her contributions include being the first lighting designer to use a computer lighting system on Broadway. Her Broadway debut was the premier of *A Long Day's Journey Into The Night* in 1956. She has designed plays and many notable musicals and operas throughout the world, and often consults with architects such as Webb & Knapp on lighting for buildings at colleges, universities and theatre complexes. One of the dominant lighting designers on Broadway, she has been nominated for numerous Tony Awards

and received Tonys for *Follies*, *A Chorus Line* and *Dreamgirls*. She has lectured widely on lighting design, been the subject of many articles, and influenced scores of assistants and colleagues.

Lighting Designs:

1956: *Long Day's Journey Into Night* 1957: *Makropoulos Secret, The*; *Monique*; *Shinbone Alley* 1958: *Firstborn, The*; *J.B.*; *Shadow of a Gunman, The* 1959: *Five Finger Exercise*; *Only in America*; *Rivalry, The* 1960: *Long Dream, The*; *Tumbler, The* 1961: *Garden of Secrets, The* 1962: *Calculated Risk*; *Giants, Sons of Giants*; *Nowhere To Go But Up* 1963: *Andorra*; *Here's Love*; *Marathon '33*; *Mother Courage and Her Children* 1964: *Alfie*; *Any Wednesday*; *Crucible, The*; *Golden Boy*; *Seagull, The* 1965: *All in Good Time*; *Flora, the Red Menace*; *Kelly*; *Minor Miracle* 1966: *Delicate Balance, A*; *Great Indoors, The*; *Lion in Winter, The*; *Malcolm*; *Mame* 1967: *After the Rain*; *Birthday Party, The*; *Everything in the Garden*; *Hallelujah, Baby!*; *Imaginary Invalid, The*; *Promise, The*; *Tonight At 8:30*; *Touch of the Poet, A* 1968: *Maggie Flynn* 1969: *Fig Leaves Are Falling, The*; *Gingham Dog, The* 1970: *Applause*; *Blood Red Roses*; *Boy Friend, The* 1971: *Follies*; *On the Town*; *Prisoner of 2nd Avenue, The*; *Trial of the Catonsville Nine, The* 1972: *Creation of the World and Other Business,*; *Night Watch*; *Sunshine Boys, The* 1973: *Good Doctor, The*; *Little Night Music, A* 1974: *Candide*; *God's Favorite*; *Good News*; *Mack and Mabel*; *Me and Bessie* 1975: *Chorus Line, A*; *Wiz, The* 1976: *1600 Pennsylvania Avenue*; *California Suite*; *Pacific Overtures* 1977: *Act, The*; *Chapter Two* 1978: *Ballroom*; *Tribute* 1979: *Last Licks*; *Romantic Comedy*; *They're Playing Our Song*; *Whose Life Is It Anyway?* 1980: *42nd Street*; *Children of a Lesser God*; *I Ought to Be in Pictures*; *Roast, The*; *Who's Life Is It Anyway?* 1981: *Dreamgirls*; *Fools*; *Moony Shapiro Song Book, The* 1982: *Special Occasions* 1983: *Brighton Beach Memoirs*; *Merlin*; *Private Lives* 1984: *Open Admissions*; *Real Thing, The* 1985: *Biloxi Blues*; *Jerry's Girls*; *Odd Couple, The* 1986: *Broadway Bound* 1987: *Dreamgirls*; *Month of Sundays, A*; *Teddy and Alice* 1988: *Rumors* 1989: *Artist Descending a Staircase*; *Welcome To The Club*

Brian Nason

After receiving an M.F.A. at New York University's Tisch School of the Arts, Brian Nason assisted Tharon Musser during the 1987-88 season. He has extensive credits off-Broadway including productions at the Jewish Repertory Theatre and Lamb's Theatre and in regional theatres. He is resident designer for both Déja Vu Dance Theatre and the Charles Ragland Dance Company. His lighting designs for *Metamorphosis* were nominated for a Tony Award. Brian Nason also designed lights for the feature film, *Sing*.

Lighting Designs:
1989: *3Penny Opera; Metamorphosis*

Richard Nelson

Richard Nelson was born on December 7, 1938 in New York City and graduated from the High School of Performing Arts in 1956. His first professional productions were *The Winslow Boy* in 1955 at the Master Institute in New York City (later Equity Library Theatre) and *Hamlet of Stepney Green* in 1958 at the Cricket Theatre off-Broadway. Since then he has designed numerous shows on and off-Broadway, in regional and international theatres. He has been principal designer and production manager for the dance companies of Merce Cunningham, José Limon, Louis Falco as well as for other dance and ballet companies. His architectural lighting projects include the Herman Miller Pavillion in Grand Rapids, Michigan, the Palm Court of the Wintergarden at the World Financial Center, and the Con Ed Energy Conservation Center in New York. He received the Tony, Drama Desk and Maharam Awards for *Sunday in the Park with George* as well as several other Drama Desk nominations. Since 1988 he has been Associate Professor of Theatre at the University of Michigan.

Lighting Designs:
1970: *Water Color/ Criss Crossing* 1971: *All Over* 1972: *Sign in Sidney Brustein's Window, The* 1974: *Magic Show, The* 1976: *So Long, 174th Street; Zalmen Or the Madness of God* 1977: *Trip Back Down, The* 1979: *Murder At the Howard Johnson's* 1980: *Censored Scenes from King Kong; Lady from Dubuque, The; Mornings At Seven; Onward Victoria* 1981: *Oh, Brother; Supporting Cast, The* 1982:

Little Family Business, A; Present Laughter; Solomon's Child 1983: *Caine Mutiny Court-martial, The; Corn Is Green, The; Five-Six-Seven-Eight...Dance!; Misanthrope, The; Tap-dance Kid, The* 1984: *Awake and Sing; Sunday in the Park with George* 1985: *Arms and the Man; Harrigan 'n Hart* 1986: *Boys in Autumn, The; Long Day's Journey into Night; Loot; Precious Sons; You Can Never Tell* 1987: *Blithe Spirit; Into The Woods; Sleight of Hand* 1988: *Mail; Night of the Iguana, The* 1989: *Cafe Crown; Secret Rapture, The*

Gertrude Newell

Gertrude Newell, born and raised in St. Johnsbury, Vermont, studied painting in Italy with Frazatti and in Allegheri's studio. She began professional life as an interior decorator. The design of a door for Grace George's production of *Major Barbara* led her to scenic, lighting and ultimately costume design. She also produced plays in New York and London.

Lighting Designs:
1916: *Pendennis*

Scenic Designs:
1915: *Earth, The* 1916: *Pendennis*

Costume Designs:
1916: *Pendennis* 1917: *Claim, The; Hamilton; Peter Ibbetson* 1920: *Little Old New York* 1921: *Fair Circassian, The* 1928: *Age of Innocence, The*

David Noling

David Noling was born on February 6, 1955 in Indianapolis, Indiana. He received a B.A. in 1977 in art and an M.F.A. in 1982 in design at Yale. He has designed off-Broadway at the New Theatre of Brooklyn, Manhattan Punch Line, Westside Arts Center, Soho Rep, Playwrights Horizon and the Manhattan Theatre Club among others. He was nominated for an Audelco Recognition Award for *Sgt. Ola and His Followers* at Soho Rep in 1987. He has many credits for regional theatres, dance companies, and as an assistant to lighting designers Frances Aronson, Thomas Skelton and Jennifer Tipton.

Lighting Designs:
1982: *Master Harold...and the Boys*

"None"

Hundreds of playbills for Broadway productions make no mention of lighting designers. This was perhaps understandable while the profession was developing during the early part of this century. Yet even as late as the early 1960s, lighting designers did not consistently receive credit on the title page of playbills. Because the focus of this book is on designers, the index of this book does not list the many plays without design credit. It cites "Ack Only" for a group of representative plays which had acknowledgements for lighting equipment companies. Plays which are not listed in the index either did not have a designer, or had only acknowledgements for lighting equipment companies in their playbills. Therefore, the focus of the index remains on those plays which credited a designer. The body of the book includes information on approximately four hundred individual designers. Some limited information about lighting equipment companies is available in the entries "Acknowledgements Only", "DuWico" and "Kliegl," among others.

Donald Oenslager

Donald Oenslager is known mainly as a scenic designer and a long-time teacher of design at Yale University, where he influenced a generation of designers. He was born in Harrisburg, Pennsylvania on May 7, 1902 and graduated from Harvard in 1923. His first sets on Broadway were seen in 1925, the same year he began teaching at Yale, and were followed by nearly two hundred additional designs for plays and operas. He wrote *Scenery Then and Now* and *Part of a Lifetime* and consulted on the design of many theatre spaces. He won a Tony Award for his set design for *A Majority of One* in 1956. He occasionally designed costumes and lighting for productions along with sets. Donald Oenslager died on June 11, 1975 at the age of 73.

Lighting Designs:
1946: *Fatal Weakness*; *On Whitman Avenue*; *Park Avenue* 1947: *Angel in the Wings*; *Eastward in Eden*; *How I Wonder*; *Lovely Me*; *Portrait in Black* 1948: *Goodbye, My Fancy*; *Leading Lady, The*; *Men We Marry, The*; *Town House* 1949: *Father, The*; *Rat Race, The*; *Smile of the World, The* 1950: *Live Wire, The* 1951: *Second Threshold* 1953: *Escapade*; *Horses in*

Midstream; *Sabrina Fair* 1954: *Dear Charles* 1955: *Janus*; *Roomful of Roses, A*; *Wooden Dish, The* 1956: *Major Barbara* 1957: *Four Winds*; *Nature's Way*; *Shadow of My Enemy, A* 1958: *Girls in 509, The*; *Man in the Dog Suit, The*; *Marriage-Go-Round, The*; *Pleasure of His Company, The* 1959: *Highest Tree, The*; *Majority of One, A* 1961: *Blood, Sweat and Stanley Poole*; *Call on Kuprin, A*; *Far Country, A*; *First Love* 1962: *Venus At Large* 1963: *Case of Libel, A*; *Irregular Verb to Love, The* 1964: *One By One* 1967: *Love in E-Flat*; *Spofford* 1968: *Avanti!* 1969: *Wrong Way Light Bulb, The*

Scenic Designs:
1925: *Bit of Love, A*; *Morals*; *Sooner Or Later* 1927: *Good News*; *Pinwheel* 1928: *Anna*; *New Moon, The* 1929: *Follow Through*; *Heads Up*; *Stepping Out* 1930: *Girl Crazy*; *Overture* 1931: *America's Sweetheart*; *East Wind*; *Free for All*; *Rock Me, Juliet*; *You Said It* 1932: *Adam Had Two Sons*; *Thousand Summers, A*; *Whistling in the Dark* 1933: *Forsaking All Others*; *Keeper of the Keys*; *Uncle Tom's Cabin* 1934: *Anything Goes*; *Dance with Your Gods*; *Divided By Three*; *Gold Eagle Guy*; *Lady from the Sea, The* 1935: *First Lady*; *Something Gay*; *Sweet Mystery of Life*; *Tapestry in Gray* 1936: *200 Were Chosen*; *Johnny Johnson*; *Matrimony RFD*; *Red, Hot and Blue*; *Russet Mantle*; *Stage Door*; *Sweet River*; *Ten Million Ghosts*; *Timber House*; *You Can't Take It with You* 1937: *Doll's House, A*; *Edna His Wife*; *I'd Rather Be Right*; *Miss Quis*; *Robin Landing* 1938: *Circle, The*; *Fabulous Invalid*; *Good, The*; *I Am My Youth*; *Spring Meeting*; *Spring Thaw*; *Woman's a Fool To Be Clever, A* 1939: *American Way, The*; *From Vienna*; *I Know What I Like*; *Man Who Came to Dinner, The*; *Margin for Error*; *Off to Buffalo*; *Skylark* 1940: *Beverly Hills*; *My Dear Children*; *My Sister Eileen*; *Old Foolishness, The*; *Retreat to Pleasure*; *Young Couple Wanted* 1941: *Claudia*; *Doctor's Dilemma*; *Lady Who Came to Stay, The*; *Mr. Bib*; *Pie in the Sky*; *Spring Again*; *Theatre* 1942: *Flowers of Virtue, The* 1943: *Hairpin Harmony* 1945: *Pygmalion* 1946: *Born Yesterday*; *Fatal Weakness*; *Land's End*; *Loco*; *On Whitman Avenue*; *Park Avenue*; *Present Laughter*; *Three to Make Ready*; *Years Ago* 1947: *Angel in the Wings*; *Eagle Has Two Heads, The*; *Eastward in Eden*; *How I Wonder*; *Lovely Me*; *Message for Margaret*; *Portrait in Black* 1948: *Goodbye, My Fancy*; *Leading Lady,*

The; *Life with Mother; Men We Marry, The;*
Town House **1949:** *At War with the Army; Fa-*
ther, The; Rat Race, The; Smile of the World,
The; Velvet Glove, The **1950:** *Liar, The; Live*
Wire, The **1951:** *Constant Wife, The; Second*
Threshold; Small Hours, The **1952:** *Candida;*
Paris '90; To Be Continued **1953:** *Escapade;*
Horses in Midstream; Prescott Proposals, The;
Sabrina Fair **1954:** *Dear Charles* **1955:** *Janus;*
Roomful of Roses, A; Wooden Dish, The **1956:**
Major Barbara **1957:** *Four Winds; Nature's*
Way; Shadow of My Enemy, A **1958:** *Girls in*
509, The; Man in the Dog Suit, The; Marriage-
Go-Round, The; Pleasure of His Company, The
1959: *Highest Tree, The; Majority of One, A*
1960: *Dear Liar* **1961:** *Blood, Sweat and Stan-*
ley Poole; Call on Kuprin, A; Far Country, A;
First Love **1962:** *Venus At Large* **1963:** *Case*
of Libel, A; Irregular Verb to Love, The **1964:**
One By One **1967:** *Love in E-Flat; Spofford*
1968: *Avanti!* **1969:** *Wrong Way Light Bulb,*
The **1974:** *Good News*

Costume Designs:
1925: *Sooner Or Later* **1927:** *Grand Street*
Follies; Pinwheel **1933:** *Uncle Tom's Cabin*
1934: *Dance with Your Gods; Gold Eagle Guy;*
Lady from the Sea, The **1935:** *Tapestry in*
Gray **1936:** *Sweet River* **1937:** *Doll's House,*
A **1938:** *Good, The; I Am My Youth* **1941:**
Lady Who Came to Stay, The **1946:** *Land's*
End **1947:** *Eastward in Eden* **1948:** *Life with*
Mother **1953:** *Escapade; Horses in Midstream*
1957: *Four Winds; Shadow of My Enemy, A*

Toshiro Ogawa

Toshiro Ogawa, a native of Tokyo, came to the
United States in 1963. He studied at the Ham-
burg Opera and the Berlin Technical University.
He has been lighting designer for the Stuttgart
Ballet, the Chautauqua Opera, and American
Ballet Theatre and has taught at the Univer-
sity of California at Berkeley and the Ohio State
University.

Lighting Designs:
1980: *Goodbye Fidel*

Robert O'Hearn

Robert O'Hearn, a designer of settings, costumes and lights for the opera, ballet and theatre, is best known for his opera sets. He was

born on July 19, 1921 in Elkhart, Indiana and
studied at Indiana University and the Art Students League. He designed his first play in 1948
for the Brattle Theatre Company in Cambridge,
Massachusetts, where he subsequently designed
sixty productions. His first opera was *Falstaff*
with Sarah Caldwell in 1951, and since that time
he has designed for every major opera company
in the United States and several in Austria and
Germany. His debut at the Metropolitan Opera
was *L'Elisir d'Amore* (1960) and was followed
by many more including his most recent, *Porgy*
and Bess (1985). He credits Robert Messel as
an influential figure in his career. His designs
have been widely exhibited and he has taught
at Lester Polakov's Studio and Forum of Stage
Design. In 1987 he was appointed Professor and
Chair of Design at the Indiana University School
of Music.

Lighting Designs:
1955: *Festival* **1956:** *Apple Cart, The; Child of*
Fortune **1964:** *Abraham Cochrane*

Scenic Designs:
1950: *Relapse, The* **1953:** *Date with April, A*
1955: *Festival* **1956:** *Apple Cart, The; Child of*
Fortune **1964:** *Abraham Cochrane*

Costume Designs:
1950: *Relapse, The*

Julia Trevelyan Oman

Julia Trevelyan Oman, a British designer of sets
and costumes for television, film, and stage, was
born in Kensington, England on July 11, 1930.
She attended the Royal College of Art and is
married to designer Roy Strong. Her first professional design of sets and costumes, *Brief Lives*,
played in both London and New York. She has
also designed operas and exhibitions, and has
created film and television designs in collaboration with her husband.

Lighting Designs:
1974: *Brief Lives*

Scenic Designs:
1967: *Brief Lives* **1974:** *Brief Lives*

Costume Designs:
1967: *Brief Lives* **1974:** *Brief Lives*

Hector Orezzoli

A native of Argentina, Hector Orezzoli attended
the University of Buenos Aires before studying

design at the University of Belgrano. He has designed sets and costumes for many productions in Europe and South America. His collaborations with Claudio Segovia have resulted in the production of several music spectaculars, including a version of *Flamenco Puro* in Seville in 1980, a second version in Paris in 1984, and a Broadway production in 1986. *Tango Argentino* resulted from his continuing collaboration with Mr. Segovia and was honored with a Tony nomination for costume design. Their scenic designs for *Black and Blue* were nominated for a Tony Award in 1989.

Lighting Designs:
1986: *Flamenco Puro*

Scenic Designs:
1985: *Tango Argentino* 1986: *Flamenco Puro*
1989: *Black and Blue*

Costume Designs:
1985: *Tango Argentino* 1986: *Flamenco Puro*
1989: *Black and Blue*

Robert Ornbo

A British designer of lights, Robert Ornbo was born in Hessle, Yorkshire, England on September 13, 1931 and studied at Hull University. He began designing in London in 1959 with *Urfaust* and has since designed many productions, including operas and plays throughout Europe. He designed lights for the opening production in the Sydney (Australia) Opera House. Together with Richard Pilbrow through the company Theatre Projects, Inc., he has been instrumental in the development of the profession of lighting design in the United Kingdom. He designed lights for the 1967 production of *As You Like It* at the National Theatre directed by Clifford Williams.

Lighting Designs:
1970: *Company* 1974: *As You Like It*; *London Assurance*; *Travesties*

Curt Ostermann

Curt Ostermann was born on July 20, 1952 in Detroit, the son of G. William and Barbara Ostermann. He received a B.A. with distinction at the University of Michigan and an M.F.A. at New York University Tisch School of the Arts, where he now teaches. From 1978 to 1980 he

assisted Tharon Musser whom he credits along with John Gleason and Roger Morgan as a mentor. He received a nomination for Best Lighting Designer for *A Streetcar Named Desire* from the American Theatre Wing. International credits include productions for the Stuttgart Ballet, the Netherlands Opera, the Theatre Royal de la Monnaie Opera, Toronto's Royal Alexandra Theatre, the Spoleto Festival in Italy and Theatre an der Wein in Vienna. He has also designed at the New York City Opera and in regional theatres throughout the United States.

Lighting Designs:
1988: *Devil's Disciple, The*; *Streetcar Named Desire, A*

A. A. Ostrander

Albert A. Ostrander designed sets, lights and costumes for the theatre and fashion shows during his career. He initially worked as a technical director for Norman Bel Geddes before designing shows. He staged several *Fashions of the Times* productions in the late 1940s and also designed for three years for the Ringling Brothers and Barnum & Bailey Circus. A.A. Ostrander died in New York on September 29, 1964 at age sixty-one.

Lighting Designs:
1944: *Sleep No More*

Scenic Designs:
1939: *Where There's a Will* 1940: *Case of Youth, A* 1943: *All for All* 1944: *Sleep No More* 1946: *Duchess Misbehaves, The*

Costume Designs:
1944: *Sleep No More*

Dennis Parichy

Dennis Parichy has been resident lighting designer for the Circle Repertory Company since 1976. He began his professional design career in 1959 with a production of *Richard II* at Eagles Mere Playhouse in Eagles Mere, Pennsylvania. He was born on November 10, 1938 in Melrose Park, Illinois, the son of Theodore and Eva Parichy. He received a B.S. in 1960 from Northwestern University where he worked with Alvina Krause, and studied at Lester Polakov's Studio and Forum of Stage Design. His mentors include Alvina Krause, Theodore Fuchs and

Thomas Skelton. He has received many awards including a Marharam Award for *Talley's Folly* and *The Fifth of July*, a Drama Desk and Obie for *Talley's Folly*, Drama Logue Awards for *Tally's Folly*, *Picnic* and *Burn This*, and Village Awards for *Devour The Snow* and *Angels Fall*. Recent designs include *The Sum of Us* at the Off-Broadway Cherry Lane Theatre. Married to Barbara Ann Begun, Dennis Parichy and his wife have two sons, David and Adam.

Lighting Designs:
1976: *Knock Knock* 1978: *Best Little Whorehouse in Texas, The*; *Water Engine, The/ Mr. Happiness* 1979: *Devour the Snow* 1980: *Fifth of July*; *Talley's Folly* 1981: *Crimes of the Heart*; *Duet for One* 1982: *Best Little Whorehouse in Texas, The*; *Curse of An Aching Heart, The* 1983: *Angels Fall* 1985: *As Is*; *Dancing in the End Zone* 1987: *Burn This*; *Coastal Disturbances*; *Nerd, The*; *Penn & Teller* 1989: *Love Letters*; *Tenth Man, The*

Chris Parry

Chris Parry designed one set in 1987 on Broadway. A British designer, he has designed operas and tours throughout the United Kingdom. He is also deputy head of stage lighting at the Royal Shakespeare Company, Stratford-upon-Avon.

Lighting Designs:
1987: *Les Liaisons Dangereuses*

William Pennington

The director of the scenic department of the Washington Square Players, William E. Pennington designed sets for a Broadway play in 1918. He was stage manager of the Bandbox Theatre, 520 E. 77th Street, New York City in 1916. In the early 1930s he was associated with Robert W. Bergman Studios at 142 West 39th Street as secretary of the corporation. His father was the British actor, W.H. Pennington, who had appeared as Hamlet at Sadler's Wells in 1872, in productions for the Drury Lane Theatre, and in recitals of Shakespeare for Prime Minister Gladstone at Carlton House Terrace.

Lighting Designs:
1918: *Hitchy Koo 1918*

Conrad Penrod

Conrad Penrod designed a set in 1971 on Broadway.

Lighting Designs:
1971: *No Place to be Somebody*

Monroe Pevear

Monroe (Moe) Pevear was an early pioneer in the use of color in stage lighting. In his 1924 book, *History of Stage Lighting*, Theodore Fuchs credits him with the first use of primary colors of light in combination with clear tinting to achieve any possible color. Monroe Pevear also developed specialized instruments for direct and indirect light. The Pevear Color Speciality Company, "Theatrical Designers and Lighting Engineers," was located in Boston. An undated brochure advertising the company says "The Pevear Color Speciality Company have been the originators of many unique and successful devices for the lighting of the theatre and pageant field, combining the science of light and color with highly effecient and practical light projections of many types."

Lighting Designs:
1925: *Edgar Allan Poe*

Andy Phillips

The British lighting designer Andy Phillips has been designing lights on Broadway since 1974. He was resident lighting designer at the Royal Court Theatre for seven seasons from 1965 to 1972, designing nearly eighty shows during his tenure. He has numerous credits in the West End, at the National Theatre, and for plays and major opera houses in Europe and the United States. In 1960 he formed the theatre company Group One in Brighton, England. He is also a playwright, with *The Orange Balloon* and *Cars* among his works.

Lighting Designs:
1974: *Equus* 1975: *Misanthrope, The* 1976: *Equus* 1977: *Merchant, The* 1981: *Rose* 1983: *Glass Menagerie, The* 1988: *M. Butterfly* 1989: *3Penny Opera*

Tim Phillips

Tim Phillips has designed lights and scenery for many off-Broadway productions and has worked

as a scenic painter. He has received two Audelco Awards, one for the scenic design for *Winti
Train* in 1978 and a second for the lighting design of *Inacent Black* in 1979.

Lighting Designs:
1981: *Inacent Black*

Ben Phlaum

Ben Phlaum (a.k.a. Benjamin F. Pflaum) designed lights for one play in 1925. He was associated with the New York Calcium Company,
a supplier of theatrical lighting equipment. In
1925 he resided at 124 Convent Avenue in New
York City.

Lighting Designs:
1925: *Book of Charm, The*

Richard Pilbrow

Richard Pilbrow has designed over two hundred
productions in London and also produced plays
in New York and Moscow since his debut in
1958. He founded Theatre Projects in 1957,
assembling a team of young lighting designers
to encourage the development of the profession
and introduce American and German methods
and equipment to the United Kingdom. He began his career as a lighting designer and a stage
manager. He has also a consulted on developing lighting systems for the Hammersmith Lyric
Theatre restoration, the National Theatre, the
Barbican, A Contemporary Theatre in Seattle,
and the Bayfront Center in Toronto among others. He believes continuing to design is critical
to effective theatre consulting. His book *Stage
Lighting* was published in 1970.

Lighting Designs:
1967: *Rosencrantz and Guildenstern Are Dead*
1968: *Zorba* **1970:** *Rothschilds, The* **1973:**
Shelter

Scott Pinkney

Scott Pinkney designs lights for the theatre and
has extensive industrial lighting design credits for clients such as IBM, Estée Lauder, and
BMW. He was born on April 7, 1953 in Pittsburgh the son of Marjorie L. Pinkney, an ac-
countant, and Ellwood E. Pinkney, an interior
designer and planner from whom he learned

drafting and a visual sense. His wife, Debra
Smith Pinkney, is a former dancer with Bal-
letWest and a founder of and teacher at the
Cape Cod Dance Center. He received a B.F.A.
from Boston University in 1976 in lighting design and assisted Richard Winkler for three
years. He has also studied and admired designs
by Tharon Musser. His first design in the professional world was *The Revels* at the Sanders
Theatre in Cambridge, Massachusetts in 1974.
His designs have been honored with a Denver
Drama Critics Circle Award for lighting design
for *Don Juan*, and a Phoebe Award for lighting
design for *My Fair Lady* at Theatre Virginia in
Richmond.

Lighting Designs:
1982: *Torch Song Trilogy*

William Pitkin

William Pitkin was born in Omaha, Nebraska
on July 15, 1925. A scenic designer, he also occasionally contributed costume and lighting designs to productions. After attending colleges in
the United States and serving in the Army Air
Force, he studied in Paris with Christian Bérard
at the École Paul Colin. He designed settings
in summer stock beginning in 1947 and was a
staff designer for Raymond Loewy Associates in
1953. His first New York production was *The
Threepenny Opera* starring Lotte Lenya at the
Theatre de Lys in 1954. He also designed for
opera and extensively for ballet. Mr. Pitkin
won an Emmy Award in 1978 for the costumes
for *Romeo and Juliet* on PBS. He died on May
10, 1990.

Lighting Designs:
1962: *Beauty Part, The; Seidman and Son*

Scenic Designs:
1957: *Cave Dwellers, The; Moon for the Misbegotten, A; Potting Shed, The* **1960:** *Invitation
to a March* **1961:** *Conquering Hero, The* **1962:**
*Beauty Part, The; Seidman and Son; Something
About a Soldier* **1965:** *Impossible Years, The*
1968: *Guide, The* **1970:** *Chinese, The/ Dr.
Fish*

Costume Designs:
1956: *Child of Fortune* **1962:** *Seidman and
Son; Something About a Soldier* **1968:** *Guide,
The*

Livingston Platt

Livingston Platt was born in Plattsburg, New York in 1874 and went to Europe to develop his skills as a painter. While in Paris he became acquainted with many actors and managers who introduced him to theatre and its possibilities. He first designed for a small theatre in Bruges, Belgium, which led to designs for several opera productions. He returned to the United States in 1911 and became head of design at the Toy Theatre in Boston, where in 1914 he designed four productions for Margaret Anglin. He preferred to be called a "stage decorator" and designed numerous settings in New York, many of them before 1915, occasionally contributing costume and lighting designs to these same productions.

Lighting Designs:
1932: *When Ladies Meet*

Scenic Designs:
1915: *Beverly's Balance* 1917: *Billeted* 1918: *East Is West*; *Electra* 1919: *Abraham Lincoln*; *First is Last*; *Lusmore*; *Shakuntala* 1920: *Bad Man, The*; *Thy Name Is Woman* 1921: *Bluebeard's Eighth Wife*; *Children's Tragedy, The*; *Eyvind of the Hills*; *Launcelot and Elaine*; *Mary Stuart*; *Two Blocks Away*; *White Villa, The* 1922: *Banco*; *Ever Green Lady, The*; *First 50 Years, The*; *It Is the Law*; *Lady Christilinda, The*; *Madame Pierre* 1923: *Floriani's Wife*; *In Love with Love*; *Robert E. Lee* 1924: *Catskill Dutch*; *Cock O' the Roost*; *Far Cry, The*; *Goose Hangs High, The*; *No Other Girl*; *Outsider, The*; *Outward Bound*; *Tantrum, The*; *Youngest, The* 1925: *Aloma of the South Seas*; *Backslapper, The*; *Dark Angel, The*; *Holka Polka*; *It All Depends*; *Oh! Mama*; *Pierrot the Prodigal*; *School for Scandal, The*; *She Had to Know*; *Stolen Fruit*; *Stronger Than Love*; *Two Married Men* 1926: *Creaking Chair, The*; *Daisy Mayme*; *Devils*; *Great Gatsby, The*; *Kitty's Kisses*; *Puppy Love*; *Slaves All*; *Sport of Kings, The*; *Witch, The* 1927: *A La Carte*; *Baby Mine*; *Behold the Bridegroom*; *Dark, The*; *Electra*; *House of Shadows*; *L'Aiglon*; *Lally*; *Legend of Leonora, The*; *Puppets of Passion*; *Savage Under the Skin*; *Storm Center*; *Strawberry Blonde, The*; *Venus* 1928: *Carry On*; *Distant Drum, A*; *Elmer Gantry*; *Free Soul, A*; *Great Power, The*; *In Love with Love*; *Lady Dedlock*; *Outsider, The*; *Pleasure Man*; *Queen's Husband, The*; *Say When*; *Tomorrow...* 1929: *Abraham Lincoln*;

First Mrs. Fraser, The; *Flight*; *Maggie the Magnificent*; *Merry Andrew*; *Precious*; *Strong Man's House, A*; *Thunder in the Air* 1930: *Greeks Have a Word for It, The*; *Launcelot and Elaine* 1931: *Berlin*; *Church Mouse, A*; *Guest Room, The* 1932: *Alice Sit By the Fire/ The Old Lady Shows*; *Dinner At Eight*; *Domino*; *Lilly Turner*; *Mademoiselle*; *Man Who Reclaimed His Head, The*; *Round-Up, The*; *Stork Is Dead, The*; *We Are No Longer Children* 1933: *£25.00 an Hour*; *For Services Rendered*; *Hangman's Whip*; *Her Tin Soldier*; *Party, A*; *Saturday Night, A*; *Three and One*

Costume Designs:
1918: *Electra*; *Freedom* 1919: *Abraham Lincoln*; *First is Last*; *Lusmore*; *Shakuntala* 1921: *Eyvind of the Hills*; *Mary Stuart* 1922: *Banco*; *First 50 Years, The* 1925: *Aloma of the South Seas*; *Holka Polka*; *Stronger Than Love* 1926: *Creaking Chair, The*; *Sport of Kings, The* 1927: *Electra*; *L'Aiglon* 1928: *Elmer Gantry* 1930: *Launcelot and Elaine* 1931: *Guest Room, The* 1933: *Pursuit of Happiness, The*

H.R. Poindexter

H.R. Poindexter was a scenic and lighting designer who worked principally on the West Coast. He was production supervisor and lighting designer for the American Ballet Theatre, the Martha Graham Company, and the Dallas Civic Opera Company. He was technical supervisor at the Mark Taper Forum in Los Angeles from 1969 to 1974, and at the time of his death on September 24, 1977 was technical supervisor for the Ahmanson Theatre. He received a Tony Award for *Paul Sills' Story Theatre* in 1971 and a Los Angeles Drama Critics' Award for *Metamorphoses*, one of many lighting designs created for the Mark Taper Forum. He also created scenery and lighting for many national tours. Two productions he designed, *Paul Robeson* and *Vincent Price in Diversions and Delights*, were on tour prior to their Broadway openings when he died in 1977 at age 41.

Lighting Designs:
1970: *Ovid's Metamorphoses*; *Paul Sills' Story Theatre* 1971: *Abelard and Heloise* 1972: *Evening with Richard Nixon, An*; *Funny Thing Happened on the Way to the Forum, A* 1974: *Henry Fonda As Clarence Darrow* 1975: *Henry Fonda As Clarence Darrow*; *Private Lives* 1976:

Belle of Amherst, The; *Music Is*; *Night of the Iguana, The* **1978**: *Vincent Price in Diversions and Delights*

Scenic Designs:

1974: *Henry Fonda As Clarence Darrow* **1975**: *Henry Fonda As Clarence Darrow* **1976**: *Belle of Amherst, The*; *Night of the Iguana, The* **1978**: *Paul Robeson*; *Vincent Price in Diversions and Delights*

Lester Polakov

Lester Polakov was born in Chicago in 1916 and studied painting in New York with George Grosz, stagecraft with Milton Smith at Columbia University, and drafting with Emeline Roche. He began his career designing sets in summer stock. His New York debut was a 1935 production of *White Trash* at Columbia University, and in 1938 he designed scenery for *The Mother*, making his Broadway debut. He assisted Harry Horner on many productions and credits him as his mentor. After service in the Army Air Corps in World War II he resumed designing and had several exhibitions. In 1958 Polakov established the Lester Polakov Studio of Stage Design, now known as the "Studio and Forum of Stage Design," where he employs some of the best-known designers of sets, lights and costumes to teach design. In addition to teaching and overseeing the operation of this school he continues to design sets and costumes for stage and film.

Lighting Designs:

1950: *Golden State, The* **1953**: *Emperor's Clothes, The* **1961**: *Great Day in the Morning*

Scenic Designs:

1938: *Mother, The* **1946**: *Call Me Mister* **1950**: *Golden State, The*; *Member of the Wedding, The* **1952**: *Mrs. McThing* **1953**: *Emperor's Clothes, The* **1954**: *Winner, The* **1955**: *Skin of Our Teeth, The* **1961**: *Great Day in the Morning* **1980**: *Charlotte*

Costume Designs:

1940: *Reunion in New York* **1941**: *Crazy with the Heat* **1947**: *Crime and Punishment* **1950**: *Member of the Wedding, The*

Helen Pond

Helen Pond was born on June 26, 1924 in Cleveland and is the daughter of Ralph Herbert and Charlotte Waters Pond. She studied at Ohio State and Columbia Universities. She began designing at the Chagrin Falls Summer Theatre in Ohio with *Papa is All* and made her New York debut in 1955 with *The House of Connelly*. Since then she has created numerous scenic and lighting designs throughout the United States, including productions for the Paper Mill Playhouse and the Cape Playhouse, Dennis, Massachusetts for twenty-plus seasons. Opera designs include numerous credits as principal designer for the Opera Company of Boston since 1970 and additional productions for the New York City Opera. She often works in collaboration with Herbert Senn.

Lighting Designs:

1963: *Double Dublin* **1964**: *Roar Like a Dove*; *What Makes Sammy Run?*

Scenic Designs:

1963: *Double Dublin* **1964**: *Roar Like a Dove*; *What Makes Sammy Run?* **1968**: *Noel Coward's Sweet Potato* **1973**: *No Sex Please, We're British* **1981**: *Macbeth* **1983**: *Show Boat* **1986**: *Oh Coward!*

Nananne Porcher

The small number of lighting design credits on the Broadway stage do not reveal the scope of the lighting designs created by Nananne Porcher for ballet, opera, and theatre throughout the United States. She was born on December 14, 1922 in LaGrange, Georgia and studied at the University of North Carolina at Chapel Hill and with Jean Rosenthal. Ultimately she has focused her talents on theatre consulting, including major projects at the Carolina Theatre of the North Carolina School of the Arts, and the George Street Playhouse in New Brunswick, New Jersey among many, many others. She has been President of Jean Rosenthal Associates since 1975 and like Jean Rosenthal is an avid proponent of renovating spaces for theatre. In addition she has served as resident designer for American Ballet Theatre and designed lights for major opera companies throughout the United States. World premieres of operas include *Beatrix Cenci* at Opera Society of Washington, D.C. in 1971 and Barber's *Antony and Cleopatra* at the Metropolitan Opera in 1966.

Lighting Designs:

1971: *Ari* **1974**: *Treemonisha*

John Pratt

John Pratt mainly designed costumes on Broadway but also created scenery and lights on for Broadway productions between 1938 and 1955. A naturalized United States citizen, he was born in Saskatchewan, Canada and graduated from the University of Chicago. His credits designing for dance were numerous and include costumes for Agnes De Mille, Ruth Page, Miriam Winslow and his wife, Kathryn Dunham. He worked with the Federal Theatre Project and usually designed both sets and costumes for productions. Mr. Pratt died at age 74 on March 26, 1986.

Lighting Designs:
1946: *Bal Negre*

Scenic Designs:
1955: *Kathryn Dunham and Her Company*

Costume Designs:
1938: *Swing Mikado, The* 1946: *Bal Negre* 1948: *Look Ma, I'm Dancin'* 1950: *Katherine Dunham and Her Company* 1955: *Kathryn Dunham and Her Company*

Shirley Prendergast

Shirley Prendergast received the first Estelle Evans Award presented by Black Women in the Theatre. She has designed lights for many theatre companies off-Broadway and in regional theatres, among them the New Federal Theatre, the Negro Ensemble Company, Buffalo's Studio Arena, Washington D.C.'s Arena Stage, Roundabout Theatre Company, George Street Playhouse and the Whole Theatre. Dance designs include lighting for the Alvin Ailey American Dance Theatre and the Dance Theatre of Harlem.

Lighting Designs:
1968: *Summer of the 17th Doll* 1973: *River Niger, The* 1982: *Waltz of the Stork* 1983: *Amen Corner* 1987: *Don't Get God Started* 1988: *Paul Robeson*

William Price

William Price designed lights on Broadway in the 1920s. He was also associated with Display Stage Lighting Company in the early 1920s, serving as secretary/treasurer of the company.

Lighting Designs:
1923: *Fashions of 1924* 1925: *Cape Smoke*

Peter Radmore

Peter Radmore is Chief Electrician of the Olivier Theatre and has been on the staff of the National Theatre since the mid-1960s. He designed lighting for *Beaux Stratagem, Trelawney of the Wells* and *Hamlet* for Rose Bruford College at Collegiate Theatre, and the British tours of *Heartbreak House, Blithe Spirit, Marriage of Figaro* and others.

Lighting Designs:
1979: *Bedroom Farce*

Robert Randolph

Robert Randolph, a scenic designer, was born on March 9, 1926 in Centerville, Iowa, and received both B.F.A. and M.A. degrees at the University of Iowa. Before designing professionally he worked as an architect and industrial designer and taught at Iowa State University. He designed on Broadway for the first time in 1954, creating both sets and costumes for *The Saint of Bleecker Street*. Since that time he has designed numerous shows, concentrating his efforts on scenery but occasionally designing costumes and lights as well. His designs have been nominated for Tony Awards for *Golden Rainbow* and *Applause*, and he has also designed settings for the Tony Award ceremonies.

Lighting Designs:
1961: *How to Succeed in Business Without Really Trying* 1962: *Bravo Giovanni; Little Me* 1963: *Sophie* 1964: *Foxy; Funny Girl; Something More!* 1965: *Skyscraper; Xmas in Las Vegas* 1966: *It's a Bird...It's a Plane...It's Superman; Sweet Charity; Walking Happy* 1967: *Henry, Sweet Henry; Sherry!* 1968: *Golden Rainbow* 1969: *Angela* 1971: *70, Girls, 70* 1973: *Good Evening; No Hard Feelings* 1974: *Gypsy* 1975: *Norman Conquests, The* 1986: *Sweet Charity*

Scenic Designs:
1954: *Saint of Bleecker Street, The* 1960: *Bye, Bye, Birdie* 1961: *How to Succeed in Business Without Really Trying* 1962: *Bravo Giovanni; Calculated Risk; Little Me* 1963: *Sophie* 1964: *Any Wednesday; Foxy; Funny Girl; Something More!* 1965: *Anya; Minor Miracle; Skyscraper; Xmas in Las Vegas* 1966: *It's a Bird...It's a Plane...It's Superman; Sweet Charity; Walking Happy* 1967: *Henry, Sweet Henry; How to Be*

a *Jewish Mother, Sherry!* **1968:** *Golden Rainbow* **1969:** *Angela; Teaspoon Every Four Hours, A* **1970:** *Applause* **1971:** *70, Girls, 70; Ari* **1973:** *Good Evening; No Hard Feelings* **1974:** *Gypsy; Words and Music* **1975:** *Norman Conquests, The; We Interrupt This Program* **1976:** *Porgy and Bess* **1982:** *Seven Brides for Seven Brothers* **1986:** *Sweet Charity*

Costume Designs:
1954: *Saint of Bleecker Street, The* **1955:** *Desperate Hours, The* **1973:** *Good Evening* **1974:** *Words and Music*

Judy Rasmuson

Judy Rasmuson was born in Anchorage, Alaska on August 2, 1945 and studied economics for three years at Smith College prior to beginning her career as a lighting designer. She has also worked in summer stock and off-Broadway as an electrician and assistant lighting designer, and off-off-Broadway as a lighting designer. A protégée of Ronald Wallace, Judy Rasmuson has been influenced by "the Impressionist painters, rock music and the 1960s." Her first design was *Brecht on Brecht* at the Austin Riggs Center in Stockbridge, Massachusetts in 1967, and her professional debut was *Heartbreak House* at the Long Wharf Theatre in New Haven, Connecticut in 1970. She has designed in regional theatres from coast to coast for twenty years and in the early 1970s also designed rock concerts.

Lighting Designs:
1977: *Annie* **1981:** *Twice Around the Park*

David Read

David Read designed lighting for a Broadway production in 1965.

Lighting Designs:
1965: *Marat/Sade*

Jane Reisman

Lighting designer Jane Reisman was born on March 25, 1937 in New York City, the daughter of Lillian and Leo Reisman, an orchestra leader and conductor. She graduated from Vassar College in 1959, studied at Lester Polakov's Studio and Forum of Stage Design, at Bayreuth

and with an I.I.E. grant. She has designed off-Broadway, in regional theatres, and for dance companies including the Rome Opera Ballet, American Ballet Theatre, the Banff Festival Ballet and The Pennsylvania Ballet. She also has over fifty design credits for opera including productions for the Manhattan School of Music, San Diego Opera, Lake George Opera, Opera Society of Washington, and the Opera Metropolitana de Caracas. She was Visiting Professor of Lighting Design at Emerson College from 1980 to 1982, and is currently on the Dance and Drama faculty at Bennington College. She founded and chairs the Lighting Internship Program for United Scenic Artists.

Lighting Designs:
1973: *Warp* **1974:** *Fifth Dimension, The* **1976:** *Me Jack, You Jill* **1989:** *Black and Blue*

Marvin Reiss

Marvin Reiss was born on August 29, 1923 in St. Louis and received a B.F.A. at the Art Institute of Chicago. He began his career designing for summer stock theatres in Oconomowoc, Wisconsin, Fitchburg, Massachusetts, and Westport, Connecticut. He is art director and original designer for the television series *All My Children.* He was also art director for the soap opera *The Doctors.* Well known as a scene designer, he has created scenic and lighting designs for many Broadway shows and has occasionally contributed costume designs as well. His New York debut was *An Evening with Mike Nichols and Elaine May* off-Broadway. Mr. Reiss worked for many years as a chargeman in New York City shops.

Lighting Designs:
1954: *Home Is the Hero* **1958:** *Back to Methuselah; Party with Betty Comden and Adolph Green* **1961:** *New Faces of '62* **1963:** *Love and Kisses* **1968:** *Portrait of a Queen*

Scenic Designs:
1954: *Home Is the Hero* **1958:** *Back to Methuselah; Party with Betty Comden and Adolph Green; Third Best Sport* **1959:** *Requiem for a Nun* **1960:** *Thurber Carnival, A* **1961:** *New Faces of '62* **1963:** *Love and Kisses* **1968:** *Portrait of a Queen*

Costume Designs:
1954: *Home Is the Hero* **1959:** *Highest Tree, The*

Frank Rembach

Frank Rembach designed sets and lights for a 1966 Broadway production. He has designed in South Africa for Krishna Shah and also in London.

Lighting Designs:
1966: *Wait a Minim!*

Scenic Designs:
1966: *Wait a Minim!*

Marilyn Rennagel

Marilyn Rennagel has both a B.A. and M.F.A. in Theatre Arts from the University of California at Los Angeles. Since 1971 she has been a active lighting designer and consultant working throughout the United States on rock concerts, special events, fashion shows, dances, and operas. Born on June 4, 1943 in Los Angeles, she includes electricians Charles Brown and Jim Seagrove and lighting designer Tharon Musser as major influences. She recently was design assistant to Tharon Musser on the ill-fated *Ziegfeld*. Her New York debut was *Mission* at Playwrights's Horizon in 1975. She has been resident designer for the Michigan Opera Theatre and consultant on lighting systems for the Criterion Center. Her Broadway debut was *Ice Dancing* featuring John Curry. Since 1988 she has pursued a career change and began taking classes at the New York Botanical Garden in landscape design. She designed the Duffy Square winter planting in 1988 and is currently enrolled as a full-time student at Rutgers University in landscape architecture.

Lighting Designs:
1979: *Faith Healer; Peter Allen "Up in One"* 1980: *Clothes for a Summer Hotel* 1981: *Woman of the Year* 1982: *Do Black Patent Leather Shoes Really Reflect Up?* 1986: *Social Security* 1989: *Run For Your Wife*

Adams T. Rice

Adams T. Rice designed lights for one production in 1920 and the set for another in 1923. He also wrote *Pinocchio, A Fantastic Comedy In Eight Scences*, published by Samuel French in 1931. He was appointed technical director of the Children's Theatre in the 1930s after working for the Detroit Civic Theatre, the Washington Square Players, the Theatre Guild, and for his own company, the Detroit Players.

Lighting Designs:
1920: *Youth*

Scenic Designs:
1923: *Enchanted Cottage, The*

William Richardson

William Richardson designed lights for one production on Broadway in 1942.

Lighting Designs:
1942: *Little Darling* 1944: *Bell for Adano, A*

Richard Riddell

Richard Riddell was raised in Missouri and is Chair of the Drama Department at the University of California at San Diego. He designed sets and lights for the premiere of *Satyagraha* by Philip Glass. He also collaborated on the libretto of *Akhnaten*, again by Philip Glass. He has also designed productions at The Guthrie Theatre, the English National Opera, the Royal Shakespeare Company, the Oregon Shakespeare Festival and in Berlin.

Lighting Designs:
1985: *Big River* 1988: *Walk in the Woods, A*

Kevin Rigdon

Kevin Rigdon, a lighting and set designer, was born on February 17, 1956 and raised in Highland Park, Illinois. He studied at Drake University and was an intern at The Guthrie Theatre during the 1975-76 season. He was resident scenic and lighting designer for the Steppenwolf Company in Chicago from 1976 to 1982, the Goodman Theatre from 1982 to 1983, and for Mordine and Company Dance Company from 1983 to 1984. He has designed for the Virginia Museum Theatre, the Williamstown Theatre Festival and other regional theatres. Honors include Joseph Jefferson Awards in Chicago for *Balm in Gilead* (1981), *Tooth of Crime* (1982), and *Moby Dick* (1983). He also received the American Theatre Design Award for lighting in 1985 and in 1990, and the American Theatre

Wing Award (formerly the Marharam) for the scenic design of *The Grapes of Wrath*. His first Broadway play, *Glengarry Glen Ross*, started at the Goodman and transferred to Broadway. Other designs in New York include *The Shawl*, *Prairie du Chien*, *Clara* and *I Can't Remember Anything* at the Mitzi Newhouse Theatre with the director Gregory Mosher, who has helped shape his design style.

Lighting Designs:
1984: *Glengarry Glen Ross* 1986: *Caretaker, The* 1988: *Our Town* 1989: *Ghetto* 1990: *Grapes of Wrath, The*

Scenic Designs:
1986: *Caretaker, The* 1990: *Grapes of Wrath, The*

William Ritman

William Ritman was well known as a set designer with dozens of Broadway shows to his credit during his twenty-five year theatre career, including *Morning's at 7*, *Who's Afraid of Virginia Woolf?* and *Happy Days*. He also designed lights and occasionally costumes for productions for which he designed the settings. A native of Chicago, he graduated from the Goodman School of Theatre and designed professionally for the first time in 1959, contributing sets and lights to the revival of *On the Town*. Prior to designing for the theatre he was active in television. He was producer of the Rebekah Harkness Dance Festival at the New York Shakespeare Festival for eight years, and also taught design at Yale and Buffalo Univerisities. Mr. Ritman died on May 6, 1984 at age 56.

Lighting Designs:
1962: *Who's Afraid of Virginia Woolf?* 1964: *Absence of a Cello* 1965: *Entertaining Mr. Sloane* 1967: *Come Live with Me; Johnny No-trump* 1968: *Loot; Playwrights Repertory—One Acts* 1969: *Mundy Scheme, The* 1970: *Sleuth* 1972: *Last of Mrs. Lincoln, The* 1974: *Noel Coward in Two Keys* 1975: *P.S. Your Cat Is Dead* 1976: *Who's Afraid of Virginia Woolf?*

Scenic Designs:
1962: *Who's Afraid of Virginia Woolf?* 1963: *Riot Act, The* 1964: *Absence of a Cello; Tiny Alice* 1965: *Entertaining Mr. Sloane* 1966: *Delicate Balance, A; Malcolm* 1967: *Birthday Party, The; Come Live with Me; Everything in*

the Garden; Johnny No-trump; Promise, The 1968: *Loot; Playwrights Repertory—One Acts; We Bombed in New Haven* 1969: *Gingham Dog, The; Mundy Scheme, The; Penny Wars, The; Play It Again, Sam* 1972: *Evening with Richard Nixon, An; Last of Mrs. Lincoln, The; Moonchildren; Sign in Sidney Brustein's Window, The; Six Rms Riv Vu* 1974: *Find Your Way Home; God's Favorite; My Fat Friend; Noel Coward in Two Keys* 1975: *P.S. Your Cat Is Dead* 1976: *California Suite; Eccentricities of a Nightingale, The; Who's Afraid of Virginia Woolf?; Zalmen Or the Madness of God* 1977: *Chapter Two* 1978: *Death Trap; Tribute* 1979: *Last Licks; Once a Catholic* 1980: *Mornings At Seven; Onward Victoria; Roast, The* 1981: *Lolita; Supporting Cast, The* 1983: *Corn Is Green, The*

Costume Designs:
1962: *Who's Afraid of Virginia Woolf?* 1964: *Tiny Alice* 1965: *Entertaining Mr. Sloane* 1967: *Birthday Party, The; Everything in the Garden; Johnny No-trump* 1968: *Playwrights Repertory—One Acts*

William Riva

William Riva, known primarily as a set designer, also contributed costumes to two Broadway plays in the early 1950s. In 1955 he was active in forming the Stamford Playhouse in Stamford, Connecticut.

Lighting Designs:
1950: *Telephone, The and The Medium* 1951: *Razzle Dazzle*

Scenic Designs:
1950: *Telephone, The and The Medium* 1951: *Razzle Dazzle*

Costume Designs:
1950: *Telephone, The and The Medium* 1951: *Razzle Dazzle*

Jesse J. Robbins

Jesse J. Robbins designed lights for one production in 1917. As an actor he appeared in the film *A Lucky Dog*. In 1922 Jess Robbins Productions was located at 220 West 42nd Street in New York City.

Lighting Designs:
1917: *Yes Or No*

Ruth Roberts

Ruth Roberts designed lights for the world premiere of *The Abduction of Figaro* by Peter Schickele (P.D.Q. Bach) in 1984. She has designed for the theatre and opera in the United States and abroad, and has numerous off-Broadway productions to her credit, as well as four Radio City Music Hall extravaganzas.

Lighting Designs:

1980: *Fearless Frank* 1985: *King and I, The*

Clarke Robinson

Clarke Robinson, who created designs for many productions between 1921 and 1941, was born in Bradford, Pennsylvania on November 26, 1894. He studied voice in Europe and debuted at the age of fifteen singing in opera, light opera and vaudeville. He designed scenery at the Roxy, Rialto and Capitol theatres, and for the Music Box Revues. He replaced Robert Edmund Jones as art director at Radio City Music Hall and was replaced by his assistant, James Morcom, after six months. He also appeared on radio shows and created television shows. Between World War I and World War II he wrote novels and biographies, designed sets and occasionally lights and costumes, raised horses and became an authority on turf. He died on January 18, 1962 at age 67.

Lighting Designs:

1927: *Delmar's Revels*; *New Yorkers, The* 1931: *Billy Rose's Crazy Quilt*

Scenic Designs:

1921: *Music Box Revue* 1922: *Music Box Revue* 1923: *Music Box Revue* 1924: *Music Box Revue* 1925: *Dearest Enemy*; *Greenwich Village Follies*; *Gypsy Fires*; *Just Beyond*; *Young Blood* 1926: *No Trespassing*; *Peggy Ann* 1927: *Delmar's Revels*; *Enchantment*; *Patience*; *Revery*; *Rufus LeMaire's Affairs* 1928: *Jarnegan*; *Rain Or Shine* 1929: *Fioretta*; *Ghost Parade, The*; *Murray Anderson's Almanac*; *Woof, Woof* 1930: *Nine-Fifteen Revue* 1933: *Roberta* 1934: *Keep Moving*; *Say When* 1935: *Earl Carroll's Sketch Book* 1936: *Broadway Sho-Window*; *Granite*; *Mainly for Lovers* 1937: *Call Me Ziggy* 1941: *Viva O'Brien*

Costume Designs:

1925: *Just Beyond* 1927: *Patience*; *Revery*

John Root

John Root was born in Chicago in 1904 and met his wife, actress Margaret Mullin, during the run of one of his more than fifty Broadway shows, *Red Harvest*. He also designed television, notably *The Armstrong Circle Theatre*, *The Perry Como Show* for several years, and commercials. Prior to working in New York he designed for the Red Barn Theatre, Locust Valley, Long Island. In the early 1960s he changed careers and formed his own company, John Root, Inc. Real Estate, in Lumberville, Pennsylvania. John Root died on March 13, 1990 at age 85 in Doylestown, Pennsylvania.

Lighting Designs:

1949: *Mrs. Gibbon's Boys* 1951: *Not for Children*

Scenic Designs:

1934: *Piper Paid* 1935: *Ceiling Zero*; *Crime Marches On*; *Cross Ruff*; *Hell Freezes Over*; *If This Be Treason*; *Substitute for Murder*; *There's Wisdom in Women* 1936: *Seen But Not Heard*; *So Proudly We Hail* 1937: *Angel Island*; *Chalked Out*; *Now You've Done It*; *One Thing After Another*; *Red Harvest*; *Sun Kissed* 1938: *All That Glitters*; *Brown Danube*; *Greatest Show on Earth, The*; *Kiss the Boys Goodbye*; *Run Sheep Run* 1939: *Pastoral*; *Ring Two*; *Sea Dogs* 1940: *George Washington Slept Here*; *Glamour Preferred*; *Lady in Waiting*; *Out from Under* 1941: *Cuckoos on the Hearth* 1942: *Cat Screams, The*; *Janie*; *Jason* 1943: *Counterattack*; *Get Away Old Man*; *Kiss and Tell*; *Nine Girls*; *Pillar to Post* 1944: *Doctors Disagree*; *Harvey*; *Highland Fling, A*; *Snafu* 1945: *Boy Who Lived Twice, A* 1947: *It Takes Two*; *Tenting Tonight* 1949: *Love Me Long*; *Mrs. Gibbon's Boys* 1950: *Mr. Barry's Etchings* 1951: *Not for Children*

Jean Rosenthal

Jean Rosenthal is usually recognized as one of the pioneers of lighting design. She emerged as a specialist in lighting at a time when the lighting of a production was handled by a set designer or an electrician, and in the course of her career made lighting designers crucial members of production teams. Born Eugenia Rosenthal on March 16, 1912 in New York City, she was the daughter of two doctors who were Romanian immigrants. After studying acting and dance at the Neighborhood Playhouse from 1929 to 1930 she became a technical assistant to faculty member Martha Graham, the beginning of a life long association between them. She studied at Yale with Stanley McCandless and joined the Federal Theatre Project in 1935, where she launched her professional career. After working with Orson Welles' Mercury Theatre, she formed Theatre Production Service in 1940 and Jean Rosenthal Associates in 1958, for consulting on major theatre and architectural projects. During her career she designed over two hundred Broadway shows for Martha Graham, the New York City Ballet, and the Metropolitan Opera. Among her major contributions were the elimination of stage shadows by using rich floods of upstage lighting, revising the use of light plots, and controlling angles and mass of illumination to create contrasts without shadows. She died at age 57 on May 1, 1969 after a long battle with cancer, ten days after attending the opening of Martha Graham's *Archaic Hours*. She received the Outer Critics Circle Award for contributions to stage design in 1968-69 and the Henrietta Lord Memorial Award from the Yale School of Drama in 1932. In 1972 her book *The Magic of Light* was published, the result of a collaboration begun much earlier between Jean Rosenthal and Lael Wertenbaker.

Lighting Designs:

1938: *Danton's Death* **1942:** *Rosalinda* **1943:** *Richard III* **1947:** *Telephone, The and The Medium* **1948:** *Joy to the World; Sundown Beach* **1949:** *Caesar and Cleopatra* **1952:** *Climate of Eden, The* **1954:** *House of Flowers; Ondine; Quadrille; Saint of Bleecker Street, The* **1956:** *Great Sebastian, The* **1957:** *Dark At the Top of the Stairs, The; Hole in the Head, A; Jamaica; West Side Story* **1958:** *Disenchanted, The; Winesburg, Ohio* **1959:** *Destry Rides Again; Redhead; Saratoga; Sound of Music, The; Take Me Along* **1960:** *Becket; Caligula; Dear Liar; Taste of Honey, A; West Side Story* **1961:** *Conquering Hero, The; Daughter of Silence; Gay Life, The; Gift of Time, A; Night of the Iguana, The* **1962:** *Funny Thing Happened on the Way to the Forum, A; Lord Pengo* **1963:** *Ballad of the Sad Cafe, The; Barefoot in the Park; Beast in Me, The; Jennie; On An Open Roof* **1964:** *Chinese Prime Minister, The; Fiddler on the Roof; Hamlet; Hello, Dolly; Luv; Poor Bitos* **1965:** *Baker Street; Odd Couple,*

The **1966:** *Apple Tree, The; Cabaret; I Do! I Do!; Ivanov; Show Boat; Star Spangled Girl, The; Time for Singing, A* **1967:** *Hello, Dolly; Illya Darling* **1968:** *Exercise, The; Happy Time, The; Plaza Suite; Weekend* **1969:** *Dear World* **1980:** *West Side Story*

Scenic Designs:
1961: *Conquering Hero, The* **1963:** *Beast in Me, The; On An Open Roof*

Stephen Ross

Stephen Ross was born on August 18, 1949 in St. Louis, Missouri, the son of David and Ellen Ross. He received a B.A. at Southern Illinois University and an M.F.A. at the University of Wisconsin under Gilbert Hemsley, who influenced his career. His first professional design was *Benvenuto Cellini* with Sarah Caldwell for the Opera Company of Boston. Based in Toronto, he designs primarily for opera in Canada and the United States and has been nominated for three Dora Mavor Moore Awards in Toronto.

Lighting Designs:
1989: *Shenandoah*

Joseph Roth

Joseph Roth designed lights for a Broadway production in 1925. In the early 1920s he was vice president of Lenox Electric Company, Inc., electricians, located at 396 Lenox Avenue, New York City.

Lighting Designs:
1925: *Paid*

Wolfgang Roth

Wolfgang Roth came to the United States in 1938 from Berlin. Born in the German capital on February 10, 1910, he studied at Berlin's Academy of Art and worked with the Piscator Theatre and Bertolt Brecht. He designed numerous sets and occasionally costumes as well. His designs for opera were seen in major houses around the world including the Metropolitan Opera and the New York City Opera. He also designed for television and film, painted, illustrated and worked as an architect. Wolfgang

Wolfgang Roth died on November 11, 1988 in New York City.

Lighting Designs:
1960: *Deadly Game, The*

Scenic Designs:
1943: *First Million, The* 1945: *Too Hot for Maneuvers* 1946: *Pound on Demand* 1947: *Yellow Jack* 1948: *Oh, Mr. Meadowbrook* 1950: *Now I Lay Me Down to Sleep* 1951: *Twentieth Century* 1953: *Porgy and Bess* 1958: *Portofino* 1960: *Deadly Game, The* 1979: *Strider*

Costume Designs:
1946: *Pound on Demand* 1947: *Yellow Jack* 1960: *Deadly Game, The*

Charles E. Rush

Charles E. Rush designed lights for a Broadway show in 1924. He also designed in London, creating lights for *Lilac Time* in 1928 at Daly's Theatre.

Lighting Designs:
1924: *Hassard Short's Ritz Revue*

Oscar Ryan

Oscar Ryan designed lighting for one Broadway production in 1938. He was co-author of *Eight Men Speak, A Political Play in Six Acts* presented by the Progressive Arts Club of Canada. The play dramatized the attempted murder of one Tim Buck in his cell at Kingston Penitentiary in 1933 and the reluctance of authorities to investigate.

Lighting Designs:
1938: *Swing Mikado, The*

Albert Rybeck

Albert Rybeck (a.k.a. Albert J. Ribicki) designed lights in 1925 for a Broadway show. Albert J. Rybicki was a photo-engraver active in New York from the teens through the thirties.

Lighting Designs:
1925: *George White's Scandals* 1942: *Once Over Lightly*

Pierre Saveron

Pierre Saveron designed lighting for a Broadway production in 1958.

Lighting Designs:
1958: *Theatre National Populaire*

George Schaaf

George Schaaf was lighting designer for two Broadway plays in the mid-1920s.

Lighting Designs:
1923: *Hamlet* 1924: *Madame Pompadour*

George Schaefer

George Schaefer, a director and producer with many Broadway and television shows to his credit, was born on December 16, 1920 in Wallingford, Connecticut. He received a B.A. in 1941 from Lafayette College and attended the Yale University School of Drama for one year. His directorial debut in New York was *Hamlet* with Maurice Evans in 1945, followed by an illustratious career full of prize-winning plays. He directed numerous productions, beginning in 1953 for the *Hallmark Hall of Fame* and continuing for two decades. He won eight Emmy Awards, the Sylvania Award, three Radio Television Daily Awards and three Directors' Guild of America Awards. In 1947 he was associate director and lighting designer for *Man and Superman* with Maurice Evans, with whom he later produced *Teahouse of the August Moon*.

Lighting Designs:
1947: *Man and Superman*

Nancy Schertler

Nancy Schertler has had a long association with the Arena Stage where she spent eight years as an electrician and assistant lighting designer. Her association with mentors Garland Wright and Allen Lee Hughes stem from the Arena Stage as does her professional debut as lighting designer, for *Quartermaines Terms*. She was born in Washington, D.C. on December 16, 1954, the daughter of Jean and Leon Schertler, and received a B.A. in speech and theatre at the College of St. Catherine in St. Paul, Minnesota. She has received ten nominations for

Helen Hayes Awards and a Tony Award nomination for *Largely New York*.

Lighting Designs:
1989: *Largely New York*

Douglas Schmidt

Douglas Schmidt has designed sets for numerous shows both on and off-Broadway and in regional theatres around the United States. Born on October 4, 1942 in Cincinnati, he studied at Boston University with Horace Armistead and Raymond Sovey and with Lester Polakov at the Studio and Forum of Stage Design. His theatre experience includes directing and stage management and occasionally costume design. He began designing with *The Thirteen Clocks* by James Thurber at High Mowing School in Wilton, New Hampshire in 1960 and in summer stock. Design activity in regional theatres includes Cincinnati Playhouse in the Park, Center Stage in Baltimore, the Old Globe, the Ahmanson Theatre, the Mark Taper Forum and The Guthrie Theatre. He has designed numerous sets for operas at the Tanglewood Festival and the Juilliard School. Often honored for outstanding scenic design, Mr. Schmidt received a Maharam Award for *Enemies* in 1973, and Drama Desk Awards for *Veronica's Room* and *Over Here!*. He has also designed sets for television and José Limon. *Nick and Nora*, with settings by Douglas W. Schmidt, is scheduled for the 1990-91 Broadway season.

Lighting Designs:
1972: *Country Girl, The*

Scenic Designs:
1970: *Paris Is Out* **1972:** *Country Girl, The*; *Grease*; *Love Suicide At Schofield Barracks, The* **1973:** *Measure for Measure*; *Streetcar Named Desire, A*; *Veronica's Room* **1974:** *American Millionaire, An*; *Fame*; *Over Here*; *Who's Who in Hell* **1975:** *Angel Street* **1976:** *Herzl*; *Robber Bridegroom, The* **1977:** *Threepenny Opera, The* **1978:** *Runaways*; *Stages* **1979:** *Most Happy Fella, The*; *Peter Allen "Up in One"*; *Romantic Comedy*; *They're Playing Our Song* **1981:** *Frankenstein* **1983:** *Porgy and Bess* **1985:** *Dancing in the End Zone* **1986:** *Smile*

Costume Designs:
1972: *Love Suicide At Schofield Barracks, The* **1976:** *Let My People Come*

Tom Schraeder

Tom Schraeder is Lighting Director for the Hilberry Repertory Theatre and Professor of Lighting Design at Wayne State University in Detroit, Michigan. Born on January 29, 1959 in Chicago, he received a B.A. in 1974 from Loyola University and an M.F.A. in 1978 from the Yale University School of Drama. Career influences include Thomas Skelton, Ming Cho Lee and Bill Warfel. He has designed sets and lights for numerous off-Broadway and regional theatre productions. Since 1986 he has been set and lighting designer for the *Stephen Foster Story*, an outdoor historical drama in Bardstown, Kentucky. The production toured Japan in 1985 and was broadcast on Japanese television.

Lighting Designs:
1979: *Wings*

Duane Schuler

Duane Schuler was planning to major in engineering at the University of Wisconsin-Madison when he took a course in lighting design from Gilbert Hemsley, which led to a three year stint as his assistant and a career in lighting design. He was born in Wisconsin on June 20, 1950 and received his B.S. in 1972. He has designed lights for major regional theatres and opera companies throughout the United States. After serving as resident lighting designer at the Guthrie Theatre from 1974 to 1978 he became Resident Lighting Designer at the Lyric Opera of Chicago. He is also a theatre consultant and an architectural lighting designer. Duane Schuler received a Drama Desk Nomination for *Teibele and her Demon* and a Hollywood Drama Critic Award for *Uncle Vanya* at A.C.T.

Lighting Designs:
1979: *Teibele and Her Demon* **1987:** *South Pacific*

Harry Sears

Harry Sears designed lights for one play in 1920. The 1920 playbill for *What's in a Name* has this acknowledgement: "All of the mechanical effects invented by Harry Sears and the entire scenic construction was under his direction." He resided at 1642 Madison Avenue, New York City in 1920.

Lighting Designs:
1920: *Pitter Patter*

David F. Segal

David F. Segal was born on June 2, 1943 in New York City, the son of Rabbi Samuel Michael Segal and Cynthia Shapiro Segal. He attended the University of Pennsylvania and received a B.A. from New York University, in 1964. He also attended Lester Polakov's Studio and Forum of Stage Design. As Tharon Musser's first assistant (under a United Scenic Artists contract) he was inspired and influenced by the woman he considers the greatest American lighting designer. His New York debut was *Say Nothing* at the Jan Hus Theatre in 1965. He has designed throughout the United States and for the Stratford (Ontario) Festival and has won numerous Hollywood Critic's Dramalogue Awards. A partial list of credits include *Happy Birthday Wanda June* and *That's Entertainment* at the Edison Theatre.

Lighting Designs:
1969: *World's a Stage, The* 1971: *Oh! Calcutta!*; *Twigs* 1973: *Irene* 1974: *Summer Brave* 1976: *Heiress, The*; *Robber Bridegroom, The* 1977: *Basic Training of Pavlo Hummel, The* 1979: *Loose Ends*; *Sarava* 1980: *Manhattan Showboat* 1981: *Hey, Look Me Over!*; *Lolita*

Claudio Segovia

Claudio Segovia was born in Buenos Aires where he studied scenery and painting at the Academia Naçional de Artes Visuales. He has designed sets and costumes for plays and operas around the world since 1965. In addition he creates productions using popular music and folk traditions such as *Flamenco Puro*, performed for the first time in Seville, Spain, and in a second edition in 1984 in Paris. Mr. Segovia often collaborates as a director, creator, and set and costume designer with Hector Orezzoli. *Tango Argentino* resulted from his continuing collaboration with Mr. Orezzoli and was honored with a Tony nomination for costume design. Their scenic designs for *Black and Blue* were nominated for a Tony Award in 1989.

Lighting Designs:
1986: *Flamenco Puro*

Scenic Designs:
1985: *Tango Argentino* 1986: *Flamenco Puro* 1989: *Black and Blue*

Costume Designs:
1985: *Tango Argentino* 1986: *Flamenco Puro* 1989: *Black and Blue*

Herbert Senn

(Charles) Herbert Senn was born on October 9, 1924 in Ilion, New York and studied at Columbia University with his mentor Woodman Thompson. He began designing while in high school and made his debut in London's West End with *The Boys From Syracuse* at the Drury Lane Theatre in November 1963. He often designs in collaboration with Helen Pond, concentrating on sets but occasionally designing lights. The team has designed extensive productions off-Broadway, for numerous summer seasons at the Cape Play House, Dennis, Massachusetts, and for operas and ballets throughout the United States.

Lighting Designs:
1963: *Double Dublin* 1964: *Roar Like a Dove*; *What Makes Sammy Run?*

Scenic Designs:
1963: *Double Dublin* 1964: *Roar Like a Dove*; *What Makes Sammy Run?* 1968: *Noel Coward's Sweet Potato* 1973: *No Sex Please, We're British* 1975: *Musical Jubilee, A* 1981: *Macbeth* 1983: *Show Boat* 1986: *Oh Coward!*

William Sheafe

William Sheafe, Jr. designed both scenery and lighting on Broadway during the teens. In collaboration with George H. Skelton he ran a design business, Sheafe & Skelton at 1547 Broadway in New York City in 1919. He resided at 64 West 9th Street in 1922.

Lighting Designs:
1919: *Phantom Legion, The*

Scenic Designs:
1916: *Six Who Passed While the Lentils Boiled*

Hassard Short

(Hubert) Hassard Short was born in Edlington, Lincolnshire, England on October 15, 1877 and made his acting debut at the Drury Lane Theatre in 1895. He came to the United States in 1901 and continued acting but became interested in directing and producing. In 1920 he directed *Honeydew*, the first of more than fifty hit musicals. He installed his own lighting system at the Music Box Theatre for *Honeydew* and often designed lights and occasionally scenery for plays he also directed. He produced many popular musicals such as *Roberta*, *Show Boat*, *Music Box Revues*, *The Great Waltz* and *As Thousands Cheer*. An innovative director, he used colored lights and other effects and is considered by many to be the first to replace footlights with lights hung from the ceiling over the audience and directed toward the stage. Hassard Short died in Nice, France on October 9, 1956.

Lighting Designs:
1920: *Honey Girl* 1933: *Roberta* 1934: *Great Waltz, The* 1937: *Frederika* 1939: *American Way, The; From Vienna* 1941: *Banjo Eyes; Lady in the Dark* 1943: *Carmen Jones; Lady in the Dark* 1944: *Mexican Hayride; Seven Lively Arts* 1947: *Music in My Heart* 1948: *Make Mine Manhattan* 1950: *Michael Todd's Peep Show*

Scenic Designs:
1924: *Hassard Short's Ritz Revue*

Costume Designs:
1920: *Honey Girl*

Harry Silverglat

Harry Silverglat has designed lights for rock concerts and musical events. He also designed the national tours of *Equus* and *Bubbling Brown Sugar*. In 1980 he designed scenery for *Fortune* off-Broadway.

Lighting Designs:
1976: *Oh! Calcutta!*

Pat Simmons

Pat Simmons was lighting designer in 1970 for a Broadway play. Additional credits include lights for the 1983-84 season production of *When Hell Freezes Over, I'll Skate* at the Coconut Grove Playhouse.

Lighting Designs:
1970: *Cherry Orchard, The*

Lee Simonson

Lee Simonson, a designer of sets, costumes and occasionally lights, was born on June 26, 1888 in New York City and was graduated from Harvard in 1909. He designed scenery for the Washington Square Players from 1917 until drafted into the service a year later. After World War I he helped found the Theatre Guild and served as one of its directors from 1919 to 1940. He debuted on Broadway with the Theatre Guild's production of *The Faithful*. He designed sets and costumes for numerous plays and operas and also taught design. In 1947 he designed Wagner's *Ring Cycle* for the Metropolitan Opera, one of his many designs there. He wrote several books about scene design, including *The Art of Scenic Design, The Stage is Set* and an autobiography, *Part of a Lifetime* published in 1943. This talented, prolific designer died at age 78 on January 23, 1967. His second wife was the costume designer Carolyn Hancock.

Lighting Designs:
1924: *Carnival* 1933: *American Dream* 1946: *Joan of Lorraine*

Scenic Designs:
1919: *Faithful, The; Moliere* 1920: *Cat Bird, The; Heartbreak House; Jane Clegg; Martinique; Mirage, The; Power of Darkness, The; Treasure, The* 1921: *Don Juan; Liliom; Mr. Pim Passes By; Tangerine* 1922: *Back to Methuselah; From Morn Till Midnight; He Who Gets Slapped; Lucky One, The; R.U.R.; Tidings Brought to Mary, The; World We Live In, The* 1923: *Adding Machine, The; As You Like It; Failures, The; Peer Gynt; Spring Cleaning* 1924: *Carnival; Fata Morgana; Man and the Masses; Mongrel, The; Sweet Little Devil* 1925: *Arms and the Man; Glass Slipper, The* 1926: *Goat Song; Juarez and Maximillian* 1927: *Mr. Pim Passes By; Road to Rome, The* 1928: *Marco Millions; Road to Rome, The; Volpone* 1929: *Camel Through the Needle's Eye; Carnival; Damn Your Honor; Dynamo* 1930: *Apple Cart, The; Elizabeth the Queen; Hotel Universe; Marco Millions; Roar China; Volpone* 1931: *Lean Harvest; Miracle At Verdun* 1932: *Collision; Good Earth, The; Red Planet* 1933: *American Dream; Mask and the Face, The; Masks and Faces; School for Husbands* 1934: *Days Without End; Jigsaw; Rain from Heaven; Sleeping Clergyman, A; They Shall Not Die* 1935: *Parade; Simpleton of the Unexpected Isles* 1936: *Call It a Day; End of*

Summer; Idiot's Delight; Prelude to Exile 1937: Amphitryon 38; Madame Bovary; Masque of Kings, The; Virginia 1938: Lorelei; Wine of Choice 1944: Streets Are Guarded, The 1945: Foxhole in the Parlor 1946: Joan of Lorraine

Costume Designs:

1919: *Faithful, The* **1920:** *Jane Clegg; Martinique; Power of Darkness, The; Treasure, The* **1921:** *Don Juan; Liliom* **1922:** *Back to Methuselah; He Who Gets Slapped; R.U.R.; Tidings Brought to Mary, The* **1923:** *Adding Machine, The; As You Like It; Failures, The; Peer Gynt* **1924:** *Fata Morgana; Man and the Masses* **1925:** *Arms and the Man; Glass Slipper, The* **1926:** *Goat Song; Juarez and Maximillian* **1927:** *Road to Rome, The* **1928:** *Marco Millions; Road to Rome, The; Volpone* **1929:** *Camel Through the Needle's Eye; Damn Your Honor; Dynamo* **1930:** *Apple Cart, The; Elizabeth the Queen; Marco Millions; Roar China; Volpone* **1932:** *Collision* **1933:** *School for Husbands* **1934:** *Sleeping Clergyman, A* **1935:** *Parade; Simpleton of the Unexpected Isles* **1936:** *Prelude to Exile* **1937:** *Madame Bovary; Masque of Kings, The* **1945:** *Foxhole in the Parlor* **1946:** *Joan of Lorraine*

Noble Sissle

Noble Sissle, a composer and lyricist, teamed with Eubie Blake to perform in vaudeville and create songs for hit musicals. In 1921 he helped create the first black musical to play at a Broadway theatre in the regular season, *Shuffle Along*. The partnership with Eubie Blake ultimately ended but each continued successful careers. Sissle was born on July 10, 1889 in Indianapolis, Indiana and after the death of his father sang with the Jubilee Singers on the Chautauqua Circuit. He served in World War I in the 369th Regiment and was in their orchestra along with Blake. Sissle was founder and first President of the Negro Actors Guild and a member of the American Society of Composers, Authors and Publishers. In 1972 he received an Ellington Medal at Yale University along with thirty black instrumentalists and singers. He died at age 86 on December 17, 1975 in Tampa, Florida. In 1948 he directed and designed *Harlem Calvacade* on Broadway in collaboration with Ed Sullivan.

Lighting Designs:

1942: *Harlem Cavalcade*

Thomas R. Skelton

Thomas R. Skelton entered the field of lighting design as an apprentice electrician under Jean Rosenthal while on a scholarship at the American Dance Festival. Interestingly he later influenced the career of lighting designer Jennifer Tipton under similar circumstances. He was born in Bridgetown, Maine on September 24, 1927 and received a B.F.A. at Middlebury College. His New York debut was *The Enchanted* in 1958, soon followed by an extensive list on and off-Broadway and throughout the United States. He has been associated with major dance companies such as the Joffrey Ballet, New York City Ballet, Paul Taylor, and José Limon and is co-founder and associate artistic director of the Ohio Ballet. Primarily a lighting designer, he has occasionally designed sets. Recent productions include *Papa*, starring George Peppard as Ernest Hemingway, and *Songs Without Words, Printemps, Cotillion, Clowns* and *Nutcracker* for the Joffrey Ballet. During the course of his career Thomas Skelton has been instrumental in making lighting designers indispensable members of production teams and fostering the talents of new generations of lighting designers.

Lighting Designs:

1963: *Oh Dad, Poor Dad, Mamma's Hung You...* **1964:** *Wiener Blut (Vienna Life); Zizi* **1968:** *Jimmy Shine; Mike Downstairs* **1969:** *Coco; Come Summer; Does a Tiger Wear a Necktie?; Indians; Patriot for Me, A* **1970:** *Henry V; Lovely Ladies, Kind Gentlemen; Purlie* **1972:** *Lincoln Mask, The; Purlie; Secret Afairs of Mildred Wild, The; Selling of the President, The* **1973:** *Gigi; Status Quo Vadis; Waltz of the Toreadors, The* **1974:** *Absurd Person Singular; Where's Charley?* **1975:** *All God's Chillun Got Wings; Death of a Salesman; First Breeze of Summer, The; Glass Menagerie, The; Musical Jubilee, A; Shenandoah* **1976:** *Days in the Trees; Guys and Dolls; Kings; Lady from the Sea, The; Legend; Matter of Gravity, A* **1977:** *Caesar and Cleopatra; King and I, The; Romeo and Juliet* **1978:** *Kingfisher, The; November People, The* **1979:** *Oklahoma!; Peter Pan; Richard III* **1980:** *Brigadoon; Camelot; Filumena* **1981:** *Camelot; Can-Can; West Side Waltz, The* **1982:** *Seven Brides for Seven Brothers* **1983:** *Dance a Little Closer; Mame; Peg; Show Boat* **1984:** *Death of a Salesman* **1985:** *Iceman Cometh, The* **1986:**

Lillian **1989:** *Few Good Men, A*

Scenic Designs:

1962: *Tiao Ch'in, or The Beautiful Bait*

Oliver Smith

Oliver Lemuel Smith was born in Wawpawn, Wisconsin on February 13, 1918 and graduated from the Pennsylvania State University in 1939. Known primarily as a scenic designer, he first designed professionally for the Ballet Russe de Monte Carlo performance at the Metropolitan Opera in 1941, making his debut on Broadway the following year with the scenic design for *Rosalinda*. Since that time he has designed sets for over four hundred productions for ballet, opera, theatre and film, and occasionally contributed costume and lighting designs to those productions. The recipient of Tony Awards for scenic design for *My Fair Lady, West Side Story, The Sound of Music, Becket, Camelot, Hello, Dolly* and *Baker Street*, he received many other nominations. He was also nominated for an Academy Award for *Guys and Dolls* and has produced many of the shows he has designed. From 1945 to 1981 he was co-director of the American Ballet Theatre with Lucia Chase, returning as Artistic Co-Director in 1989 following the departure of Mikhail Baryshnikov.

Lighting Designs:

1963: *Children from Their Games*

Scenic Designs:

1942: *Rosalinda* **1944:** *On the Town; Perfect Marriage, The; Rhapsody* **1945:** *Billion Dollar Baby* **1946:** *Beggar's Holliday* **1947:** *Brigadoon; High Button Shoes; Topaz* **1948:** *Look Ma, I'm Dancin'* **1949:** *Along Fifth Avenue; Gentlemen Prefer Blondes; Miss Liberty; Miss Liberty* **1950:** *Bless You All* **1951:** *Paint Your Wagon* **1952:** *Pal Joey* **1953:** *Carnival in Flanders; In the Summer House* **1954:** *Burning Glass, The; On Your Toes* **1955:** *Will Success Spoil Rock Hunter?* **1956:** *Auntie Mame; Candide; Mr. Wonderful; My Fair Lady* **1957:** *Clearing in the Woods, A; Eugenia; Jamaica; Nude with Violin; Time Remembered; Visit to a Small Planet, A; West Side Story* **1958:** *Flower Drum Song; Present Laughter; Say, Darling; Winesburg, Ohio* **1959:** *Cheri; Destry Rides Again; Five Finger Exercise; Goodbye Charlie; Juno; Sound of Music, The; Take Me Along* **1960:** *Becket; Camelot; Taste of Honey, A;*

Under the Yum-Yum Tree; Unsinkable Molly Brown, The; West Side Story **1961:** *Daughter of Silence; Gay Life, The; Mary, Mary; Night of the Iguana, The; Sail Away; Show Girl* **1962:** *Come On Strong; Lord Pengo; Romulus; Tiger Tiger Burning Bright* **1963:** *110 Degrees in the Shade; Barefoot in the Park; Children from Their Games; Girl Who Came to Supper, The; Natural Affection* **1964:** *Bajour; Beeckman Place; Ben Franklin in Paris; Chinese Prime Minister, The; Dylan; Hello, Dolly; I Was Dancing; Luv; Poor Richard; Slow Dance on the Killing Ground* **1965:** *Baker Street; Cactus Flower; Kelly; Odd Couple, The; On a Clear Day You Can See Forever; Very Rich Woman, A* **1966:** *Best Laid Plans, The; I Do! I Do!; Show Boat; Star Spangled Girl, The* **1967:** *Hello, Dolly; How Now Dow Jones; Illya Darling; Song of the Grasshopper* **1968:** *Darling of the Day; Exercise, The; Plaza Suite; Weekend* **1969:** *But, Seriously; Come Summer; Dear World; Indians; Jimmy; Last of the Red Hot Lovers; Patriot for Me, A* **1970:** *Lovely Ladies, Kind Gentlemen* **1971:** *Four in a Garden* **1972:** *Little Black Book, The; Lost in the Stars* **1973:** *Gigi; Tricks; Women, The* **1974:** *All Over Town* **1975:** *Don't Call Back; Hello, Dolly (Starring Pearl Bailey); Royal Family, The* **1976:** *Heiress, The; My Fair Lady* **1978:** *Do You Turn Somersaults?; First Monday in October; Hello, Dolly* **1979:** *Carmelina* **1980:** *Clothes for a Summer Hotel; Lunch Hour; Mixed Couples; West Side Story* **1981:** *My Fair Lady; Talent for Murder, A* **1982:** *84 Charing Cross Road*

Costume Designs:

1955: *Will Success Spoil Rock Hunter?* **1959:** *Five Finger Exercise* **1961:** *Daughter of Silence; Sail Away*

Hans Sondheimer

Hans Sondheimer was born in Gelnhausen, Germany on December 6, 1901 and worked as an engineer and in the technical departments of theatres in Germany. He moved to the United States in 1939 and joined Erwin Piscator's New School Dramatic Workshop. He spent most of his professional life with the New York City Opera beginning in the inaugural season of 1944, and serving as technical director, lighting designer and production coordinator until he retired in 1980. During that time, he designed lights for the majority of the company's productions. A founding member of the United States Institute of Theatre Technology (USITT), he was an active theatre consultant and designer and was technical consultant, designer and manager for other companies. After his retirement, until the time of his death on September 1, 1984, he remained active with New York City Opera as a technical consultant.

Lighting Designs:
1942: *Winter Soldiers*

Raymond Sovey

Raymond Sovey was a prolific scenic designer who followed the common practice of his time of creating costumes for productions he was engaged to design. He occasionally also designed lights. Born in 1897 in Torrington, Connecticut, he studied at Columbia University and taught art in Baltimore before beginning his association with the theatre. He began as an actor, appearing on Broadway in 1919 before designing his first production in 1920. The following forty years were busy ones for him, filled with designs for numerous plays. Mr. Sovey died at age 72 on June 25, 1966. He received Tony Award nominations for his scenic designs for *The Great Sebastians* and for his costume designs for *All the Way Home*.

Lighting Designs:
1948: *Edward, My Son; Grandma's Diary* **1950:** *Cocktail Party; Ring 'Round the Moon* **1954:** *Living Room, The* **1955:** *Chalk Garden, The* **1959:** *Look After Lulu*

Scenic Designs:
1920: *George Washington; Mirage, The* **1921:** *Iphigenia in Aulis* **1923:** *Icebound; Jolly Roger, The; Saint Joan; White Desert; You and I* **1924:** *Cheaper to Marry; Dear Sir; Mask and the Face, The; Nancy Ann; New Toys* **1925:** *Butter and Egg Man, The; Harvest; Puppets; Something to Brag About* **1926:** *Adorable Liar, The; Gentlemen Prefer Blondes; Glory Hallelujah; Ladder, The; Proud Woman, A; Ramblers, The* **1927:** *Brother's Karamazov, The; Coquette; Letter, The; Mikado, The; Wild Man of Borneo, The* **1928:** *Animal Crackers; Command Performance, The; Front Page, The; Goin' Home; Hotbed; Little Accident; She's My Baby; Three Cheers; Tonight At 12; Wings Over Europe* **1929:** *Meteor; Other Men's Wives;*

Scarlet Pages; Strictly Dishonorable; Top Speed **1930:** *Art and Mrs. Bottle; As Good As New; Inspector General, The; Strike Up the Band; That's the Woman; Twelfth Night; Vinegar Tree, The; Waterloo Bridge* **1931:** *After All; Cloudy with Showers; Counsellor-At-Law; Fast Service; Green Grow the Lilacs; Left Bank, The; Way of the World, The; Wiser They Are, The; Wonder Boy* **1932:** *Black Sheep; Counsellor-at-Law; Here Today; Hey, Nonny Nonny; Honeymoon; I Loved You Wednesday; Men Must Fight; She Loves Me Not; Wild Waves* **1933:** *Blue Widow, The; Conquest; Doctor Monica; Her Master's Voice; Lone Valley; She Loves Me; Shooting Star* **1934:** *Distaff Side, The; Oliver! Oliver!; Portrait of Gilbert; Post Road; Ragged Army; Wooden Slipper, The* **1935:** *Bright Star; Distant Shore, The; Dominant Sex, The; Eldest, The; Fly Away Home; Libel; Life's Too Short; May Wine; Most of the Game; Petrified Forest, The* **1936:** *Alice Takat; Promise, The; Star Spangled; Sweet Aloes; Tovarich* **1937:** *Amazing Dr. Clitterhouse; And Now Good-Bye; Babes in Arms; French Without Tears; Loves of Women; Yes, My Darling Daughter* **1938:** *Dance Night; If I Were You; Knights of Song; Once Is Enough; Oscar Wilde; Our Town* **1939:** *Miss Swan Expects; Woman Brown, The* **1940:** *Delicate Story; Grey Farm; Jupiter Laughs; Ladies in Retirement* **1941:** *Arsenic and Old Lace; Boudoir; Happy Days, The; Letters to Lucerne; Ring Aroung Elizabeth; Village Green; Walrus and the Carpenter, The; Your Loving Son* **1942:** *Broken Journey; Counsellor-at-Law; Damask Cheek, The; Flare Path; Guest in the House; Strip for Action* **1943:** *Another Love Story; Murder Without Crime; Outrageous Fortune; Tomorrow the World; Vagabond King, The* **1944:** *Feathers in a Gale; For Keeps; Jackpot; Lower North; Over Twenty-One; Sleep, My Pretty One; Soldier's Wife* **1945:** *And Be My Love; Hasty Heart, The; Mermaids Singing; Place of Our Own, A; Rich Full Life, The; Ryan Girl, The; State of the Union; Therese* **1946:** *Antigone; Apple of His Eye; Temper the Wind; This, Too, Shall Pass; Wonderful Journey* **1947:** *For Love Or Money; Heiress, The; I Gotta Get Out; Love Goes to Press; Parlor Story* **1948:** *Edward, My Son; Grandma's Diary; Hallams, The; Harvest of Years* **1949:** *Traitor, The* **1950:** *Cocktail Party; Ring 'Round the Moon* **1951:** *Four Twelves Are 48; Gigi; Gramercy*

Ghost; *Remains to Be Seen* **1952**: *One Bright Day* **1954**: *Living Room, The*; *Witness for the Prosecution* **1956**: *Great Sebastian, The*; *Reluctant Debutant, The* **1957**: *Under Milkwood* **1958**: *Patate*

Costume Designs:
1920: *George Washington* **1921**: *Macbeth* **1923**: *Saint Joan* **1924**: *Flame of Love* **1927**: *Coquette*; *Mikado, The* **1928**: *Command Performance, The*; *Jealous Moon, The*; *La Gringa*; *She's My Baby* **1930**: *As Good As New*; *Second Little Show, The*; *Twelfth Night* **1931**: *Third Little Show, The*; *Way of the World, The* **1932**: *Here Today*; *Hey, Nonny Nonny*; *Wild Waves* **1933**: *Her Master's Voice* **1934**: *Portrait of Gilbert*; *Ragged Army* **1935**: *Distant Shore, The* **1936**: *Tovarich* **1938**: *Oscar Wilde* **1939**: *Woman Brown, The* **1940**: *Grey Farm*; *Jupiter Laughs* **1942**: *Damask Cheek, The* **1944**: *Lower North* **1945**: *Hasty Heart, The*; *Therese* **1951**: *Gramercy Ghost* **1954**: *Living Room, The*; *Witness for the Prosecution* **1960**: *All the Way Home*

John Spradbery

John Spradbery designed lights in 1974 for a Broadway production.

Lighting Designs:
1974: *Flowers*

Allan Stitchbury

Allan Stitchbury, a Canadian designer of lights, has designed productions throughout Canada. He graduated from the University of Alberta, where he began designing, and spent two years as resident lighting designer for Victoria's Bastion Theatre. As resident designer for Edmonton's Northern Light Theatre he has designed *Wings, Side by Side by Sondheim, Overruled, Take Me Where the Water's Warm* and *Piaf* among others. He also produced daily highlights of the Commonwealth Games for the Canadian Broadcasting Company.

Lighting Designs:
1980: *Mister Lincoln*

Frederick Stover

Although primarily a designer for film and television, Frederick Stover designed sets and lights on Broadway during the 1940s. He was one of the first students in the graduate program at Yale University where he studied with Donald Oenslager. He was an active designer on the West Coast and was chief designer of the Los Angeles unit of the Federal Theatre Project.

Lighting Designs:
1949: *Harlequinade, A and The Browning Version*

Scenic Designs:
1940: *Meet the People* **1945**: *Hamlet* **1947**: *Man and Superman* **1949**: *Browning Version, The and A Harlequinade*

Stephen Strawbridge

Stephen Strawbridge was born on October 24, 1954 in Baltimore. He graduated from Towson State University where he became involved with theatre, and received a Master of Fine Arts from the Yale University School of Drama. He is an active designer in regional theatres including the Goodman Theatre, The Guthrie Theatre, Center Stage and La Jolla, and off-Broadway including productions for the Theatre for The New City, American Place Theatre and the New York Shakespeare Festival. Recent credits include *When We Dead Awaken* with Robert Wilson and *End of the World* with Richard Foreman at American Repertory Theatre. He was nominated for a Helen Hayes Award for *Macbeth* at the Folger Theatre, and for an American Theatre Wing Award for *Ice Cream with Hot Fudge* at the New York Shakespeare Festival. He has assisted Jennifer Tipton, whom he considers his mentor.

Lighting Designs:
1989: *Mastergate*

Jason Sturm

Jason Sturm, who has designed lighting extensively on the West Coast, made his East Coast and Broadway debut with *Chu Chem* in 1989. He was born in Miami Beach, Florida on August 12, 1951 and received a B.A. in liberal arts from the University of New Mexico. He credits a college teacher in New Mexico, John Malolepsy, and designer Bob Mitchell as influences on his career. Although a brother tried to involve him in backstage activity at a local college theatre when he was growing up, he received little formal training in the theatre and spent a number of years in other professions before finding himself drawn into the theatre. His professional debut was *The Fantastiks* for the Albuquerque Civic Light Opera Association. He has also designed for the New Mexico Repertory Theatre, Opera Southwest, and the Vortex Theatre, where he has also served on the Board of Directors.

Lighting Designs:
1989: *Chu Chem*; *Miss Margarida's Way*

Dennis Sullivan

Dennis Sullivan designed a Broadway set in 1916. An interior decorator, he resided at 141 East 50th Street, New York City in 1918. He died on January 31, 1940 at age 46.

Lighting Designs:
1916: *Queen's Enemies, The*

John Sullivan

John Sullivan designed lights in 1946 and 1948 for several productions on Broadway.

Lighting Designs:
1946: *Critic, The*; *Henry IV, Part II*; *Henry IV, Part I*; *Oedipus*; *Uncle Vanya* 1948: *Oedipus Rex*

Paul Sullivan

Paul Sullivan has designed lights for theatres in Canada, Mexico, France and Germany as well as for the Pennsylvania Ballet Company, Brooklyn Academy of Music, Dance Theatre of Harlem, The Kennedy Center in Washington, D.C. and Carnegie Hall. Additional productions in New York City include *Broadway Soul*.

Lighting Designs:
1968: *New Faces of 1968* 1972: *Heathen!*; *Lost in the Stars*; *Mother Earth* 1984: *Wiz, The*

Victor En-Yu Tan

See En-Yu Tan, Victor

John Tedesco

John Tedesco was born in New York City on October 13, 1948, the son of Pasquale and Marie Tedesco. He studied at New York University, receiving a B.F.A. in theatre in 1970, and acknowledges Jules Fisher as his mentor. He has designed productions in New York City since his 1971 debut, *The House of Blue Leaves*. He was responsible for the 1986 lighting design of the Statue of Liberty, and designed and supplied special effects for the Han River Festival opening ceremonies of the 1988 Olympics in Seoul, South Korea. He is the owner of Phoebus Lighting in San Francisco.

Lighting Designs:
1972: *Grease* 1973: *Bette Midler*

Rouben Ter-Arutunian

Rouben Ter-Arutunian, a scenic and costume designer, was born on July 24, 1920 in Tiflis, Russia. He studied concert piano in Berlin and art in both Berlin and Paris. His first design was for *The Bartered Bride* in Dresden in 1941, followed by costumes for the Berlin State Opera Ballet. In 1951 he moved to the United States, becoming a citizen in 1957. His extensive designs include scenery, costumes and occasionally lights for ballets, operas and theatres in the United States and around the world. He has been staff designer for the three major television networks and has also designed variety shows and specials. Mr. Ter-Arutunian received an Emmy Award for art direction in 1957 for *Twelfth Night*, an Outer Critics Circle Award for *Who Was that Lady I Saw You With?* in 1958, as well as a Tony Award for costume design for *Redhead* in 1959.

Lighting Designs:
1957: *New Girl in Town* 1963: *Arturo Ui*

Scenic Designs:
1957: *New Girl in Town* 1958: *Maria Golovin*; *Who Was That Lady I Saw You With?* 1959: *Redhead* 1960: *Advise and Consent* 1961: *Donnybrook!* 1962: *Passage to India, A* 1963: *Arturo Ui*; *Hot Spot* 1964: *Deputy, The*; *Milk Train Doesn't Stop Here Anymore, The* 1965: *Devils, The* 1966: *Ivanov* 1968: *Exit the King*; *I'm Solomon* 1969: *Dozens, The* 1971: *All Over* 1975: *Goodtime Charley* 1976: *Days in*

the Trees; Lady from the Sea, The **1980:** *Good-bye Fidel; Lady from Dubuque, The*

Costume Designs:
1957: *New Girl in Town* **1959:** *Redhead* **1961:** *Donnybrook!* **1962:** *Passage to India, A* **1963:** *Arturo Ui; Hot Spot* **1964:** *Milk Train Doesn't Stop Here Anymore, The* **1966:** *Ivanov* **1969:** *Dozens, The* **1971:** *All Over* **1976:** *Days in the Trees; Lady from the Sea, The*

Max Teuber

Max Teuber designed lights in 1929 and scenery in 1933 on Broadway. A theatrical producer, he resided at 203 West 103rd Street, New York City in 1925.

Lighting Designs:
1929: *Earl Carroll's Sketch Book*

Scenic Designs:
1933: *Murder At the Vanities*

Cheryl Thacker

Cheryl Thacker is from Birmingham, Alabama, where she was born on August 18, 1948. She received a B.A. at Birmingham Southern College in 1970 (cum laude, Phi Beta Kappa) and an M.F.A. from New York University Tisch School of the Arts in theatre design in 1973. Her New York debut was the lighting design for the Laura Foreman Dance Company in 1973 at the American Laboratory Theatre. In recent years most of her work has been in television. She was staff lighting designer at NBC-TV for fourteen years and lit the first one thousand David Letterman Shows. She was also lighting director for the Simon and Garfunkel Reunion concert in Central Park, working with lighting designer Jules Fisher.

Lighting Designs:
1976: *Runner Stumbles, The* **1977:** *Unexpected Guests*

Frank Thomas

Frank Thomas designed lights for a 1917 Broadway production. A specialist in stage effects, he lived at 1547 Broadway, New York City in 1922.

Lighting Designs:
1917: *Going Up*

William Thomas

William Thomas designed lights in the 1920s and 1940s on Broadway. An interior decorator, he resided at 135 West 97th Street, New York City in 1918.

Lighting Designs:
1924: *Marjorie* **1945:** *Lady Says Yes, A; Many Happy Returns*

Woodman Thompson

Woodman Thompson was a scenic designer who also created costumes and occasionally lights. He began his theatrical career in 1918 and worked steadily in the theatre until his death on August 30, 1955 at the age of 66. He was a member of the faculty at Carnegie Tech when the undergraduate theatre program was established, but left for New York City in 1921, a move that would prove permanent. He was resident designer for the Theatre Guild, the Actor's Theatre, and the Equity Theatre and taught design both privately and at Columbia University. A member of United Scenic Artists from 1923, he served his fellow designers as President, Vice President and Treasurer at various times.

Lighting Designs:
1946: *Hear the Trumpet*

Scenic Designs:
1922: *Malvaloca; Rivals, The; Why Not?* **1923:** *Business Widow, The; Chastening, The; Neighbors; Queen Victoria; Roger Bloomer; Sweet Nell of Old Drury* **1924:** *Admiral, The; Beggar on Horseback; Candida; Close Harmony; Expressing Willie; Firebrand, The; Habitual Husband, The; Hedda Gabler; Macbeth; Marjorie; Minick; New Englander, The; What Price Glory?* **1925:** *Beggar on Horseback; Candida; Cocoanuts, The* **1926:** *Desert Song, The; God Loves Us; Hedda Gabler; Importance of Being Earnest, The; Iolanthe; Pirates of Penzance, The; Shelf, The; White Wings* **1927:** *Iolanthe; Pirates of Penzance, The* **1928:** *Merchant of Venice, The; These Few Ashes* **1929:** *Primer for Lovers, A* **1930:** *Merchant of Venice, The; Midnight; This One Man* **1932:** *Dangerous Corner; Warrior's Husband, The* **1933:** *Dangerous Corner* **1934:** *Lady Jane* **1935:** *Bishop Misbehaves, The; Tomorrow's a Holiday* **1936:** *Plumes in the Dust* **1937:** *Candida; Ghost of Yankee Doodle, The*

1942: *Candida* 1946: *Candida; Hear the Trumpet; Magnificent Yankee*

Costume Designs:
1922: *Malvaloca* 1923: *Neighbors; Queen Victoria; Sweet Nell of Old Drury* 1924: *Beggar on Horseback; Firebrand, The; Hedda Gabler* 1925: *Beggar on Horseback; Candida* 1926: *Iolanthe; Pirates of Penzance, The; Shelf, The* 1928: *Merchant of Venice, The* 1930: *Merchant of Venice, The* 1932: *Warrior's Husband, The* 1936: *Plumes in the Dust* 1937: *Candida* 1942: *Candida* 1946: *Hear the Trumpet; Magnificent Yankee*

Clarke W. Thornton

Clarke W. Thornton is active in regional theatres and has designed the national tours of *Man of La Mancha, Fiddler on the Roof,* and *Anything Goes.* He designed *Gotta Getaway* and other productions at Radio City Music Hall as well as productions off-Broadway. For three years he was resident designer for the Dance Theatre of Harlem. He is also a consultant for new and renovated theatres.

Lighting Designs:
1979: *Meeting in the Air, A*

James F. Tilton

James F. Tilton began designing while in the United States Army Special Services Division (1959-1962) as Resident Designer at the Frankfurt (West Germany) Playhouse. After his discharge in 1963 he became principal designer for the APA Repertory. From 1963 to 1971 he designed numerous plays for APA, including the first production at the Phoenix Theatre, *Scapin.* He has designed for many regional theatres, industrial shows, and for other New York theatres. In 1970 he designed his first film, *Dear Dead Delilah.* He concentrates on the design of scenery and lights and only rarely designs costumes. James Tilton was born in Rochelle, Illinois on July 30, 1937 and received a B.A. at the University of Iowa in 1959.

Lighting Designs:
1965: *You Can't Take It with You* 1967: *Pantagleize; Show-Off, The* 1968: *Cherry Orchard, The; Cocktail Party, The; Exit the King; Misanthrope, The; Pantagleize; Show-Off, The* 1969: *Cock-a-doodle Dandy; Hamlet; Private Lives* 1970: *Harvey* 1971: *Grass Harp, The; School for Wives, The* 1975: *Seascape* 1977: *Vieux Carre* 1983: *You Can't Take It with You*

Scenic Designs:
1965: *You Can't Take It with You* 1966: *Right You Are...; School for Scandal, The; We, Comrades Three* 1967: *Pantagleize; Show-Off, The; War and Peace; Wild Duck, The; You Can't Take It with You* 1968: *Cherry Orchard, The; Cocktail Party, The; Misanthrope, The; Pantagleize; Show-Off, The* 1969: *Cock-a-doodle Dandy; Hamlet; Private Lives* 1970: *Harvey* 1971: *Grass Harp, The; Oh! Calcutta!; School for Wives, The* 1975: *Seascape* 1976: *Comedians; Oh! Calcutta!* 1977: *Vieux Carre* 1981: *Twice Around the Park* 1983: *You Can't Take It with You*

Jennifer Tipton

Few contemporary lighting designers have the versatility of Jennifer Tipton, who designs not only for theatre but for dance and opera as well. She was born in Columbus, Ohio on September 11, 1937 and received a B.A. at Cornell University in 1958. Though initially a dance student at Connecticut College, she studied lighting design under Thomas Skelton. Her first design was a dance piece by Pauline De Groot at the Connecticut College School of Dance. She began her professional career with Paul Taylor and Twyla Tharp and has designed for most major modern and ballet companies and choreographers. Her theatre design includes productions at The Guthrie Theatre, Goodman Theatre, Yale Repertory Theatre and in London's West End, the Spoleto Festival in Italy and the Netherlands Dans Theatre. She maintains an on-going collaboration with Robert Wilson for whom she has designed *CIVIL warS, Alcestes,* and *Hamletmachine* at the Lyric Opera of Chicago and *Parsifal* at the Hamburg Opera. Her designs have been honored with many awards: Tonys for *Jerome Robbins' Broadway* and *The Cherry Orchard,* two Drama Desks, Obies, Bessie Awards, the 1989 American Theatre Wing Design Award, a Brandeis Arts Award, Medal in Dance, Joseph Jefferson Awards, a Kudo Award, a Commonwealth Award, a 1991 *Dance Magazine* Award and a Guggenheim.

Lighting Designs:
1969: *Our Town* 1975: *Habeas Corpus; Murder Among Friends* 1976: *For Colored Girls Who Have Considered Suicide; Rez* 1977: *Cherry Orchard, The; Happy End* 1978: *Runaways* 1979: *Bosoms and Neglect; Goodbye People, The* 1980: *Lunch Hour* 1981: *Pirates of Penzance, The; Sophisticated Ladies* 1982: *Alice in Wonderland; Wake of Jamie Foster, The* 1984: *Hurlyburly; Whoopi Goldberg* 1985: *Singin' in the Rain* 1988: *Ah, Wilderness!; Long Day's Journey Into Night* 1989: *Jerome Robbins' Broadway*

James Trittipo

James Trittipo was known mainly as a set designer and art director for television. He was born in Ohio and graduated from the Carnegie Institute of Technology. He began designing for television in its early days, for both live variety shows and dramatic productions. The recipient of three Emmys for his designs for *Hollywood Palace*, which he designed for eight years, he also worked in theatre on the West Coast. As a set designer his work was often seen on Broadway and included *On the Town*, which he designed just prior to his death in 1971 at the age of 43.

Lighting Designs:
1962: *Captains and the Kings, The*

Scenic Designs:
1962: *Captains and the Kings, The* 1970: *Ovid's Metamorphoses* 1971: *On the Town* 1972: *Funny Thing Happened on the Way to the Forum, A*

Costume Designs:
1962: *Captains and the Kings, The*

Martin Tudor

Martin Tudor spent two years as an assistant to Jennifer Tipton. He has designed many off-Broadway productions including *I'm Getting My Act Together and Taking It On The Road* and *Marie and Bruce*. He was born on December 17, 1954 in Jersey City, New Jersey and graduated from The Bergen School. He attended Rutgers University and studied at Lester Polakov's Studio and Forum of Stage Design. He designed Barry Manilow's European Tour and produced and designed the Meat Loaf World

Tour. He is also president and executive producer of B&D Communications, a film and television production company.

Lighting Designs:
1977: *Miss Margarida's Way*

Vannio Vanni

Vannio Vanni designed lights for a Broadway production in 1964.

Lighting Designs:
1964: *Rugantino*

Fred Voelpel

Fred Voelpel was born in Peoria, Illinois and attended the University of Illinois and Yale, where he studied with Donald Oenslager and Frank Poole Bevan. He has been designing costumes, lights and sets since his first efforts in 1943 when he debuted at both Peoria Players Little Theatre and Peoria Central High School. He has been designing professionally since 1956 for television and the theatre. In 1959 he debuted in New York with the costume designs for *On the Town*. Additional costume credits include *Seascape* and *The Effect of Gamma Rays on Man-in-the-Moon Marigolds*. He has won two New York Critics Circle Awards for set design, an Obie Award for *The Effect of Gamma Rays on Man-in-the-Moon Marigolds*, a Variety Poll Award, an Esquire Dubious Achievement Award for *Oh, Calcutta*, and a Miami (Florida) L.O.R.T. Award for *Seascape*. He has been a master teacher of design at New York University's Tisch School of the Arts since 1964, and from 1966 to 1988 designed for the National Theatre for the Deaf. He has been Resident Designer for the National Playwrights' Conference since 1965 and on the faculty of the National Theatre Institute since its founding in 1970. From 1964 to 1987 he designed sets and costumes for Paul Green's *The Lost Colony*, the nation's longest running outdoor drama, located at Manteo, North Carolina.

Lighting Designs:
1960: *From A to Z* 1961: *Young Abe Lincoln*

Scenic Designs:
1960: *From A to Z; Vintage '60* 1961: *Young Abe Lincoln* 1969: *Home Fires/ Cop Out* 1970: *Sganarelle* 1971: *And Miss Reardon Drinks a*

Little 1972: *Hurry, Harry* 1975: *Very Good, Eddie* 1981: *Einstein and the Polar Bear*

Costume Designs:

1960: *From A to Z* 1961: *Young Abe Lincoln* 1963: *Sophie* 1964: *Absence of a Cello*; *Murderer Among Us, A*; *Sign in Sidney Brustein's Window, The* 1965: *Drat! the Cat!*; *Peterpat* 1969: *Home Fires/ Cop Out* 1970: *Sganarelle*; *Songs from Milkwood*; *Two By Two* 1971: *Oh! Calcutta!* 1975: *Seascape* 1981: *Bring Back Birdie*

Susan Wain

Susan Wain designed scenery and costumes for a 1977 Broadway play. She has served as director of costumes and make-up for Roy Cooney Productions, Ltd. in England.

Lighting Designs:

1977: *Ipi Tombi*

Costume Designs:

1977: *Ipi Tombi*

Walter Walden

Walter Walden conceived costume, lighting and particularly scenic designs for Broadway productions in the 1920s and 1930s.

Lighting Designs:

1928: *Dark Mirror, The*

Scenic Designs:

1928: *Dark Mirror, The* 1929: *Subway, The*; *Vegetable, The* 1930: *At the Bottom*; *Life Line, The*; *Seagull, The* 1932: *Lost Boy* 1934: *Jayhawker* 1937: *Swing It* 1938: *Prologue to Glory*

Costume Designs:

1930: *At the Bottom*; *Troyka*

Billy B. Walker

Billy B. Walker is head electrician and resident lighting designer at Radio City Music Hall where he has designed lights for approximately three hundred productions. He graduated from the University of Illinois. His professional career began with sound design and he created the first sound system for the Indianapolis 500 auto race. After serving as technical director for *Skating Vanities*, he moved to New York City in the mid-1950s and has spent most of the last thirty years

at Radio City. His responsibilities at Radio City include not only the stage lighting system but the entire electrical operations.

Lighting Designs:

1979: *New York Summer*

Ronald Wallace

Ronald Wallace began his association with the Long Wharf Theatre when it was formed in 1965. He has extensive credits at the Long Wharf Theatre, off-Broadway (especially for the New York Shakespeare Festival), at the Edinburgh International Festival of the Arts and in London's West End. His designs have also been seen at the Kennedy Center and in regional theatres including the Cleveland Playhouse, the Actors Theatre of Louisville, and StageWest.

Lighting Designs:

1971: *Solitaire/ Double Solitaire* 1973: *Changing Room, The* 1974: *National Health, The*; *Sizwe Banzi is Dead* 1975: *Ah, Wilderness* 1976: *Comedians*; *Pal Joey* 1977: *Gin Game, The*; *Shadow Box, The* 1979: *Strangers* 1980: *Watch on the Rhine* 1983: *American Buffalo*; *Passion*; *View from the Bridge, A* 1985: *Joe Egg*; *Requiem for a Heavyweight* 1987: *All My Sons* 1988: *Checkmates*

Ward and Harvey Studios

Ward and Harvey Studios, comprised of designers Herbert Ward and Walter Harvey, received credit for the scenic design of Broadway productions from 1921 to 1932.

Lighting Designs:

1930: *Vanderbilt Revue, The*

Scenic Designs:

1927: *Oh, Ernest*; *Talk About Girls*; *White Lights* 1928: *Atlas and Eva*; *Divorce a La Carte*; *Present Arms* 1929: *Booster, The*; *Crooks Convention, The*; *Lady Fingers*; *Silver Swan, The* 1930: *Bad Girl*; *Lew Leslie's Blackbirds*; *So Was Napoleon* 1931: *Old Man Murphy* 1932: *Surgeon, The*

William B. Warfel

William B. Warfel was born on February 12, 1933 in Amherst, Massachusets. He received both a B.A. (1955) and an M.F.A. (1957) at Yale University studying lighting design with Stanley McCandless. Since 1967 he has been Lighting Director at Yale Repertory, where he has amassed many credits and also taught and influenced numerous students. He has earned great respect and developed an expertise as a theatre consultant and is president of Systems Design Associates. This consulting company for performance spaces is comprised of William B. Warfel, Ming Cho Lee, John R. Hood, and Eugene C. Leitermann.

Lighting Designs:
1985: *Blood Knot*

William Washcoe

William (Will) Washcoe designed lights in 1941 on Broadway.

Lighting Designs:
1941: *They Walk Alone*

Perry Watkins

Perry Watkins worked as a flower seller, journalist and insurance salesman before taking a trip to New York City and discovering scene design. He broke the color barrier by becoming the first black member of United Scenic Artists in the late 1930s. He designed several productions for the Harlem unit of the Federal Theatre Project, including *S.S. Glencairn*, *Androcles and the Lion*, *Horse Play* and others. He worked as a producer, beginning with *Beggars' Holiday* in 1946 and *Moon of Mah'no'men* in 1947, working through Production Associates with Thomas Ward Lanyan and Dale Wasserman. He was also a director and art director for films and was preparing to go to Africa to make a film at the time of his death. Mr. Watkins died in Newburgh, New York at age 67 on August 14, 1974.

Lighting Designs:
1940: *Big White Fog* **1945:** *Blue Holiday* **1949:** *Forward the Heart*

Scenic Designs:
1937: *Moon of the Caribees, Etc.* **1938:** *Haiti*; *Pinocchio* **1939:** *Mamba's Daughter's* **1940:** *Big White Fog*; *Mamba's Daughter's* **1942:** *Heart of a City*; *Three Men on a Horse*; *You'll See the Stars* **1943:** *Bright Lights of*

1943; *Manhattan Nocturne*; *Run, Little Chillun* **1944:** *Take It As It Comes* **1945:** *Blue Holiday* **1949:** *Forward the Heart* **1954:** *Integration Show Case, The* **1956:** *Harbour Lights*

Costume Designs:
1935: *Three Men on a Horse* **1938:** *Androcles and the Lion* **1939:** *Mamba's Daughter's* **1940:** *Mamba's Daughter's* **1942:** *Three Men on a Horse* **1943:** *Bright Lights of 1943*; *Run, Little Chillun* **1945:** *Blue Holiday*

David Watson

David Watson was born on March 13, 1941 in London and was orphaned by the death of his parents in the 1941 London blitz. He was adopted by Leonard and Vera Watson and studied music on scholarship at Westminster Abbey School and the Royal Academy of Music. Known as an actor and singer, he appeared in the London productions of *West Side Story* and *The Fantasticks* prior to moving to the United States and appearing on television and in the theatre. He also designed lights in 1974 for a Broadway production.

Lighting Designs:
1974: *Scapino*

Lee Watson

Leland Hale Watson worked steadily in the theatre after his professional debut at the Provincetown Playhouse in 1950. He was principally a lighting designer who worked in theatre, ballet, opera and television. Born on February 18, 1926 in Charleston, Illinois, he received an M.F.A. at Yale in 1951 after service in World War II and work as a radio engineer. His interest in the theatre began in high school. Occasionally Mr. Watson also designed scenery for plays and more rarely costumes. He served as lighting director for CBS-TV from 1951 to 1955, and taught design in many universities and at Lester Polakov's Studio and Forum of Stage Design. He also wrote articles about lighting design and two books, beginning with *Theatrical Lighting Practice* in 1955. *Lighting Design Handbook*, one of the few comprehensive books about lighting design, was published posthumously in 1990. His awards included an Obie for *Machinal* in 1957. Lee Watson died on December 10, 1989.

Lighting Designs:
1955: *Diary of Anne Frank, The; View from the Bridge, A* **1956:** *Girls of Summer; Harbour Lights; Protective Custody* **1957:** *Cave Dwellers, The; Mask and Gown; Miss Isobel; Moon for the Misbegotten, A* **1958:** *Next President, The-A Musical Salamagundi; Night Circus, The; Portofino* **1959:** *Legend of Lizzie* **1960:** *Lovely Night, A* **1961:** *Do You Know the Milky Way?; Importance of Being Oscar, The* **1962:** *Moby Dick*

Scenic Designs:
1958: *Next President, The-A Musical Salamagundi* **1960:** *Lovely Night, A* **1961:** *Importance of Being Oscar, The*

Costume Designs:
1958: *Next President, The-A Musical Salamagundi* **1961:** *Importance of Being Oscar, The*

John Watt

John Watt, a mechanical engineer by training, designs primarily for television and occasionally for theatre. His career in television began in 1958.

Lighting Designs:
1983: *Edmund Kean*

Byron Webb

Byron Webb designed lights on Broadway in 1938. He worked as technical director for the Federal Theatre Project in New York and designed lights for the FTP production of *Androcles and the Lion.*

Lighting Designs:
1938: *Haiti*

Gil Wechsler

Gil Wechsler is from Brooklyn, New York where he was born on February 5, 1942, the son of Arnold and Miriam Wechsler. In 1964 he received a B.S. from New York University and in 1967 an M.F.A. from the Yale University School of Drama. He assisted Jo Mielziner on *Mata Hari* in 1967 and toured with the Harkness Ballet prior to working for various ballet comapnies, The Guthrie Theatre, and the Shaw and Stratford Fesivals in Canada. Since 1976 he has been

principal lighting designer for the Metropolitan Opera where he has designed nearly one hundred operas in the repertory, reworked earlier designs, and supervised lighting for many television productions of operas at the Met. Prior to 1976 he was resident lighting designer for the Lyric Opera of Chicago for four years. He credits Charles Elson as a major influence on his career.

Lighting Designs:
1968: *Staircase* **1972:** *There's One in Every Marriage*

Marc B. Weiss

Marc B. Weiss studied biology in college but soon discovered theatre, first as an avocation and subsequently as a career. His professional debut was the set design for the Washington Ballet at Arena Stage in Washington, D.C., followed by designs (principally for lights) for dozens of productions. He designed the international tour of *My One and Only* and *The Flying Karamazov Brothers* on Broadway and television. He has designed for television, regional theatres, nightclub acts, and productions for the American Shakespeare Festival. He recently designed lights for *The March on Russia,* presented by the Chelsea Stage in association with the Cleveland Playhouse. His combined credits number over two hundred. Marc Weiss is also an international theatre consultant.

Lighting Designs:
1972: *Six Rms Riv Vu* **1973:** *Medea* **1974:** *Cat on a Hot Tin Roof; Find Your Way Home; Words and Music* **1975:** *Hughey/ Duet; We Interrupt This Program* **1976:** *Eccentricities of a Nightingale, The* **1977:** *Ladies At the Alamo* **1978:** *Death Trap* **1979:** *Break a Leg; Once a Catholic* **1980:** *Horowitz and Mrs. Washington; Life, A* **1981:** *Animals; First, The; One Act Play Festival, The; Shakespeare's Cabaret; To Grandmother's House We Go* **1982:** *84 Charing Cross Road; Othello* **1983:** *Zorba* **1984:** *Design for Living; Moon for the Misbegotten, A; Rink, The* **1986:** *Raggedy Ann; Uptown...It's Hot* **1987:** *Cabaret* **1988:** *Macbeth*

John Wenger

John Wenger was born in Elizabeth, Odessa, Russia on June 16, 1891. He studied at the

Imperial Art School in Odessa and the National Academy of Design. After moving to the United States in 1903 he found work as a jewelry designer and scenic artist. He designed settings for the Boston Opera Company, the Metropolitan Opera, and the Greenwich Village Theatre and was art director for the Rivoli, Capital and Roxy movie theatres. His film designs included *Paramount on Parade* in 1929. He was the first designer to use gauze backdrops and lateral moving scenery, for *Good Boy* in 1928. This innovative designer and watercolorist died on August 24, 1976 in Manhattan at age 89. His designs and paintings are in the permanent collections of the Museum of the City of New York, the Metropolitan Museum of Art, and The Museum of Modern Art.

Lighting Designs:
1946: *Walk Hard*

Scenic Designs:
1921: *Poppy God, The* 1922: *George White's Scandals* 1924: *Great Music; Round the Town; Ziegfeld Follies: 1924* 1925: *Bridge of Distances; Master of the Inn, The; Monkey Talks, The; Tip Toes* 1926: *No Foolin'; Oh, Kay* 1927: *Funny Face; Hit the Deck; Piggy; Spring Song* 1928: *Good Boy; Here's Howe; Oh, Kay; Ups-A-Daisy* 1929: *Spring Is Here* 1933: *Pardon My English* 1946: *Walk Hard*

Roland West

Roland West was a film director who began acting in plays and vaudeville in his native Cleveland, Ohio. He began writing some of his own sketches prior to joining the Lowe circuit as a producer of short acts and skits. His first film was the silent *Lost Souls*, which he directed and co-produced. Later films included several starring Norma Talmadge. The first talkie he directed was *Alibi* with Chester Morris in 1928. He died on March 31, 1952 in Santa Monica, California at age 65.

Lighting Designs:
1918: *Unknown Purple, The*
Scenic Designs:
1918: *Unknown Purple, The*

Peter Wexler

Peter Wexler received a B.S. in design in 1958 from the University of Michigan, where he majored in photography and painting. He attended graduate school at Yale University. Born on October 31, 1936 in New York City, he began designing with sets, costumes and lights for the New York Shakespeare Festival's production of *Anthony and Cleopatra* in 1959. Since then he has amassed extensive credits for plays, operas, television and films throughout the United States. In the early 1970s he began producing and programming after many years of designing theatrical events. Beginning with the Promenades and Rug Concerts at the New York Philharmonic, his company has produced, programmed, and directed museum exhibitions, concerts, public spaces, and media events for major symphony orchestras, opera companies, museums, government agencies and the private sector. His models and drawings have been widely collected and exhibited. Peter Wexler has been married to Emmy award winning costume designer Constance Ross Wexler since 1962.

Lighting Designs:
1966: *Joyful Noise, A*

Scenic Designs:
1966: *Joyful Noise, A* 1968: *Happy Time, The* 1970: *Minnie's Boys* 1971: *Trial of the Catonsville Nine, The* 1978: *Broadway Musical, A*

John Whalen

John J. Whalen was an electrician who worked for Shubert Enterprises, particularly on productions at the Lyric Theatre. He also created special effects. He was active on Broadway in the teens and probably was responsible for more productions than those for which he received credit. He resided at 563 West 170th Street, New York City in 1915.

Lighting Designs:
1915: *Alone At Last; Hands-Up; Taking Chances* 1916: *Fixing Sister*

Michael J. Whitfield

Michael J. Whitfield was born on April 11, 1944. He received a B.A. from the University of Victoria, British Columbia in 1967, an M.A. from Villanova University in 1970, and attended the University of Illinois at Champaign-Urbana from

1971 to 1974. From 1974 to 1976 he was assistant to his mentor, Gil Wechsler, at the Stratford (Ontario) Festival. His first professional design was for the Third Stage Season for the Stratford Festival in 1974. He has remained with the company since then and is currently Resident Lighting Designer. He is also a regular designer for the Canadian Opera Company in Toronto. He received the Dora Award in 1988 for the lighting design of *Observe the Sons of Ulster Marching Towards the Somme*.

Lighting Designs:
1987: *Mikado, The*

Vantile Whitfield

Vantile Whitfield was born on September 8, 1930 in Washington, D.C. and received a B.A. at Howard University and a M.A. at the University of California. In his varied career as an administrator and designer he has held positions such as art director for Ad Graphics in Hollywood, general manager of the American Theatre of Being, and set designer for Universal Studios. He has also served as program director, Expansion Arts, at the National Endowment for the Arts in Washington, D.C.

Lighting Designs:
1965: *Amen Corner, The*

Scenic Designs:
1965: *Amen Corner, The*

Costume Designs:
1965: *Amen Corner, The*

Richard Whorf

Richard Whorf, who was born in Winthrop, Massachusetts on June 4, 1906, worked in the theatre as an actor, director and designer. He first appeared on stage in 1921 in Boston. He had an active career as an actor and director for theatre and film and ocasionally also designed costumes and lights. He began designing in the early 1940s and in 1949 played the role of Richard III in the play *Richard III*, while also designing the costumes and scenery. He also directed numerous television programs, including episodes of *Gunsmoke, Alfred Hitchcock* and *The Beverly Hillbillies*. In 1954 he received both a Donaldson Award and a Tony Award for his costume design for *Ondine*. Richard Whorf died in 1966.

Lighting Designs:
1957: *Genius and the Goddess, The*

Scenic Designs:
1940: *Fledgling; Old Acquaintance; There Shall Be No Night* **1944:** *But Not Goodbye* **1949:** *Richard III* **1957:** *Genius and the Goddess, The*

Costume Designs:
1949: *Richard III* **1954:** *Ondine*

Bolton Wilder

Bolton Wilder designed lights for a Broadway production in 1939.

Lighting Designs:
1939: *Once Upon a Time*

Robert T. Williams

Robert T. Williams designed sets for Broadway in the 1960s and early 1970s. For one production he also designed lights.

Lighting Designs:
1967: *Warm Body, A*

Scenic Designs:
1964: *Girl Could Get Lucky, A* **1965:** *Glass Menagerie, The* **1967:** *Warm Body, A* **1970:** *Charley's Aunt*

Andrea Wilson

Andrea Wilson designed lights in 1977 on Broadway.

Lighting Designs:
1977: *Party with Betty Comden and Adolph Green*

Joseph P. Wilson

Joseph P. Wilson designed lights for plays on Broadway in 1914, long before the profession was formally developed. He was an actor and manager, born in Dublin, Ireland on February 16, 1858. His stage debut was in Leeds, England in 1885. From 1904 to 1914 he was manager of the Tivoli Theatre. He died on December 4, 1940 at age 84.

Lighting Designs:
1914: *Mix-Up, A* **1917:** *Have a Heart* **1918:** *Toot-Toot!* **1920:** *Lady Billy* **1922:** *Clinging Vine, The* **1923:** *Magic Ring, The; White Desert* **1925:** *Lass O'Laughter; Lucky Break, A*

Kathryn Wilson

Kathryn Wilson designed lights for a play in 1936. A decorator, she worked for A.M. Kemper at 1441 Broadway, New York City in 1932.

Lighting Designs:
1936: *Living Newspaper, The*

E. Carlton Winckler

The lighting designer E. Carlton Winckler was born on January 20, 1908 in Jersey City, New Jersey. For twenty years he worked with John Murray Anderson, who encouraged his interest in lighting design while they created "units" for Paramount Movie Theatres. He worked for producer Billy Rose for nearly thirty years while also designing lights throughout the United States for theatre and films. He designed numerous shows for which he did not receive program credit, working at a time when the profession of lighting design was only beginning to emerge. He was also an active designer during the period when United Scenic Artists and IATSE Local One struggled over jurisdiction of theatrical lighting design. He designed the lights for Walt Disney's *Fantasia*, pioneering new techniques in film lighting. In 1943 he became involved in television, working in New York and on the West Coast, and in 1951 became General Manager of the Program Department for CBS-TV, where he remained until retirement in 1973. He then joined Imero Fiorentino Associates as senior production consultant and director of the Education Division. In 1977 the Society of Motion Picture and Television Engineers honored him with their Progress Award Gold Medal for contributions to television's development.

Lighting Designs:
1929: *Murray Anderson's Almanac* **1940:** *Earl Carroll's Vanities*; *Louisiana Purchase* **1941:** *Ah, Wilderness*; *Clash By Night*; *Hope for a Harvest*; *Liberty Jones*; *Sunny River* **1942:** *New Faces of 1943*; *R.U.R.* **1943:** *Counterattack* **1944:** *Seven Lively Arts* **1945:** *Assassin, The*; *Concert Varieties*; *Hamlet* **1946:** *Duchess Misbehaves, The*; *If the Shoe Fits* **1948:** *Light Up the Sky*

Scenic Designs:
1927: *Lace Petticoat*

Richard Winkler

Richard Winkler was born on June 20, 1948 in Detroit, Michigan, the son of Edith and Leslie Winkler. He received a B.S. at the University of Michigan and continued his study at Lester Polakov's Studio and Forum of Stage Design and with Tharon Musser, who has had a major influence on his career. His first design was for *Once Upon A Mattress* at the University of Michigan. He has received a Helen Hayes Nomination for *A Midsummer Night's Dream* at the Folger Theatre in Washington, D.C., and a Hollywood Dramalogue Award for Best Lighting for *Once in a Lifetime* at the La Jolla Playhouse.

Lighting Designs:
1973: *Play's the Thing, The* **1976:** *Best Friends*; *George Abbott...a Celebration*; *Something's Afoot* **1978:** *Neighborhood Playhouse At 50-A Celebration* **1980:** *Your Arms Too Short to Box with God* **1982:** *Your Arms Too Short to Box with God* **1985:** *Loves of Anatol, The* **1986:** *Corpse!* **1987:** *Barbara Cook: A Concert for the Theatre*

Ed Wittstein

Ed Wittstein was born in Mt. Vernon, New York on April 7, 1929 and received a B.S. at New York University. He also studied at the Parsons School of Design, Cooper Union, and Erwin Piscator's Dramatic Workshop in New York City, where he first designed in 1947. He has designed sets for numerous plays and in addition often designs costumes and/or lights. He has also designed sets and costumes for operas, ballets and television. Designs include the long-running off-Broadway play *The Fantasticks*, *The Adams Chronicles* on television, and the films *Endless Love* and *Fame*. He received an Obie Award in 1966 for *Sergeant Musgrave's Dance* and a Maharam Award in 1974 for *Ulysses in Nighttown*.

Lighting Designs:
1963: *Enter Laughing*; *Rainy Day in Newark, A* **1969:** *Celebration*

Scenic Designs:
1961: *Kean* **1963:** *Enter Laughing*; *Rainy Day in Newark, A* **1964:** *White House, The* **1965:** *And Things That Go Bump in the Night*; *Yearling, The* **1967:** *Natural Look, The*; *You Know I Can't Hear You When the Water's Running*

1968: *Before You Go; Man in the Glass Booth, The* 1969: *Celebration* 1970: *Blood Red Roses* 1972: *Ring Round the Bathtub; Tough to Get Help* 1974: *Ulysses in Nighttown*

Costume Designs:
1961: *Kean* 1962: *Bravo Giovanni* 1963: *Enter Laughing; Rainy Day in Newark, A* 1964: *White House, The* 1965: *Yearling, The* 1969: *Celebration*

Peter Wolf

Peter Wolf debuted on Broadway as a set designer in 1947 and as a lighting designer in 1950. After forsaking acting as a career, he studied at the Grand Central School of Art and the Yale School of Drama. He then worked as an assistant for several New York-based scenic designers and at the New York City Center with Maurice Evans. A position supplying scenery for summer musicals in Dallas led to considerable travel and eventual relocation to Texas. His firm, Peter Wolf Concepts (formerly Peter Wolf Associates), began as a major scenic studio and has become a firm which designs and builds commercial buildings, industrial promotions, restaurants, exhibits, etc. He has credits for settings for hundreds of plays, musicals and operas throughout the United States.

Lighting Designs:
1950: *Devil's Disciple, The*

Scenic Designs:
1947: *Sweethearts* 1948: *Linden Tree, The* 1950: *Devil's Disciple, The* 1977: *King and I, The* 1979: *Peter Pan* 1980: *Blackstone!; Music Man, The* 1983: *Mame* 1984: *Wiz, The* 1985: *King and I, The*

John Wyckham

John Wyckham Suckling was born on May 18, 1926 in Solihull, Warwickshire, England. He first worked in theatre as a stage manager in the early 1950s and began his career as a lighting designer in 1955. He has extensive credits for lighting in the West End, for the Royal Shakespeare Company, and Sadler's Wells among others. He is senior partner in John Wyckham Associates, theatre consultants, and was a founding member of the Society of Theatre Consultants. He has also consulted on the design and renovation of many theatres in the United Kingdom.

Lighting Designs:
1963: *Oliver!* 1965: *Beyond the Fringe; Oliver!*

Scenic Designs:
1965: *Beyond the Fringe*

Nicholas Yellenti

Nicholas Yellenti, who was active on Broadway from 1923 to 1963, usually designed settings but also designed lights for one production. He also constructed sets for other designers.

Lighting Designs:
1948: *Vigil, The*

Scenic Designs:
1923: *Breaking Point, The* 1924: *Bluffing Bluffers; Flossie* 1925: *Easy Come, Easy Go; Family Upstairs, The; Mud Turtle, The; Solid Ivory; Twelve Miles Out* 1926: *Ashes of Love; Bells, The; Black Boy; Donovan Affair, The; Gertie; If I Was Rich; Just Life; Kongo; She Couldn't Say No; They All Want Something; This Woman Business; We Americans* 1927: *Bless You, Sister; Fog Bound; Fog; Her First Affairs; Jazz Singer, The; Lady in Love, A; Mystery Shop, The; Nightstick; Restless Women; Set a Thief; Shannons of Broadway, The; Skin Deep; Take My Advice; Tenth Avenue* 1928: *Adventure; Behavior of Mrs. Crane, The; Brothers; Get Me in the Movies; Golden Age, The; Happy Husband, The; Man with Red Hair, A; Mirrors; Mystery Man, The; Quicksand; Tin Pan Alley; War Song, The* 1929: *House Unguarded; Ladies Don't Lie; Scotland Yard; Veneer* 1930: *Love, Honor and Betray; Made in France; Schoolgirl; Sweet Chariot* 1931: *Her Supporting Cast; In the Best of Families; In Times Square* 1932: *Absent Feather; Web, The* 1933: *Curtain Rises, The; Family Upstairs, The* 1934: *American–Very Early; Baby Pompadour; Theodora, the Queen; When in Rome* 1935: *Good Men and True; Ragged Edge, The; Woman of the Soil, A* 1936: *Around the Corner; Arrest That Woman; Love on the Dole* 1937: *Behind Red Lights; Places Please; Something for Nothing* 1938: *Bright Rebel; Censored* 1939: *Aries Is Rising* 1948: *Vigil, The* 1963: *Golden Age, The*

Appendix 1:
The Tony Awards

Beginning in 1947, The Antoinette Perry or Tony Award is given at the end of each season for an outstanding contribution to Broadway in several categories. The award for lighting design was given for the first time in 1970. Under the auspices of the American Theatre Wing, nominees and winners are selected by members of the governing boards of professional organizations, opening night press lists, the board of directors of the American Theatre Wing, and members of the League of New York Theatres and Producers. (Winners are printed in boldface.)

1970 .... **Jo Mielziner:** *Child's Play*
Tharon Musser: *Applause*
Thomas Skelton: *Indians*

1971 .... **H.R. Poindexter:** *Story Theatre*
Robert Ornbo: *Company*
William Ritman: *Sleuth*

1972 .... **Tharon Musser:** *Follies*
Martin Aronstein: *Ain't Suppose To Die A Natural Death*
John Bury: *Old Times*
Jules Fisher: *Jesus Christ Superstar*

1973 .... **Jules Fisher:** *Pippin*
Martin Aronstein: *Much Ado About Nothing*
Ian Calderon: *That Championship Season*
Tharon Musser: *A Little Night Music*

1974 .... **Jules Fisher:** *Ulysses in Nightgown*
Martin Aronstein: *Boom, Boom Room*
Ken Billington: *The Visit (Revival)*
Ben Edwards: *A Moon for the Misbegotten*
Tharon Musser: *The Good Doctor*

1975 .... **Neil Peter Jampolis:** *Sherlock Holmes*
Chipmonck: *The Rocky Horror Show*
Abe Feder: *Goodtime Charley*
Andy Phillips: *Equus*
Thomas Skelton: *All God's Chillun*
James Tilton: *Seascape*

1976 .... **Tharon Musser:** *A Chorus Line*
Ian Calderon: *Trelawny of the "Wells"*
Jules Fisher: *Chicago*
Tharon Musser: *Pacific Overtures*

1977..............Jennifer Tipton: (Tie) *The Cherry Orchard*
John Bury: (Tie) *No Man's Land*
Pat Collins: *Threepenny Opera*
Neil Peter Jampolis: *The Innocents*

1978..............Jules Fisher: *Dancin'*
Jules Fisher: *Beatlemania*
Tharon Musser: *The Act*
Ken Billington: *Working*

1979..............Roger Morgan: *The Crucifier of Blood*
Ken Billington: *Sweeney Todd*
Beverly Emmons: *The ElephantMan*
Tharon Musser: *Ballroom*

1980..............David Hersey: *Evita*
Beverly Emmons: *A Day in Hollywood/A Night in the Ukraine*
Craig Miller: *Barnum*
Dennis Parichy: *Talley's Folly*

1981..............John Bury: *Amadeus*
Tharon Musser: *42nd Street*
Dennis Parichy: *Fifth of July*
Jennifer Tipton: *Sophisticated Ladies*

1982..............Tharon Musser: *Dreamgirls*
Martin Aronstein: *Medea*
David Hersey: *The Life and Adventures of Nicholas Nickleby*
Marcia Madeira: *Nine*

1983..............David Hersey: *Cats*
Ken Billington: *Foxfire*
Robert Bryan: *All's Well That Ends Well*
Allen Lee Hughes: *K2*

1984..............Richard Nelson: *Sunday in The Park With George*
Ken Billington: *End of the World*
Jules Fisher: *La Cage aux Folles*
Marc B. Weiss: *A Moon for the Misbegotten*

1985..............Richard Riddell: *Big River*
Terry Hands: *Cyrano de Bergerac*
Terry Hands: *Much Ado About Nothing*
Allen Lee Hughes: *Strange Interlude*

1986..............Pat Collins: *I'm Not Rappaport*
Jules Fisher: *Song & Dance*
Paul Gallo: *The House of Blue Leaves*
Thomas R. Skelton: *The Iceman Cometh*

1987..............David Hersey: *Les Miserables*
Martin Aronstein: *Wild Honey*
David Hersey: *Starlight Express*
Beverly Emmons and Chris Parry: *Les Liaisons Dangereuses*

1988..............Andrew Bridge: *The Phantom of the Opera*
Paul Gallo: *Anything Goes*
Richard Nelson: *Into the Woods*
Andy Phillips: *M. Butterfly*

1989 .... Jennifer Tipton: *Jerome Robbins' Broadway*
Neil Peter Jampolis and Jane Reisman: *Black and Blue*
Brian Nason: *Metamorphosis*
Nancy Schertler: *Largely New York*

1990 .... Jules Fisher: *Grand Hotel*
Paul Gallo: *City of Angels*
Kevin Rigdon: *The Grapes of Wrath*
Paul Pyant and Neil Peter Jampolis: *Orpheus Descending*

Appendix 2:
The Maharam Awards

The Maharam Awards (a.k.a. Marharam Award) were presented each fall to recognize distinguished design on, off- and off-off Broadway. Each award included a cash stipend and a citation, and was given as part of a yearly design seminar. These awards were sponsored by the Joseph Maharam Foundation from 1964 when they began until 1986. After 1986 the awards were sponsored by the American Theatre Wing and became known as the American Theatre Wing Design Awards. Winners of the Maharam were selected by members of the professional theatre. The Maharam Award for Lighting Design was first presented in 1977.

1977-78 .... **Jules Fisher:** *Dancin'*

1978-79 .... **Beverly Emmons:** *The Elephant Man*

1979-80 .... **Dennis Parichy:** *Talley's Folly*

1980-81 .... **Dennis Parichy:** *Fifth of July*

1981-82 .... **Tharon Musser and Robin Wagner** *Dreamgirls*

1982-83 .... **Allen Lee Hughes:** *K-2*

1983-84 .... **Richard Nelson:** *Sunday in the Park with George*
   Paul Gallo: *The Garden of Earthly Delights*

1984-85 .... **Richard Riddell:** *Big River*
   Lawrence Eichler: *The Mystery of Irma Vep*
   Blu: *Nosferatu*

Appendix 3:
The American Theatre
Wing Design Awards

The American Theatre Wing Design Awards were first given in 1986. The American Theatre Wing took responsibility for this award program from the Joseph Marharam Foundation which awarded a cash stipend and citation in recognition of distinguished design on, off and off-off Broadway beginning in 1964. Award winners in lighting design are selected by members of the professional theatre. The awards are presented each fall during a seminar on theatrical design.

1986 .... Kevin Rigdon *Ghost Stories*
1987 .... Paul Gallo *The Hunger Artist*
　　　　　　　　Jennifer Tipton *Worstward Ho*
1988 .... (No Lighting Award)
1989 .... Jennifer Tipton: *Long Day's Journey Into Night, Jerome Robbins' Broadway, Waiting for Godot,* and *The Rimers of Eldrich*
1990 .... Jules Fisher: *Grand Hotel*

Selected Bibliography

Bellman, Willard F. *Lighting the Stage: Art and Practice*. New York: Thomas Y. Crowell Co., 1974.

Bentham, Frederick P. *The Art of Stage Lighting*. London: Pitman & Sons, 1980.

Bergman, Gösta M. *Lighting in the Theatre*. New Jersey: Rowman and Littlefield, 1977.

Bowman, Wayne. *Modern Theatre Lighting*. New York: Harper & Brothers, 1957.

Fuchs, Theodore. *Stage Lighting*. Boston: Little Brown and Co., 1929.

Hays, David. *Light on the Subject*. New York: Limelight Editions, 1990.

McCandless, Stanley. *A Method of Lighting the Stage*. New York: Theatre Arts Books, 1958.

McCandless, Stanley. *A Syllabus of Stage Lighting*. 11th ed. New Haven, Conn.: Drama Book Specialists, 1964.

Ost, Geoffrey. *Stage Lighting*. London: Herbert Jenkins, Ltd., 1957.

Palmer, Richard H. *The Lighting Art: The Aesthetics of Stage Lighting Design*. Englewood Cliffs, N.J.: Prentice-Hall, 1985.

Parker, W. Oren and Harvey K. Smith. *Scene Design and Stage Lighting*. New York: Holt, Rinehart and Winston, 1979.

Pilbrow, Richard. *Stage Lighting Handbook*. New York: Van Nostrand Reinhold Co., 1970.

Rees, Terence. *Theatre Lighting in the Age of Gas*. London: Society for Theatre Research, 1978.

Reid, Francis. *Stage Lighting Handbook*. New York: Theatre Arts Books/Methuen, 1982

Rosenthal, Jean and Lael Wertenbacker. *The Magic of Light*. Boston: Little Brown and Co., 1972.

Rubin, Joel E. and Leland H. Watson. *Theatrical Lighting Practice*. New York: Theatre Arts Books, 1954.

Selden, Samuel and Hunton D. Sellman. *Stage Scenery and Lighting*. Rev. ed. New York: Appleton-Century-Crofts, 1959.

Sellman, Hunton D. *Essentials of Stage Lighting*. New York: Appleton-Century-Crofts, 1972.

Warfel, William B. *Handbook of Stage Lighting Graphics*. New York: Drama Book Specialists, 1974.

Watson, Lee. *Lighting Design Handbook*. New York: McGraw-Hill, Inc., 1990

Williams, Rollo G. *The Technique of Stage Lighting*. London: Pitman & Sons Ltd., 1952.

Index of Plays

The plays in this index can be found listed under the lighting designer's name in the main portion of the text.

Captain Brassbound's Conversion '72: Batchelder, William H.

Captain Kidd, Jr. '16: Ack Only

Captains and the Kings, The '62: Trittipo, James

Career Angel '44: Fox, Frederick

Caretaker, The '64: March, Marvin

Caretaker, The '86: Rigdon, Kevin

Carib Song '45: Mielziner, Jo

Caribbean Carnival '47: Ack Only

Carmelina '79: Feder, A.H.

Carmen Amaya and Her Company '55: Ack Only

Carmen Jones '43: Short, Hassard

Carnival '19: Ack Only

Carnival '24: Simonson, Lee

Carnival '61: Armstrong, Will Steven

Carrie '88: Hands, Terry

Carry Me Back to Morningside Heights '68: Lundell, Kert

Case of Lady Camber, The '17: Ack Only

Case of Libel, A '63: Oenslager, Donald

Castles in the Air '26: DuWico

Cat and the Canary, The '22: Ack Only

Cat and the Fiddle, The '31: Ack Only

Cat Bird, The '20: Ack Only

Cat on a Hot Tin Roof '55: Mielziner, Jo

Cat on a Hot Tin Roof '74: Weiss, Marc B.

Cat on a Hot Tin Roof '90: Henderson, Mark

Catch Me If You Can '65: Jenkins, George

Cats '82: Hersey, David

Cave Dwellers, The '57: Watson, Lee

Celebrated Case, A '15: Ack Only

Celebration '69: Wittstein, Ed

Celebrity '27: Ack Only

Censored Scenes from King Kong '80: Nelson, Richard

Century Girl, The '16: Ack Only

'Ception Shoals '17: Ack Only

Chalk Garden, The '55: Sovey, Raymond

Challenge, The '19: Ack Only

Chamberlain Brown's Scrapbook '32: Ack Only

Chameleon, The '32: Ack Only

Champagne Complex '55: Elson, Charles

Champion, The '21: Ack Only

Change in the Heir '90: Davis, Jeff

Changelings, The '23: Ack Only

Changing Room, The '73: Wallace, Ronald

Channel Road, The '29: Ack Only

Chapter Two '77: Musser, Tharon

Charlatan, The '22: Ack Only

Charley's Aunt '25: Ack Only

Charley's Aunt '40: Ack Only

Charley's Aunt '70: Dana, F. Mitchell

Charlie and Algernon '80: Lester, Hugh

Charlot Revue '25: Ack Only

Charlotte '80: Collins, Pat

Charm School, The '20: Ack Only

Charm '29: Ack Only

Chastening, The '23: Ack Only

Chauve Souris '22: Ack Only

Chauve Souris '27: Ack Only

Chauve Souris '29: Ack Only

Cheaters '78: Calderon, Ian

Cheating Cheaters '16: Ack Only

Checkerboard, The '20: Ack Only

Checking Out '76: Billington, Ken

Checkmates '88: Wallace, Ronald

Chee-Chee '28: Ack Only

Chemin De Fer '73: Billington, Ken

Cheri '59: Clark, Peggy

Cherokee Night '37: Ack Only

Cherry Orchard, The '23: Ack Only

Cherry Orchard, The '29: Ack Only

Cherry Orchard, The '68: Tilton, James

Cherry Orchard, The '70: Simmons, Pat

Cherry Orchard, The '77: Tipton, Jennifer

Chess '88: Hersey, David

Chicago '26: DuWico

Chicago '75: Fisher, Jules

Chicken Every Sunday '44: Bay, Howard

Chief, The '15: Ack Only

Chiffon Girl, The '24: Ack Only

Child of Fortune '56: O'Hearn, Robert

Child's Play '70: Mielziner, Jo

Children from Their Games '63: Smith, Oliver

Children of a Lesser God '80: Musser, Tharon

Children of Darkness '30: Ack Only

Children of Earth '15: Ack Only

Children of the Moon '23: Ack Only

Children of the Wind '73: Kerz, Leo

Children! Children! '72: Mielziner, Jo

Children's Tragedy, The '21: Ack Only

Chimes of Normandy, The '31: Ack Only

China Rose '25: Ack Only

Chinese Prime Minister, The '64: Rosenthal, Jean

Chinese, The/ Dr. Fish '70: Aronstein, Martin

Chippies '29: Ack Only

Chips with Everything '63: Herbert, Jocelyn

Chivalry '25: Ack Only

Chocolate Dandies, The '24: Greshoff, Anthony

Chocolate Soldier, The '31: Ack Only

Chocolate Soldier, The '34: Ack Only

About the Author

BOBBI OWEN is Associate Professor of Dramatic Art, University of North Carolina at Chapel Hill. The author of parallel volumes on Broadway design, *Costume Design on Broadway* (Greenwood, 1987) and *Scenic Design on Broadway* (Greenwood, 1991), she has contributed articles on design and designers to *Notable Women in the American Theatre* (Greenwood, 1989) and the forthcoming *Cambridge Guide to American Theatre*.

Recent Titles in
Bibliographies and Indexes in the Performing Arts

Memorable Film Characters: An Index to Roles and Performers, 1915-1983
Susan Lieberman and Frances Cable, compilers

Stage Lives: A Bibliography and Index to Theatrical Biographies in English
George B. Bryan, compiler

The Federal Theatre Project: A Catalog-Calendar of Productions
The Staff of the Fenwick Library, George Mason University, compilers

Victorian Plays: A Record of Significant Productions on the London Stage,
1837-1901
Donald Mullin, compiler

Costume Design on Broadway: Designers and Their Credits, 1915-1985
Bobbi Owen

Eighteenth Century British and Irish Promptbooks: A Descriptive
Bibliography
Edward A. Langhans

The German Stage: A Directory of Playwrights and Plays
Veronica C. Richel, compiler

Stage Deaths: A Bibliographical Guide to International Theatrical Obituaries,
1850 to 1990
George B. Bryan, compiler

The Stratford Festival Story: A Catalogue-Index to the Stratford, Ontario,
Festival, 1953-1990
J. Alan B. Somerset